The Wakhan Corridor-
In the Footsteps of Hsüang-tsang and Marco Polo
Nature and Inhabitants

玄奘(三蔵)法師やマルコ ポーロも辿った

ワハーン回廊
自然と棲む人たち

Go Hirai / 平位 剛

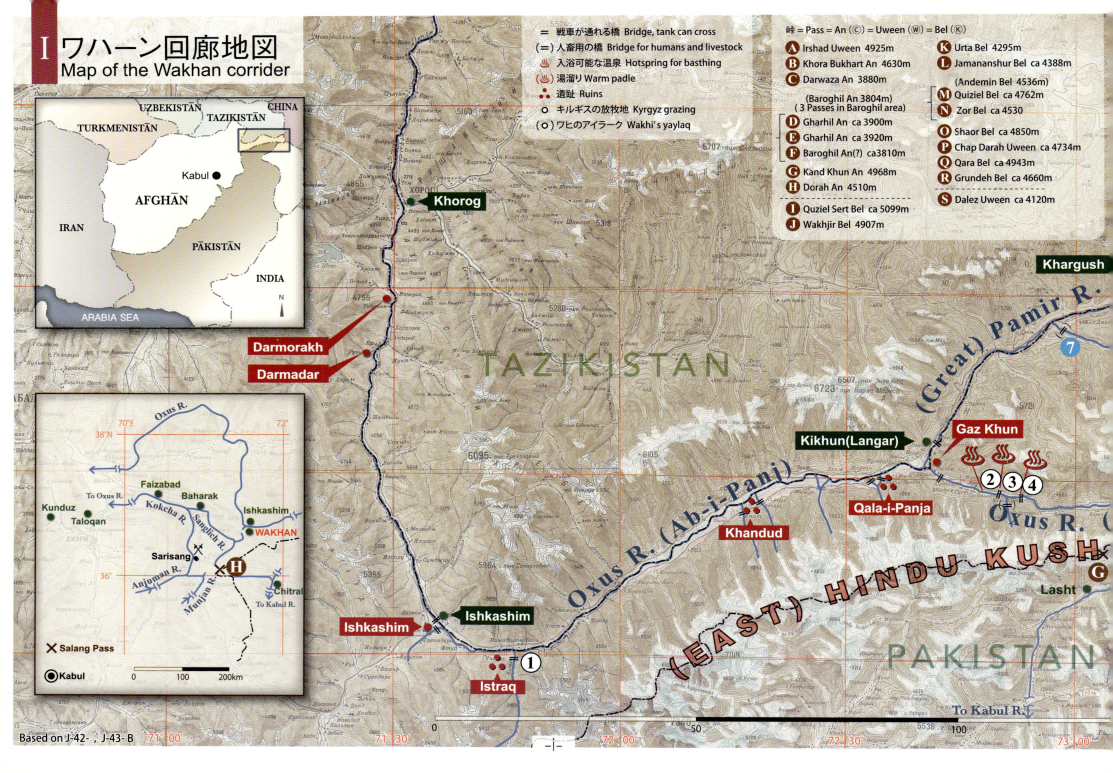

I ワハーン回廊地図
Map of the Wakhan corridor

戦車が通れる橋 Bridge, tank can cross
人畜用の橋 Bridge for humans and livestock
入浴可能な温泉 Hotspring for basthing
湯溜り Warm padle
遺趾 Ruins
キルギスの放牧地 Kyrgyz grazing
ワヒのアイラーク Wakhi's yaylaq

峠 = Pass = An Ⓒ = Uween Ⓦ = Bel Ⓚ

Ⓐ Irshad Uween 4925m
Ⓑ Khora Bukhart An 4630m
Ⓒ Darwaza An 3880m

(Baroghil An 3804m)
(3 Passes in Baroghil area)
Ⓓ Gharhil An ca 3900m
Ⓔ Gharhil An ca 3920m
Ⓕ Baroghil An(?) ca3810m
Ⓖ Kand Khun An 4968m
Ⓗ Dorah An 4510m
- - - - - - - - - - - - - - - -
Ⓘ Quziel Sert Bel ca 5099m
Ⓙ Wakhjir Bel 4907m

Ⓚ Urta Bel 4295m
Ⓛ Jamananshur Bel ca 4388m
(Andemin Bel 4536m)
Ⓜ Quiziel Bel ca 4762m
Ⓝ Zor Bel ca 4530
Ⓞ Shaor Bel ca 4850m
Ⓟ Chap Darah Uween ca 4734m
Ⓠ Qara Bel ca 4943m
Ⓡ Grundeh Bel ca 4660m
Ⓢ Dalez Uween ca 4120m

挿入地図（左上）
UZBEKISTĀN
TAZIKISTĀN
CHINA
TURKMENISTĀN
AFGHĀN
Kabul
IRAN
PĀKISTĀN
INDIA
ARABIA SEA
N

挿入地図（左下）
70°E   72°
38°N
Oxus R.
Faizabad
Baharak
Ishkashim
WAKHAN
Kunduz
Taloqan
Kokcha R.
Sanglich R.
Sarisang
Ⓗ
Anjuman R.
Munjan R.
36°
Chitral
To Oxus R.
To Kabul R.
✕ Salang Pass
◉ Kabul
0   100   200km

本図地名
Khorog
Khargush
Darmorakh
Darmadar
TAZIKISTAN
(Great) Pamir R.
7
Kikhun(Langar)
Gaz Khun
Qala-i-Panja
Khandud
Oxus R. (Ab-i-Panj)
2 3 4
Oxus R.
(EAST) HINDU KUSH
Ⓖ
Lasht
PAKISTAN
Ishkashim
Ishkashim
Istraq
1
To Kabul R.

Based on J-42- , J-43-B

0   50   100

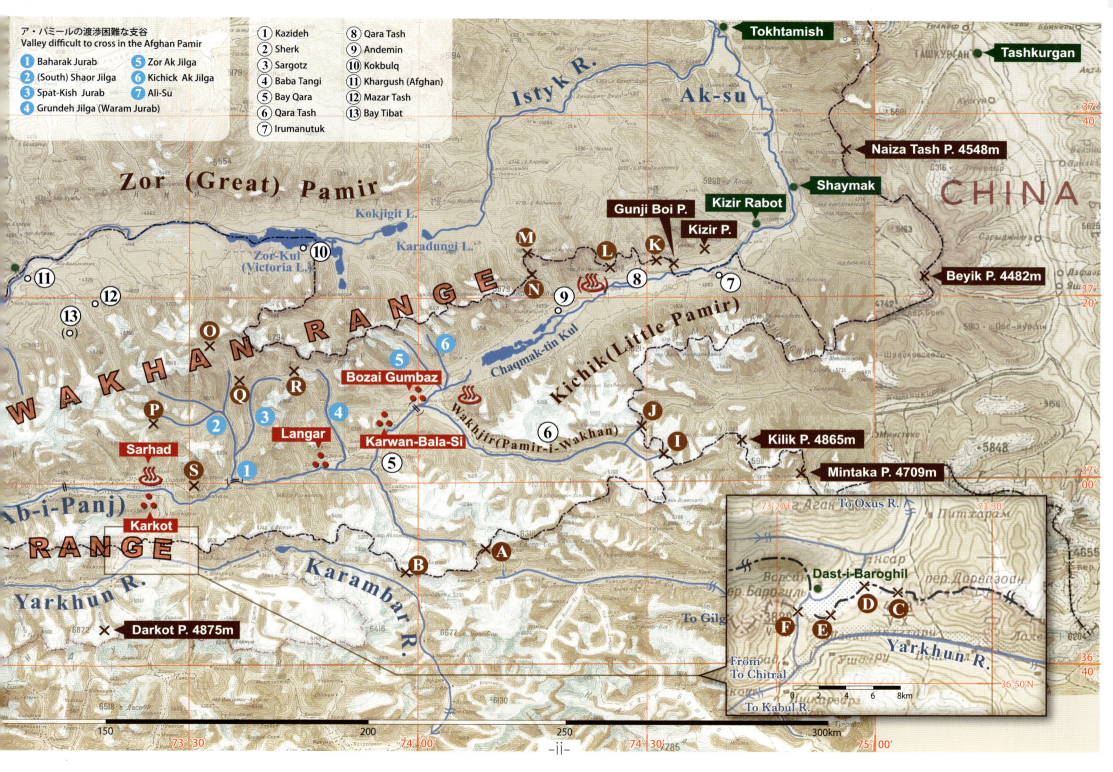

ア・パミールの渡渉困難な支谷
Valley difficult to cross in the Afghan Pamir

① Baharak Jurab   ⑤ Zor Ak Jilga
② (South) Shaor Jilga ⑥ Kichick Ak Jilga
③ Spat-Kish Jurab   ⑦ Ali-Su
④ Grundeh Jilga (Waram Jurab)

① Kazideh   ⑧ Qara Tash
② Sherk   ⑨ Andemin
③ Sargotz   ⑩ Kokbulq
④ Baba Tangi   ⑪ Khargush (Afghan)
⑤ Bay Qara   ⑫ Mazar Tash
⑥ Qara Tash   ⑬ Bay Tibat
⑦ Irumanutuk

Zor (Great) Pamir

Kokjigit L.

Karadungi L.

Zor-Kul
(Victoria L.)

Istyk R.

Ak-su

Tokhtamish

Tashkurgan

Naiza Tash P. 4548m

Shaymak

CHINA

Kizir Rabot

Gunji Boi P.

Kizir P.

M

N

L

K

8

Beyik P. 4482m

W A K H A N   R A N G E

O

R

Q

P

Sarhad

S

Karkot

(Ab-i-Panj)

R A N G E

Yarkhun R.

Darkot P. 4875m

2

3

4

5

6

Langar

Bozai Gumbaz

Karwan-Bala-Si

5

Chaqmak-tin Kul

9

7

Kichik (Little Pamir)

Wakhjir (Pamir-i-Wakhan)

6

J

I

Kilik P. 4865m

Mintaka P. 4709m

Karambar R.

A

B

To Oxus R.

Dast-i-Baroghil

D

C

F

E

To Gilg

Yarkhun R.

From
To Chitral

To Kabul R.

0 2 4 6 8km

150   200   250   300km

73° 30'   74° 00'   74° 30'   75° 00'

73° 20'E   73° 30'

37°
40'

37°
20'

37°
00'

36°
40'

36° 50'N

–ii–

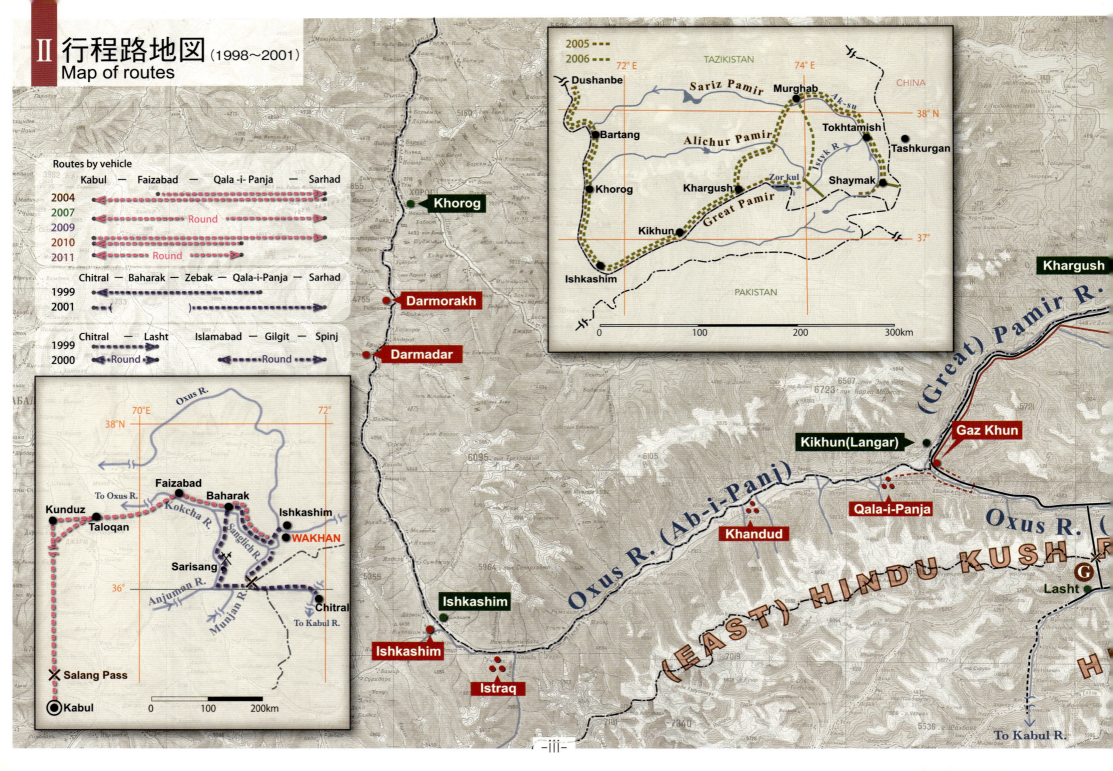

II 行程路地図 （1998〜2001）
Map of routes

Routes by vehicle

Kabul — Faizabad — Qala -i- Panja — Sarhad

2004	
2007	Round
2009	
2010	
2011	Round

Chitral — Baharak — Zebak — Qala-i-Panja — Sarhad

1999	
2001	

Chitral — Lasht   Islamabad — Gilgit — Spinj

1999	
2000	Round Round

2005
2006

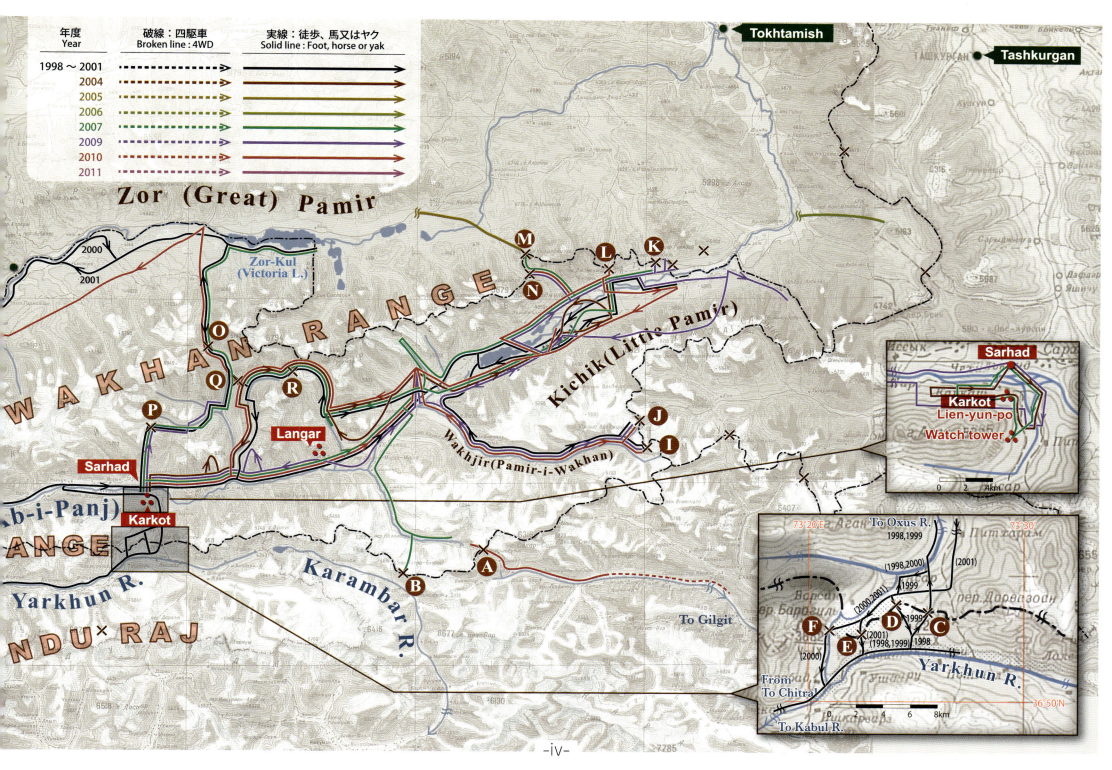

III 撮影地点表示の地図
Map showing the location
where the photographs were taken

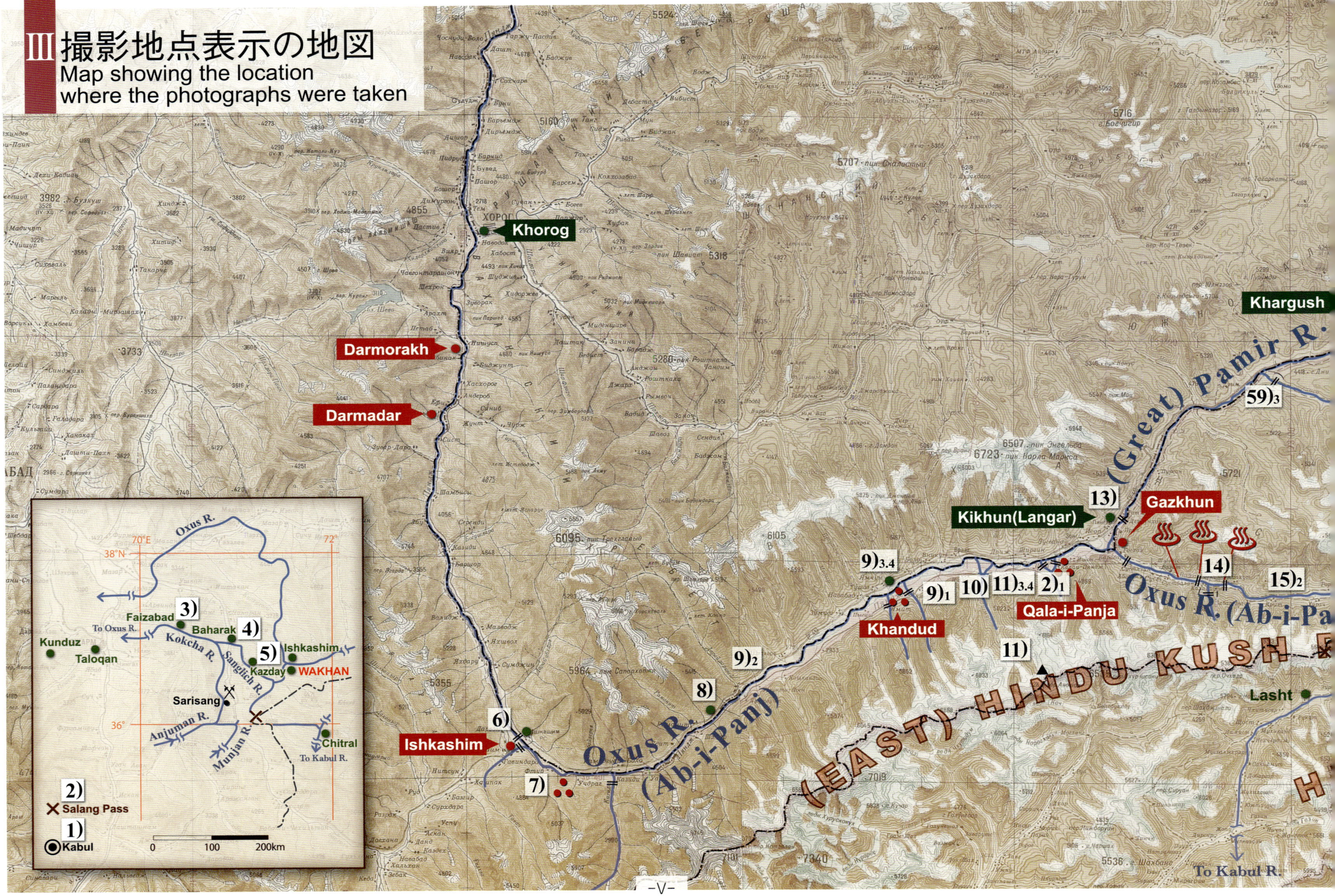

Khorog
Darmorakh
Darmadar
Ishkashim
Khargush
(Great) Pamir R.
59)3
13)
Gazkhun
Kikhun(Langar)
9)3.4
9)1
10)
11)3.4
2)1
14)
15)2
Oxus R. (Ab-i-Panj)
Khandud
Qala-i-Panja
11)
9)2
8)
6)
7)
(EAST) HINDU KUSH
Lasht
To Kabul R.
Oxus R.
70°E
72°
38°N
36°
Faizabad
3)
Baharak
4)
To Oxus R.
Kunduz
Taloqan
Kokcha R.
5)
Ishkashim
Kazday
WAKHAN
Sanglich R.
Sarisang
Anjuman R.
Munjan R.
Chitral
To Kabul R.
2)
Salang Pass
1)
Kabul
0
100
200km

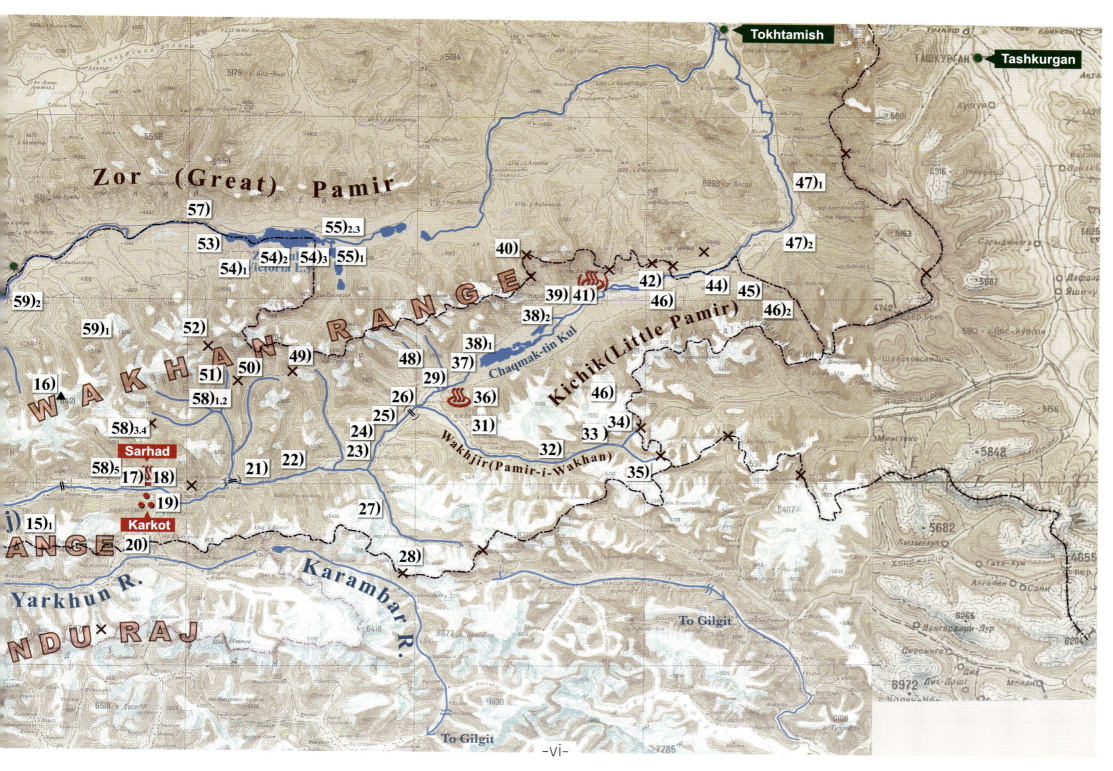

III （キリギスの生活）
The life of the Kyrgyz

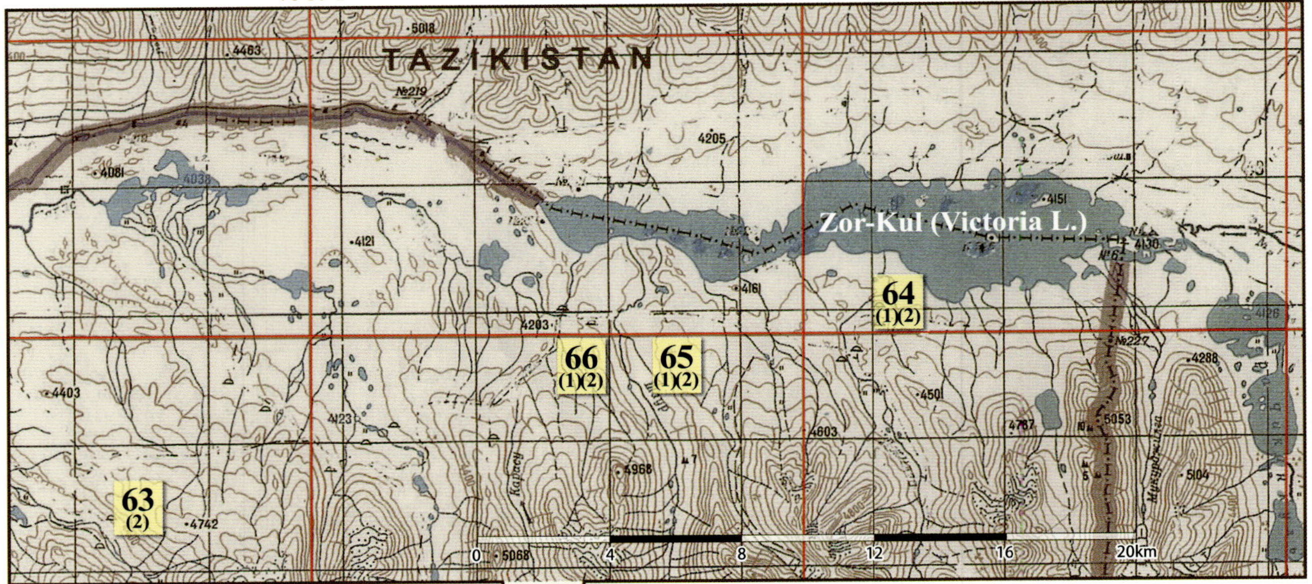

TAZIKISTAN

73°30′ E 73°40′ E 73°50′ E

37°30′ N
37°15′ N

Zor-Kul (Victoria L.)

64 (1)(2)

66 (1)(2)   **65** (1)(2)

63 (2)

0 4 8 12 16 20km

Based on J-43-XX

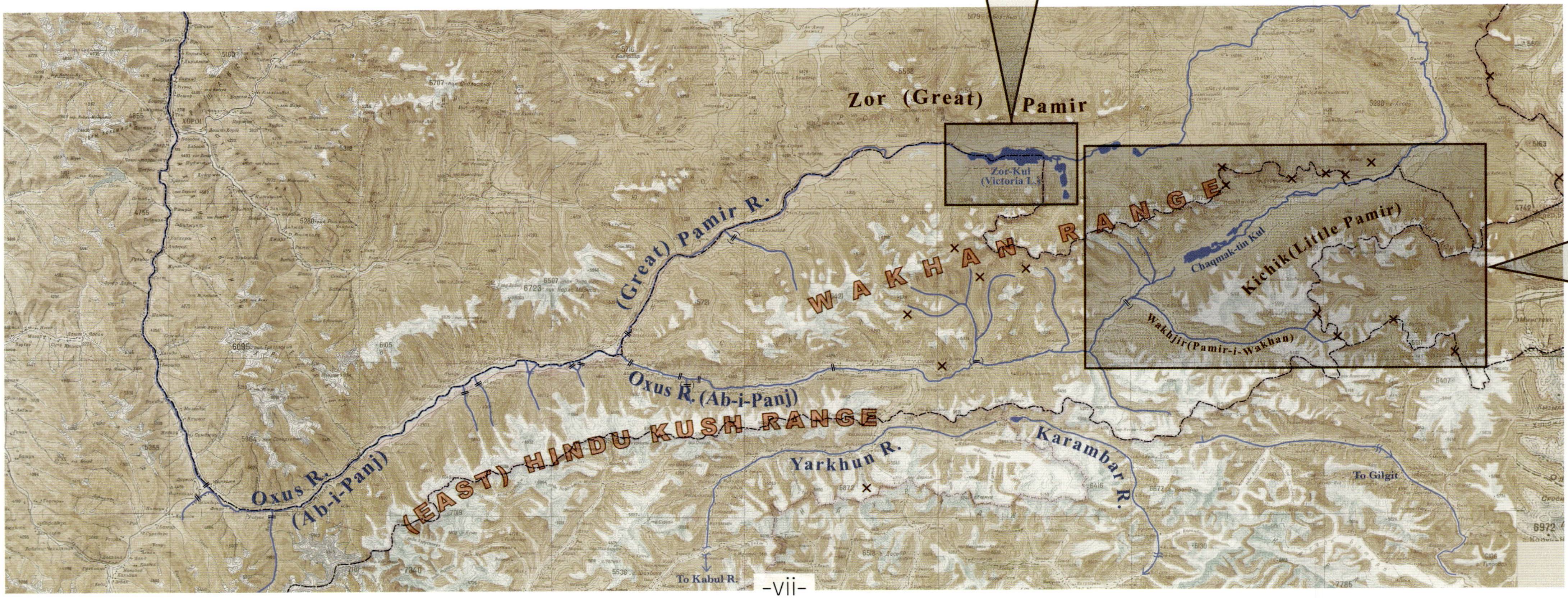

Zor (Great) Pamir

Zor-Kul (Victoria L.)

WAKHAN RANGE

Chaqmak-tin Kul

Kichik (Little Pamir)

(Great) Pamir R.

Wakhjir (Pamir-i-Wakhan)

Oxus R. (Ab-i-Panj)

(EAST) HINDU KUSH RANGE

Oxus R. (Ab-i-Panj)

Yarkhun R.

Karambar R.

To Gilgit

To Kabul R.

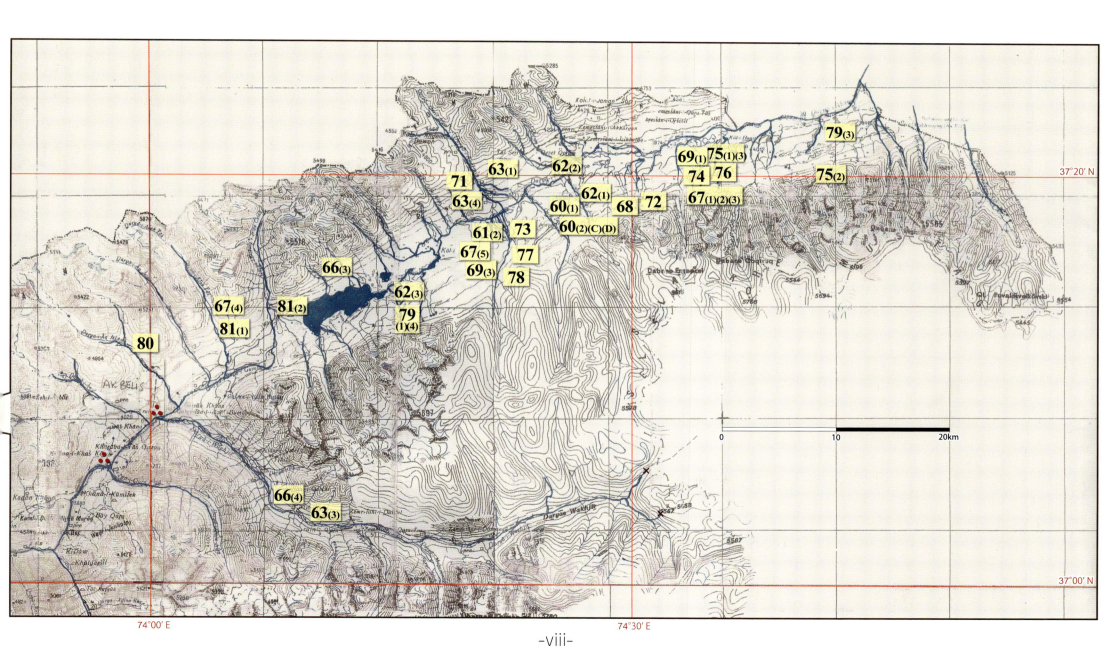

目次
Contents

目次
Contents

目次
Contents

目次
Contents

目次
Contents

目次
Contents

目次
Contents

目次
Contents

金子民雄

　今回出版される本書は、先年（2003年12月）に、『禁断のアフガーニスターン・パミール紀行』と題して出版されたものの補巻として、主に図版・地図を中心に纏めた報告書である。

　ワハーン回廊と言われても、我々にとって一体なになのか、すぐに分かる人はそう多くないであろう。中央アジアやパミールに親しんだ人でさえ、咄嗟に思い浮かばないこともあろうかと思う。それほどこの地域は今なおお秘境であり、古来訪れることのむずかしい所だった。文字通り現代の仙境で、日本人としてもこの回廊に足跡を残した人は、これまで平位氏以外ないに違いない。

　ワハーン回廊とは、アフガーニスターンの北東部、北にパミール、南にヒンズー・クシュ山脈に囲まれた細い地帯を指して呼んでいる。ここはアジアの西と東を結ぶ、いまひとつの古来のシルクロードの重要な交通ルートであったが、なにしろ場所が場所だけにそう簡単に通り抜けることもむずかしかった。しかし、古くは玄奘三蔵もマルコ・ポーロもこの通路を通過している、名前だけはよく知られた所だった。ようやく19世紀の新しい時代を迎え、今度こそ脚光を浴びるかと思いきや、南下政策をとる帝政ロシアと、インドの防衛を旗頭にする英国とのグレイト・ゲイムの舞台となり、外部の人達にとって自由な旅行が一層むずかしくなった。このことが、現在もなお続いている。

　ちょうど私がアフガーンを訪れ、ぐるりと一周したのは、1978年のことだったが、この一年半後、ソ連軍が突如アフガーンに侵攻を始め、たちまち国内は戦場と化してしまった。そしてこの混乱状態は約10年間も続くことになり、せっかくアフガーンを再訪しようという夢は、春の淡雪のように消えてしまった。

　本書の著者平位剛氏は、広島大学医学部山岳会に所属していたとき、たまたまヒンズー・クシュ山脈中の高峰の登山を始めたのだった。1960年代のアフガーニスターンは、この国の歴史の中でも稀に見るくらい平和な一時期だった。しかし、ソ連軍の侵攻と軍事支配下に入ったため、自由な旅行は不可能になり、登山も調査もずっと東方に当たる、旧インド北西部国境地帯に移さなければならなくなった。現在のパキスタンとアフガーニスターン国境地帯のチトラール地方である。このすぐ北西部がいわゆるワハーン回廊であった。

　やがて1988年には、力尽きたソ連軍もアフガーンから撤退していき、とくにアフガーン北部は平穏になりつつあり、テロ集団の影響力も小さかった。ソ連撤収後10年した1998年から、平位氏は、いよいよこのワハーン回廊部に新しい調査の的を絞ったようである。ここは危険地帯であることに変わりはなかったが、この選択は賢明だったに違いない。

　北アフガーニスターンは、南部地域のパシュトゥーン族支配と違って、外部からの日本人に対してもとかく好意的に対遇してくれたようである。これは誰に対してでもなく、とくにいたって温厚な平位氏だったからこそ、なんの問題もなく旅は可能だったのだろう。人はみな見かけは同じ様だが、辺境になればなるほどその人の性格たる人間性が重要になってくるようである。このすぐ北部のタジキスターンでは、かつて日本人の犠牲者も出ている。

　ところがこれから僅か数年した2001年9月11日、今度は予想すらしなかった例のアメリカを襲った9・11多発テロ事件が起こり、せっかく平和を取り戻したかに見えたアフガーンは、アメリカのテロ掃討戦の火中に入ってしまった。そしてふたたび夢の国は、悪夢の世界に逆戻りしてしまったのである。私は偶然にもこの9・11事件の突発の翌日、インドからカシミールのラダクのレーに向かったのだが、インドの空港はがらんとして人影もなかった。

　いつも私が感じることは、平位氏の行動に驚きを禁じ得ないことで、どんな事態に直面しても冷静に判断し、自分の意志を決して曲げないことである。一見、暴虎馮河の行いに見えるけど、どうして慎重な行動をとられていることは明らかで、でなくては来る年ごとに命など紙より薄いアフガーンに、旅など出来ないはずであるからだ。これには驚きを通り越して、頭が下がる思いがする。

　たまたまこの辺境地帯が激変する前夜に当たる2000年春、パーキスターン国境地帯沿いに北から南へとガンダーラ地方を下り、ペシャワールからハイバル峠まで、パーキスターンの兵士とアフガーン兵士と行ったことがある。辺りの情勢はかつてと一変し、この訪問の数ヶ月後、現地で聞いた予測通り、バーミアンの仏教遺跡は破壊されてしまった。このとき会った現地人たちは、仏教遺品を日本に一時避難してはどうかと、みな熱心に言ってくれたが、外交力のない日本政府など聞く耳がない。

　辺境地域の中でも辺境地ワハーンの回廊部は、アフガーンの地理と歴史を少

しぐらい聞き知ったところで、とても理解の及ぶところでない。なぜそんな僻地が重要なのかということになる。そのため文章でいくら説明したところで無理で、むしろ百万言の説明を労するより写真一枚がはるかに重要となる。

　そこで平位氏のワハーンの紀行本が出版された際、もしする意思がおありなら、この補巻としての写真と地図を中心に纏められてはどうかと、余計なことを話した。そのよい例に1908年、英国王立地理学会（RGS）から出版された、オーレル・スタインの『パミールと崑崙の山岳図集』(Aurel Stein：Mountain Panoramas from the Pamirs and Kuen Lun, London 1908) が、一つのよい参考になるのではないかと。この報告書はせいぜい40ページ足らずのものだが、パミールとクン・ルン山脈のパノラマ写真が入っていて、この地域が一望できるからで、この図版に説明や地名などが記入されている。幸い平位氏がこのことをよく憶えておられたようで、以後の旅はこの記録写真の撮影に専念されたようである。

　しかし、聞く所によると、苦心して持っていったカメラ3台が全て、機能不全になってしまった年もあったという。また別の時には、せっかく貴重な場面にぶつかったのに撮影して帰国してみたところ、なんと画面が全て消えていたという。私の乏しい体験でもこうしたことは少なからずあった。そのためスケッチをするのだが、チベットの峠で休息する度に描くにしても、スケッチは1枚描くのに最低30分はかかり、少し丁寧に描くとなると1時間以上必要となり、仲間たちがいるとこの時間の調整ができない。平位氏はいつでも単独の旅なので、旅としては最も賢明というべきであろう。

　本書に挿入された図版は、どれも珍しく貴重なものばかりである。なかでもヴィクトリア湖のパノラマや、オクサス河源流部の大小様々な支流群の記録写真は、これだけでも十分なだけの価値を持っていると思う。一見平凡に見えるかもしれないが、写真に妙な工作がないこと、それだけ一枚の写真の中に込められた著者の永年の労苦の思いを、是非お察しいただけたらと思う。友人の一人として、切にお願い致したい。

2011年1月

Pamir

Introduction

(Tamio. Kaneko)

"The Wakhan Corridor – Its Nature and Inhabitants" is a photographic travelogue of Dr. Go Hirai's travels in the Wakhan Corridor, and compliments the author's previous publication "Travels in the Forbidden Regions of Afghanistan and the Pamirs" (published in December 2003).

Most people, even those who are familiar with Central Asia and the Pamirs, would have difficulty locating the Wakhan Corridor on a map. So remote and inaccessible is this region, that a modern hermitage could be located here. Therefore I would assume that as of this date, Mr. Hirai is the only Japanese who has left his footprints in the Wakhan Corridor.

The Wakhan Corridor is a narrow strip of land wedged into the northeastern corner of Afghanistan. Buttressed by the Pamirs to the North, and by the Hindu Kush to the South, the Wakhan Corridor was an important part of the Silk Road, historically serving as a trade route that connected the East and the West. Travel has always been difficult in these parts but such notable travelers as Hsuang Tsang the Chinese monk, and Marco Polo both passed through the Wakhan Corridor, leaving records that gave an historical prominence to its name. In the 19th century, the Wakhan attracted world-wide attention when Czarist Russia's expansionist policy brought it into direct confrontation with the British Empire's interests in India. The fierce battle for hegemony between the two great powers of the 19th century became known as "The Great Game", and the Wakhan as a buffer zone was suddenly thrown into the limelight. Ever since those heady days, the Wakhan continues to be closed to foreign travelers.

In 1978 I traveled around Afghanistan, but a year and half after that visit, the Soviet invasion occurred. During the ten-year occupation of the Soviets, Afghanistan turned into a battlefield and all my hopes of revisiting that country were dashed.

The author Dr. Go Hirai was a young student when he made his first foray into the Hindu Kush in the 1960's, as a member of the Hiroshima University Mountaineering Club. At that time, Afghanistan enjoyed a rare period of peace. But when the Soviets invaded and occupied Afghanistan, travel restrictions became so tight that Dr. Hirai was forced to shift his mountaineering and research activities further east to Chitral in the Northwest Frontier Province (Currently Khyber Pakhtunkhwa) of Pakistan, near the border with Afghanistan. The Wakhan Corridor lies to the immediate northwest of Chitral.

In 1988, when the Soviet forces, considerably weakened and demoralized, withdrew from Afghanistan, peace returned to the northern parts of Afghanistan. Just 10 years after the withdrawal of the Soviet forces, in 1998 Dr. Hirai changed the focus of his research to the Wakhan Corridor, though the area remained dangerous. His choice proved to be a good one.

Unlike the southern parts of Afghanistan where the Pashtun tribes prevail, the Japanese were well received by the people of northern Afghanistan. Dr. Hirai's calm disposition must have had a particular appeal to the local residents, giving him ready access to the region. It is no wonder that Dr. Hirai was welcomed, because in remote areas travelers will be judged by their character rather than by their appearance. Just to the north in Tajikistan, a Japanese had been killed a few years earlier.

Unexpectedly the tragedy of 9/11 occurred, shattering the short period of peace that Afghanistan had enjoyed. Afghanistan became the forefront of America's war against terrorism. The country of my dreams was once again shattered and plunged into hell. By pure coincidence, the day after 9/11, I was on my way from India to Ladakh. At that time, the airport in New Delhi was completely deserted.

I am always amazed at how indefatigable a traveler Dr. Hirai is. Dr. Hirai can remain firm and in control even in the most difficult situations, and he always seems to get his way. Dr. Hirai may come across as a reckless person to some, but his prudence has underpinned his successful visits to a country where there is little regard for human life. I deeply respect Dr. Hirai for his achievements.

In the spring of 2000, shortly before this remote area of Afghanistan was to experience a major upheaval, I traveled from north to south along the border of Afghanistan and Pakistan, in the Ghandara region, visiting Peshawar and the Khyber Pass en route. On that occasion, I was guided by a soldier of the Pakistan Army who was accompanied by an Afghan soldier. The area had changed dramatically, and it was only a few months after that visit that the two giant Buddhas of Bamiyan were destroyed by the Taliban. At the time of my visit, my local contacts who had foreseen such an attack, suggested that the Buddhist archeological relics be sent to Japan for safeguarding. Unfortunately, perhaps due to lack of political clout, the Japanese government refused to consider this proposal.

The Wakhan Corridor is so remote that even those who may have some knowledge about the history and geography of Afghanistan do not understand the significance of this area. How can we encourage others to learn more about this inaccessible region? The answer was obvious. The unspoiled beauty and remoteness of this region can best be conveyed by photographs.

These were my thoughts when I suggested to Dr. Hirai that he publish a book of photographs to accompany a detailed travelogue which he had already published. I also suggested that Sir Aurel Stein's "Mountain Panoramas from the Pamirs and

Kuen Lun," (London 1908. published by the Royal Geographic Society) would be worth emulating. This short, 40 page report contains many panoramic photographs of the Pamirs and the Kun Lun Range, giving a good birds-eye view of the entire region. The photo captions and drawings contained in the report provide valuable information regarding geographical sites, names and descriptions. Fortunately, Dr. Hirai heeded my advice, and subsequently devoted his attention to taking photographs of the Wakhan area.

His efforts, however, were apparently thwarted one year when all three cameras that he had taken along with great trouble, failed him completely due to mechanical problems. Another year, Dr. Hirai had taken some valuable pictures only to find in dismay that they had disappeared from the memory device. Though I am not an experienced photographer, I have also experienced such mishaps, so when I travel, I make it a point to draw sketches. Recently when I traveled to Tibet I drew sketches whenever we took a break at the top of a pass. It takes me about 30 minutes to complete one rough sketch and more than an hour to draw a complete sketch, so when I am traveling in a group I never have enough time. Whereas I tend to travel with a group of people, Dr. Hirai always travels solo, which is the best way to travel.

Every photograph contained in this publication is valuable and novel. The panoramic photograph of Lake Victoria, and of the major and minor tributaries that form the headwaters of the Oxus River are exceedingly valuable. The photographs are impressive because they provide first hand evidence of a land that lures many, but few can hope to travel. As a friend, I am confident that each photograph will help the reader appreciate the achievements of Dr. Hirai as one of the few who have traveled so extensively in the Wakhan Corridor.

January 1, 2011

はじめに

　中央アジアに在る乾燥した地、イスラーム教徒の国,日本語表記でアフガニスタン・イスラム共和国・通称アフガーニスターン（以下アフガーン）。私達にはイラク以上に繰り返される、血生臭いテロが頻発している国と謂う響きが強い。ここ4半世紀と少しの間に、クーデターもしくは武力による8回の政権変動、うち4回は前首脳の処刑死による政権交替。しかも同一形態の政権でも、僅か1年余の間に2回もの血による交代政変。1979年に侵攻したソ連軍は1989年に完全撤退し、その後にラバニー大統領誕生、相次ぐ内戦を経て、パーキスターン軍部の後押しで1996年にはターリバーン政権樹立。

　2001年9月9日アルカイーダの差し金と思われるテロで、いわゆる北部同盟アーメード・シャー・マスウド総司令官が死亡。11日にニューヨークの多発テロ勃発。その主謀者ウサマ・ビン・ラーディンを匿うターリバーンに対し、10月にアメリカが攻撃を開始し、その助力で、北部同盟軍がターリバーンを駆逐した。その後カルザイ氏が大統領に就任し、2010年に2期目の政権を担っている。その間に国名は6度も変更されている。これほど激動した国は珍しい。

　2011年5月にはビン・ラーディンが隣国パーキスターンの首都近くの隠れ家で、アメリカ海軍特殊部隊により処刑（射殺）された。7月にはISAFからアフガーン側に治安維持権限の移譲が開始されたが、ターリバーンによる、大統領の実弟や要人、9月にはターリバーンとの和平交渉の要である、ラバニー前大統領の暗殺やアメリカ大使館への襲撃などのテロが続き、治安維持の前途は遙か遠い。

　その後も政府とタリバーン側との和平交渉は進展せず、その一方で2014年4月に任期終了のカルザイ大統領は、12月のアメリカ軍戦闘部隊の完全撤収に伴う、一連の協定に署名せず（2014年3月現在）、4月の新大統領選出まで問題は繰越される見込みである。

　そんな戦火にまみれる国のなかに、全く無縁の平和郷がある。それがワハーン回廊であり、本書の舞台でもある。アフガーンの東北端に、東西に虫垂突起（いわゆる 盲腸）のように細長く東西に延びる高所渓谷地帯がある。その形状からワハーン"回廊"とも称ばれている。西の起点イシュカシェムから東西長約300km、南北幅は狭い所でほぼ15km余、広い所でも約65kmである。

　南縁は氷雪の東部ヒンドゥクシュ山脈で旧インド（現パーキスターン）、北縁はオクサス河中流（アーブ・イ・バンジ）、支流（大）パミール河とワハーン山脈の東部で旧ロシア帝国・旧ソ連（現タジキスターン）及び東南端を旧シナ（現中国）に接している。

　アフガーンでは、イシュカシェムからオクサス河沿いに東に約150kmのサルハッドまでをワハーン、以東を小パミールとワフジールに、（大）パミール河と本流との合流点の少し上流のガズ フーン北辺（タジキスターンのキフゥンの対岸）までをワハーン、以東を大パミールとしている。また、タジキスターンでも同様に、キフゥン（この地にランガール・"聖所"が在るので、ランガールとよばれる事も多い）までをワハーンとしている。そしてここより上流域を大パミールとしている。オーレル・スタイン卿や他の19世紀末前後の報告書に、ランガール・キシュトとあるのは、この事の誤聞記であるかも知れない。なお、ここには旧ソ連軍がアフガーンに侵攻した翌1980年に、（大）パミール河に架かた唯一の（戦車が通れる）橋が残されている。G.N.カーゾン卿は、上記の部分を大・小パミールとパミール・イ・ワハーンの3部に分けている。

　これらアフガーン・パミール（以下ア・パミール）は全パミールの約10分の1を占め、全パミールの最南端に位置している。

　往時は、シルク ロードの一幹線であり、近辺の領域を含めると、紀元前に張騫氏、4世紀末に法顕法師、6世紀に宋雲と彗生法師、642年に唐の玄奘（三蔵）法師、747年に高仙芝将軍、1274年頃にベネチアのマルコ ポーロ氏などが、歴史にその名をとどめている。

　19世紀に入ると1838年2月19日、J. ウッド大尉（英印海軍）のビクトリア湖（大龍池・大湖・シル・イ・クル又はゾルクル）の（再）発見を初めとする近代的探検時代に入り、同時にこの周辺地は、グレート・ゲームの名で知られる、英・露の二大帝国の覇権角遂の場となり、1895年5〜8月、両国による国境策定委員会により、ワハーン回廊が、緩衝地帯として、アフガーン領となった。この時代のア・パミールの登場者としてT. E. ゴードン中佐（英陸軍）、F.E.ヤングハズバンド大尉（英印陸軍）、イオノフ大佐（ロシア帝国陸軍）やカーゾン卿（英）（後インド副王）など、軍人を主に少かならぬ人々がスポットされる。

以後、その地政的背景から外国人の入域は厳しく制限され、過酷な地理的環境も伴って、20世紀前半では、オーレル・スタイン卿（英）（1906年）、その周辺で同氏（1915年）、H.W.ティルマン氏（英）（1947年、不法入国で逮捕）、後半では数える程の少ない人達が入域しているに過ぎない。

1970年前後から20世紀末にかけての、ア・パミールに関する報告は身近に多くなく、1967年・1968年のミショー夫妻（仏）、1971年・1972年のC.M.ナウマン博士（カーブル大隊）ら、1971年当時の在カーブル英国大使夫妻と同行したC・グレイ・ウィルソン博士ら、1972 ～ 1974年のアフガーン・ウズベク族のM.N.M.シャラーニ博士（ワシントン大学）、グラデュー氏夫妻（仏）（1998年）ぐらいと少ない。

なおサルハッド周辺のワハーン山脈の核心部には、登山隊として1971年の私達広島大学医学部山岳会隊を初め、イタリアのC.Aピネリー博士隊、ポーランド隊、1975年のオーストリアのR.S.ドゥ・グランツ博士隊などが入域している。

前記 ゴートン中佐、ヤングハズバンド大尉、カーゾン卿とティルマン氏の記録には和訳があるが、後者を除くと現在とは相当離れている19世紀後半のものである。

近年、短期間の許可でワフジール峠やチャクマク・ティン湖など、小パミール周辺を訪れる小グループを見かけるようになった。2007年には、アフガーン トゥーリスト オーガネイションによる、ゾル クル中畔までの騎馬旅行が催されている。

20世紀後半の報告は、学術的報告か小パミールの一部でのキルギス人の生活に関する写真記録に限られている。

最近 "ワハーン" を冠した数冊が見られるが、ワハーンに関する部分は短く、綜説的な記述に終わっている。

他にオクサス河の真の水源を求めて、タジキスターン側のゾル クル、アフガーン側ではチャクマク・ティン湖周辺やワフジール峠を訪れた記録が出版されているが、地理的飛躍が大きく、記述も簡素で現地を知る私にも理解が難しい。なお回廊を縦断したとする写真集もあるが、小パミール東部の手前までのもので、大パミールへは及んでない。これらはすべて外国語によるものであり、隔靴掻痒の感を拭いえない。また東方見聞録の和訳書の中には、大湖（ゾル クル）に関する注釈で、同定に誤りがあるものも見受けられる。

私は幸運にも "あとがき" で述べるように、1969・1971年にワハーンで2度の登山ができた。その後30年の空白を圣て1999年から続けて3夏、その後も2011年までの夏までに計8回、ア・パミールを縦横に踏査することができた。2005・2006年には、同域に接するタジキスターンの地も踏め、両国に住むキルギス人の生活の違いも垣間の見聞ができた。また2010年には、ワフジール峠に南接する峠で、オクサス河の眞の源（?）かも知れない湖畔に立てた。

またこれらの間に、紀元前後と思われる拝火教徒の城趾（?）、スタイン卿が推定した、8世紀に唐の高仙芝軍の一隊が辿った "北谷" ルートと確信できろ谷路や同軍が攻略した山頂の連雲堡趾を踏めた。更に、現地住民が僅か乍ら利用している、東部ヒンドゥクシュ山脈を越えてワハーン回廊に通じる7峠、大、小パミールを結ぶワハーン山脈越えの5峠とパミール・イ・ワハーン（ワフジール）からタ-グドゥムバシュ パミール（シナ）へ向かう2峠を踏むか抜ける事が出来た。本書は学術的報告ではなく、ワハーン回廊、特にア・パミールの自然とそこに息づくキルギス人の生活・習慣の素顔を紹介したいと念じたものである。写真はアートを求めたものではなく、被写体を素直に伝えることに主眼を置いた。説明はなるべく簡単に加えた。

昔ながらの暮らしを続けてきた、ア・パミールのキルギス人の生活は、ここ数年ほどの間に、少なからぬ変化がみられる。太陽光発電による電燈とテレビの出現である。2004年7月、いづれも小パミールで、電燈は3軒のユルトで、テレビは別の1軒でお目にかかった。電燈は石油ランプと同じ程度の暗いもので、テレビは発動機発電によるビデオ専用であった。後者はラーマン クル脱国後のア・パミールで随一の富裕者となった、アパンディ ボイ（図81）（1））のユルトであった。2007年には小パミールとワフジールで、半数過ぎのユルトに電燈がつき（但し各ユルトに一ヶ）、3軒のユルトではパラボラ アンテナで近隣国からの受像ができ、電源は大型化した受光パネルに変わっていた（図68））。

科学的調査は2 ～ 3の資料を持ち帰り、専門家により同定・分析がなされ、成績は他の資料と共に83）に記載した。

蝶の採集は殆んど毎回、主にイシュムルグとサルハッドからボザイ グムバースの間およびワフジール峠で行い、酒井成司氏（日本鱗翅学会員）により分類・同定

はじめに

され、2010年分については本書に収録した。なお2010年の資料のうち、アフガーンでのタテハチョウ科ヒョウモンモドキ属の一新亜種の副模式標本（paratype of *Melitaea pallas hirai* Sakai）が、同氏のご高配により大英博物館（現ロンドン自然史博物館 The Natural History Museum, London, England）の所蔵に加えられた。

温泉に関しては、広島市衛生研究所と広島県保健環境センター、キルギス人の家畜の飼料塩に関しては、広島市衛生研究所で分析された。

カラ ビル（黒い峠）で採取した黒い小岩石は、沖村雄二博士（広島大学名誉教授・広島大学中部アフガニスタン学術調査隊員1969）により同定された。脂臀羊、マルコ ポーロ羊に関する説明には、（同じく）伊藤敏男博士にご添削を頂いた。

魚類は主にチャクマク・ティン湖及び周辺の渓流で10匹前後捕獲し、東京国立博物館新宿分館と寺島彰氏を介して（現在精査中）京都大学に保管されている。

頭痛を訴えるキルギス人達の聖皮膚動脈血ヘモグロビン酸素飽和度と血圧を測定した。

なおワフジール峠で採取したマルコ ポーロ羊の角付き頭蓋骨は広島大学総合博物館に寄贈した。

金子民雄博士には前著に続き序文を早々に賜った。本書に使用した地図は、長岡正利氏（もと国土地理院）のご高配とご指導によるものである。

山座の同定と標高はポーランドのJ.Wala氏（故吉沢一郎氏を介して）と宮森常雄氏（日本山岳会員）のご教示によった。

写真の構成および配列など本書の構成のすべては紺野昇氏（前中国新聞社写真部長、日本山岳会員）に、ご高慮とご高配を頂いた。

英文対訳は井手マヤ女史のご好意によるものである。因みに女史は日本人として初めて、タジキスターン側のビクトリア湖畔に達し（2005年7月）、厳冬期（2009年12月）の東端到達を含め、3度（いづれも本多海太郎氏同行）同湖のタジキスターン側を踏んでいる。同時にスタイン卿の著作の精通者でもある。

収載した図譜は、[　]を付したものを除いて、私の撮影によるものである。年月を記したもの以外はすべて1999年以後のものである。撮影地は写真のそばの（　）に記し、冒頭の地図IIIに写真の標題番号で示した。キルギス人の生活に関しては黄色を付した。

なお金子民雄先生のご高慮により、古い貴重な蔵書(原書)のなかから、主に19世紀のパミールとワハーンに関する文献の抄録などを頂いた。[付]として掲載させて頂いたが、本書の絶好の参考書である。

凡　例

本文中の登場人物の敬称は文の構成上省略させて頂いた。高度の標記は、数字のみのものは成書や地図に掲載されている標高（海抜）の数値で、GPSによる数値にはcaを付した。

現地語の日本語表記はなるべく現地発音に近い標記にした。アフガーニスターン（アフガニスタン）、アフガーン（アフガン）、カーブル（カブール）、ワハーン（ワハン）、アームー ダリアー（アムダリア）、ターリバーン（タリバン）などである。

なおパーミールは慣用されているパミールとした。現地語の地名や単語の末尾の（Ⓓ）はダリー、Ⓦ はワヒ、Ⓚ はキルギス語、Ⓒ はチトラール（コワール）語、又 Ⓖ はドイツ語、Ⓢ はスペイン語であることを示す。

現地語の英語化は、縄田鉄男博士（故人、東京外語大学名誉教授、広島大学中部アフガニスタン学術調査隊1969特別隊員）の御教示によるダリー以外は、専門的語学履修歴のない通訳サフューラ君によるもので、正鵠を射てないものが多々ある可能性があることをお断りし、ご叱正を頂ければ幸甚である。

2014年3月

The Islamic Republic of Afghanistan, an arid country of Muslims, lies in the heart of Central Asia. In the minds of most Japanese, Afghanistan evokes images of bloody terrorist attacks that occur so frequently that even the situation in Iraq pales in comparison. During the last twenty-five years, the government has changed eight times following armed conflict, of which four times the incumbent prime minister was executed in the aftermath of a change in government. The political situation has been so unstable that even under the same ruling party, twice within a span of one year the government was overthrown violently.

The Soviet Union, which invaded Afghanistan in 1979, was forced to withdraw in 1989. The Rabbani Government, established in the aftermath of the Soviet army withdrawal, could not contain the civil war which raged on until 1996 when the Taliban, with the backing of the Pakistan Military, took control of the government. Ahmad Shah Masoud, military commander and political leader of the Northern Alliance, was assassinated by two Arab al-Qaeda suicide bombers on September 9, 2001, just two days before the attack on the Twin Towers in New York on September 11, 2001. In retaliation, one month later in October, the US-led forces commenced their military operations in Afghanistan, routing out the Taliban with the support of the Northern Alliance. President Karzai, who was immediately installed by the US-led coalition forces, is now serving his second term in office as of 2011. During this period, the official name of the country has changed six times. There are few countries that have seen so much upheaval as Afghanistan.

In May 2011, Osama Bin Laden was executed (shot to death) in his hideout by US Marine Special Forces in the outskirts of Islamabad, the capital of Pakistan. In July, 2011 the responsibility for security in Afghan was delegated by ISAF to the Afghan police and military. Shortly after, the brother of President Karzai and other officials were assassinated by the Taliban. In September 2011, former Prime Minister Rabanni, who was instrumental in negotiating a peace settlement with the Taliban, was assassinated. At around the same time, the US embassy in Kabul was attacked by terrorists. These incidents once again highlight the difficulty of achieving peace in that country.

Since then, the Government's peace negotiations with the Taliban has not progressed.

As of March, President Karzai, whose term ends 2014 April, has refused to sign a series of status of force agreements which would allow American troops to remain in Afghanistan after the scheduled withdrawal of NATO forces from Afghanistan in the end of 2014. It is most likely that those agreements will not be finalized until the next president of Afghanistan is elected. The prospect of peace remains ever elusive.

Despite the turmoil in most areas of Afghan, there is an isolated, remote pocket where peace reigns and which is the focus of this book. The Wakhan Corridor is a high altitude valley, located in the northeastern fringe of Afghanistan. Shaped like a human appendix (hence called the Corridor) the valley thrusts from west to east starting at Ishkashim for a length of 300 kilometers and a width that varies from 15 kilometers to 65 kilometers.

The Wakhan Corridor is wedged in between the snow-covered peaks of the Eastern Hindu Kush range in Pakistan to the south (or historically with British India), and to the north by the mid-stream of the Oxus River (Ab-i-i-Panj) and its tributary, the (Great) Pamir River, and the Wakhan Mountain Range. The Wakhan Mountain Range forms the border between Tajikistan (former Soviet Union) and Afghanistan at its eastern extremety. The Wakhan is also bordered by China to the southeast. The Wakhan starts from its western gateway, Ishkashim and stretches for 150 kilometers along the main course of the Panj (Oxus) to the east until it reaches Sarhad. Regions further east beyond Sarhad are known as the (Little) Pamir and the Wakhjir. On the Afghan side, the name Wakhan is applied to the area up to Gazkhun which is slightly upstream from the confluence of the (Great) Pamir River and the Panj (right across the river from Kikhun on the Tajik side of the river). All regions east of Gazkhun are known as the Great Pamir. On the Tajikistan side, the name Wakhan is applied to the area between Ishkashim and Kikhun. (In Kikhun since there is a holy place or " Langar" , the place is also called Langar). All the areas further east are called the Great Pamir. Sir Aurel Stein, as well as most explorers who reported about this region in the late 19th century, might have mistakenly named this place Langar Kisht. At this point only one bridge remains that spans the (Great) Pamir River and which is broad enough for tanks to cross.

It was built by River and which is broad enough for tanks to cross. It was built by the former Soviet Army in 1980, one year after the Soviet invasion of Afghanistan.

Lord G.N. Curzon divides the valley into three parts, the Little Pamir, the Great Pamir and the Pamir-i-Wakhan.

The Afghan Pamirs accounts for one tenth of the entire Pamirs region in geographical area and is located along its southern rim.

Historically, the Wakhan Corridor was a major thoroughfare of the Silk Road, travelled by such historically renowned figures as Zang Qian before Christ, Fa-fian in the end of the 4th century, and Sung-yun with Hwui-sang in the 6th century. Hsü ang-tsang passed through the valley in the year A.D. 642 during the Tang dynasty, the

Preface

Chinese General Kao Hsien-chih in A.D.747, and the Venetian traveler Marco Polo in A.D. 1274.

In the 19th century a frenzy of explorations took place in this area. On February 19th, 1838, Lieutenant John Wood of the British Indian Navy became the first Westerner to reach the shore of Lake Victoria (current Zor Kul, meaning the Great Lake, and known in historical records as the Great Dragon Lake). In those days the Russian Empire and the British Empire competed fiercely for supremacy over Central Asia in a battle that was to be called "The Great Game". Between May and August 1895, the Boundary Commission designated the Wakhan Valley (Corridor) as a buffer zone to be officially recognized as Afghan territory. The Wakhan Corridor (especially the Afghan Pamirs) was subsequently visited by famous explorers, many on military expeditions led by Lieutenant Colonel T.E. Gordon, Captain F.E. Younghusband (British Indian Army), Colonel Yonoff (Czarist Russia) and Sir G.N. Curzon, who later became Viceroy of British India, among others. Since then, however, the Wakhan has been off limits to ordinary travelers because of the sensitive geopolitical situation of the region. The difficult terrain and climate ensured that the area would remain inaccessible as well. During the early 20th century, the few who did venture into this bleak, desolate valley included Sir Aurel Stein (1906), and Mr. H.W. Tillman, who was arrested for illegal entry in 1947. Even by the end of the 20th century only a few visitors had set foot in the Wakhan, and there were even fewer reports that were published regarding the Afghan Pamirs.

From around 1970 till the end of the 20th century, the region was visited sporadically by a handful of visitors, most notably by the married couple, Sabrina and Roland Michaud (France) in 1967-1968, a team led by Dr. C.M. Naumann as a member of the Kabul University Mission in 1971-1972, and Dr. C. Gray Wilson, who accompanied the UK Ambassador to Afghanistan and his wife in 1971. Dr. M.N.M. Sharani, an Uzbek Afghan (1972-1974) (Washington State University) and Mr. and Mrs. Gradue. also visited the valley in 1998.

The innermost areas of the Wakhan northwest of Sarhad have been trodden by a number of mountaineering expeditions. In 1971, the Medical Alpine Club of Hiroshima University sent one of the first mountaineering expeditions to climb the Wakhan Mountain Range, which I had the good fortune of participating in. Other pioneers included the Italian Expedition led by C.A. Pinelli, the Poland expedition and in 1975 the Austrian Expedition under R.S. Due Granz.

The Japanese translations of the exploration reports written by Lieutenant Colonel Gordon, Captain Younghusband, Sir Curzon and Mr. Tilman have been available for many years now. Most of these reports, with the exception of Tilman's, were published in the 19th century, when the situation was quite different from what they are today.

Recently I have come across small groups of tourists traveling on short-term visas to the Wakhjir Pass and to Lake Chaqmak-tin. In 2007, the Afghan Tourist Organization was offering tours on horseback to Zor Kul.

Most of the publications since the late 20th century regarding Wakhan have either been academic journal articles or photograph books focused on the lifestyles of the Kyrgyz living in the Little Pamir.

Lately I have noticed a few books with the name Wakhan in their titles, but the contents related to Wakhan are short, and only general in description.

There are also some books that have been published recently by authors who claim to have visited Zor Kul on the Tajikistan side, and Chaqmak-tin Lake and the Wakhjir Pass on the Afghan side, to confirm the source of the Oxus.

Being a frequent traveler of that area, I must say that without exception, the authors do not provide sufficient details as to the routes they took to reach these places.

Furthermore, the descriptions of the geographic sites are too inaccurate to verify. An author of a photograph book claims to have visited the entire length of the Wakhan Valley, but the photographs indicate that the author has barely reached the east part of the Little Pamir, and has obviously not entered the Great Pamir. The books which I am referring to were written by Americans, British or Europeans who obviously lack knowledge about the Wakhan There are many, different Japanese translations of "Marco Polo's Travels", some of which have footnotes that misrepresent the location of Victoria Lake or Zor Kul.

As I have written in the epilogue, I was fortunate to have had the opportunity to visit the Wakhan twice, in 1969 and in 1971, as a member of a mountaineering expedition. From 1999, thirty years later after those first visits, I spent three consecutive summers in the Afghan Pamirs, followed by a total of eight trips until the summer of 2011 when I visited many different parts of the Afghan Pamirs. In 2005 and 2006, I visited the Tajikistan side of the Wakhan, the Great Pamir and the Little Pamir, and was able to compare the different lifestyles of the Kyrgyz nomads. In 2010, I was able to reach the lake that could be the true source of the Oxus River, since it is located right under a pass that is adjacent to the southern side of the Wakhjir Pass.

Also over the years I was able to visit the ruins of a fortress that is believed to have been built by Zoroastrians around the time of Christ's birth. I also visited a valley that Sir Aurel Stein identified as being the "north valley" through which the Chinese general Kao Hsien-Chih led his troops into Wakhan, and the remains of the Tibetan stronghold Lien-yun-po perched on a hilltop, which was defeated by the Chinese general.

Furthermore, I was able to either reach the crest of, or to cross over seven passes that led into the Wakhan Corridor from the Eastern Hindu Kush Range, five passes that linked the Great Pamir to the Little Pamir via the Wakhan range, and two passes that connected the Pamir-i-Wakhan (Wakhjir) to the Taghdumbash Pamir.

This photographic travelogue is not meant to be an academic report. It is an endeavor on my part to introduce the natural environment of the Wakhan Corridor, and the lifestyle and customs of the nomadic Kyrgyz people who make this place so special.

Rather than being a work of art, the photographs are a straightforward record of the scenes and people that the camera lens has captured. The accompanying photo captions have been kept as simple as possible.

The traditional lifestyle of the Kyrgyz people living in the Afghan Pamirs has been changing over these last few years with the introduction of solar -generated electricity and television. In July 2004, in the Little Pamir I saw three yurts alight with solar-powered electricity, and one yurt even had a television. The electric lamp was as weak as a kerosene lamp. A generator powered the television which could only be used to play video recordings. The yurt with the television was owned at that time by Apandi Boi (fig. 81)(1)), the richest man in the entire Afghan Pamirs. He succeeded Rahman Qul, who lives in exile today. By 2007, more than half of all the yurts in the Little Pamir and the Wakhjir had solar -powered electricity (one for each yurt) and 3 yurts had parabolic antennas that could receive broadcast transmissions from neighboring countries, the power source of which was a large photovoltaic panel (fig. 68)).

As part of my scientific survey, I have been collecting several kinds of specimens of butterflies and fishes which have been analyzed by experts. The list of specimens collected during my visits, and the analysis of the findings can be found in 83). The butterflies were mainly captured during several visits to the vicinity of Ishmurg, between Sarhad and Bozai Gumbaz, and at the Wakhjir Pass. Mr. Seiji Sakai, a member of the Lepidopterological Society of Japan, was kind enough to analyze and categorize the butterfly specimens. The butterflies gathered during 2010 are recorded in this book. Of the butterfly specimens brought back in 2010, The Para type Melitaea Pallas hirai Sakai ssp.nov. was added to the butterfly collection of the London Natural History Museum of the British Museum as recommended by Mr. Sakai. The properties of the hot springs were analyzed by the Hiroshima City Institute of Hygiene, and the Hiroshima Prefectural Technology Research Institute Health and Environment. The salt that the Kyrgyz nomads feed to their animals was analyzed by the Hiroshima City Institute of Hygiene.

The black pebbles that I collected at Qara Bel (black pass) were analyzed by Dr. Yuuji Okimura, Professor Emeritus of Hiroshima University (a member of the Hiroshima University Scientific Expedition to Central Afghanistan 1969). Dr. Toshio Ito, Professor Emeritus of Hiroshima University (a member of Hiroshima University Scientific Expedition to Central Afghanistan 1969) kindly proof -read my explanations concerning the fat-rumped sheep, and Marco Polo sheep.

I was able to capture around 10 fish specimen in Chaqmak-tin Lake and the surrounding streams. The fish specimens were donated to the Tokyo National Museum of Nature and Science (Shinjuku Branch),and to Kyoto University through the good efforts of Mr. Akira Terashima. I measured the blood pressure and the degree of oxygen saturation of the hemoglobin in the arterial blood drawn intravenously from a number of Kirgiz who were suffering from headaches. I also donated a skull of the Marco Polo sheep with its horns attached , which I brought back from the Wakhjir Pass to the Hiroshima University Museum. from a number of Kirgiz who were suffering from headaches.

I also donated a skull of the Marco Polo sheep with its horns attached, which I brought back from the Wakhjir Pass to the Hiroshima University Museum.

My gratitude goes to Dr. Tamio Kaneko for taking the time to write the introduction for this work. Dr. Kaneko also kindly wrote the introduction for my first book. A special thanks goes to Mr. Masatoshi Nagaoka (the former a staff member of the Geographical Information Authority of Japan) for helping me prepare the maps for this book.

I am indebted to Mr. J. Wala from Poland (through Mr. Ichiro Yoshizawa, who is deceased) and Mr. Tsuneo Miyamori (a member of the Japanese Alpine Club), who were kind enough to help me identify the mountains and their altitudes

I would also like to thank Mr. Noboru Konno, the former head of the Department of Photography, Chugoku Newspaper Company, and a member of the Japanese Alpine Club, for editing and organizing the layout of the photographs.

I would like to express my appreciation to Ms. Maya Ide for her competent English translation of the Japanese text. Ms. Maya Ide (together with Mr. Kaitaro Honda) was the first Japanese to reach the shore of Lake Victoria (Zor Kul) from the Tajikistan side in August 2005. She, together with Mr. Kaitaro Honda, has visited Zor Kul three times, including a trip in mid- winter to the eastern end of Lake Zor Kul (December 2009). Ms. Ide is also an avid reader of Sir Aurel Stein's works. With first-hand knowledge of the Wakhan and Pamirs, she has proved to be the most suitable translator for this work.

All photographs shown in this book were taken by this author except when bracketed. [ ] are shown to indicate the source. The photographs were taken after 1999, unless the dates have been also specified. The location where the photographs were The mapIII shown at the beginning shows the position of the sites as well. The photographs related to the lifestyle of the Kirgiz are indicated with yellow marks.

Dr. Tamio Kaneko very kindly sent me the summaries of his collection of books, most of which are valuable originals, that are mainly related to the 19th century Pamirs and Wakhan. These are in the appendix and should provide a good reference point for this book.

Legend

The local names of places have been phonetically transcribed in Japanese with due care taken so that they are as close to the original pronunciation as possible. The original language of the words appearing in the text, is indicated as follows:

(Ⓓ) for Dali, (Ⓦ) for Wakhi, (Ⓚ) for Kyrgyz, (Ⓒ) for Chitral (kowal), (Ⓖ) for German and (Ⓢ) for Spanish.

Regarding the English transcription and translation of the local languages,with respect to Dali, I have received helpful advice from Dr. Tetsuo Naswata, Professor Emeritus of Tokyo University Foreign Studies, and a special member of the Hiroshima University Scientific Expedition to Central Afghanistan 1969, the departed. With the exception of the Dali, other local languages were translated by Safiullah John who never received a formal English education, and therefore the English transcription and translation may not always be correct. Any correction by the readers will be greatly appreciated.

2014. March

アフガーン
Afghanistan

（1）諸国に囲まれるアフガーン

アフガーンの総人口は約3,439万人[1]（2010年7月）で、アフガーンと称されるパシュトゥーン族を初め、10余の諸民族で構成される多民族国家である。2～3の統計[1)2)3)]から大まかにみると、パシュトゥーン：40～60%、ハザーラ15%、タジック：10～27%、ウズベック：6～9%、トルコメン、アイマック、ヌーリスタニなどの諸民族：8%。ワハーンに定住するワヒは約10,000人足らず、ア・パミールに住むキルギス人は、約1000人である。

言語も民族同様に多種であるが、公用語はパシュートゥーとダリー（ペルシャ語のアフガーン方言）の2つである。

国教はイスラーム教で大半がスンニ派、次いでシーア派で最も少ないのがイスマーイーリ派である。

(1) Afghan being surrounded by many countryries

As of July, 2010, the population of Afghanistan is 3439 million[1] . There are 10 different ethnic groups in Afghanistan, the distribution of which varies according to which statistic[2)3)] is being used. Pashtuns known as Afghans account for 40% to 60% of the total population, Tajiks 10% to 27%, Hazaras 15%, Uzbeks 6%-9%, and Turkmen, Aimaq, Nuristanis and other minorities combined account for 8% of the total population. There are less than 10000 Wakhis that live in Wakhan (until Sarhad) and about 1000 Kyrgyz that live in Afghan Pamirs.

Afghanistan is not only ethnically diverse but many different languages ane spoken as well. The two official languages are Pashtun and Dali (Afghan dialect of Persian)

The state religion is Islam, with the majority of the population belonging to the Sunni sect, followed by the Shiah Sect. The Ismaili sect of Islam has the least number of followers.

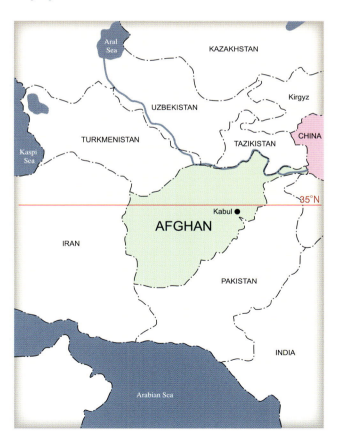

（2）オクサス河の源流　　(2) The source of the Oxus River

（図 34），35）参照）　　(Refer to fig .34),35))

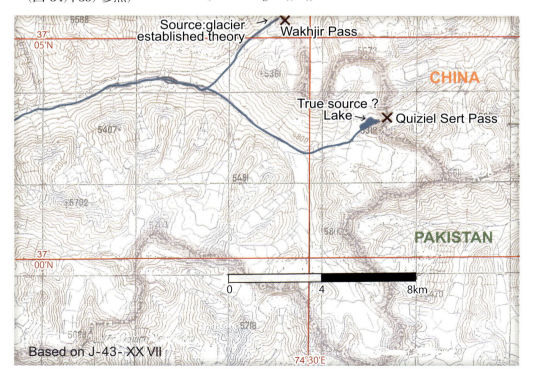

Based on J-43- XX VII

ワハーンへ
To the Wakhan

(1) 中心部の雑踏

首都カーブルの人口は年々増加し、ある新聞[4)]によると400万人（2008年）とされる。

中心部のブルー モスク周辺は、人・人・人・。40年前の静寂な佇まいからは、想像も付かない人込みだ。

(1) Mayhem in the center

The population of Kabul, the capital, is increasing year by year, which according to a Japanese newspaper,[4)] stood at 4 million as of 2008.

The Blue Mosque in central Kabul is always teeming with crowds of people so densely packed it is hard to imagine that only 40 years ago this was one of the quieter areas of Kabul.

（マスジドゥ プル ハスティ近くのバザール / A bazar near Masjide Pule Khesti）

（2）夏のカーブルは果物の宝庫

　夏には、各地から多くの果物が集荷されてくる。ハルブーザ、水瓜、葡萄、桃、杏やリンゴなど、多種の甘い果物が店頭に並ぶ。特にハルブーザ（メロンの一種）は、お奨めの一品だ。アフガーン原産の薬用植物である柘榴と人参も、店頭でジュースで飲める。

(2) Fruits abound in Kabul during the summer

　During the summer, Kabul's markets are stacked with abundant fruit that have been brought to the capital from different parts of Afghanistan. Kharbuza (D) (a type of melon), watermelons, grapes, peaches, apricots and apples are among the many sweet fruit sold at the fruit stands.TheKharbuza is particularly recommended for its succulent and delicious taste. Also, juice stands sell pomegranate, carrotand other vegetable/ fruit juice that have medicinal use.

（シャリナウ / Shar-i-・Naw）

（3）街角の女性（40年前）

　西欧式のドレスで颯爽と

(3) Urban women (40 years ago.)

　The light strides of an Afghan woman dressed in western attire.

(1969.6)

（スピンザールホテル近く /
Near the Spinzar Hotel 2009）

（4）街角の女性（現今）

　40年前に比べ、女子学生を除くと圧倒的にチャドリ姿が多い。多くはライト・ブルー色、時に黒や黄色も見られる。ターリバーン時代の影響か。

(4) Urban women (today.)

　Many more women are veiled today than was so 40 years ago. Many wear full-length veils that are usually light blue in color, but some wear black or yellow veils called Cadori (pro-nunciation, Chadri).
　Does the Taliban influence still prevail?

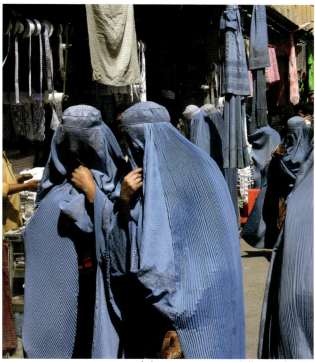

（プル ハシャティ モスク北のバザール /
The bazar north of the Pul khesti mosque）

2) Kotal-e-Salang　サーラング峠
Salang Pass

（最高地のトンネルの北直下 / Right under the northern side of the tunnel where the road reaches its highest altitude）

"コータル"（Ⓓ）は"峠"の意味。カーブルから北へ約100km。1961年に旧ソ連が建設した北に向かう幹線道路に在るサーラング峠。最高地のトンネルは標高3400m、長さ2.5km。1969年前後にカーブルの市民から、「近い内にこの道を通って、ソ連軍の戦車がやってくる」と謂う噂話を聞いた。それは10年後の1979年12月27日に悪夢の正夢となった。

泥沼戦闘の10年後、主にアメリカの援助を受けた、多くのムジャヒデイディーン(イスラーム戦士)の執拗な抵抗に、力尽きたソ連軍は、同じ道を辿り撤退して去った。パンジ シニール渓谷を守り抜いたアフメード・シャー・マスウドの名は輝いている。

Kotal "（Ⓓ）means pass. The Salang Pass is located 100 kilometers north of Kabul and is on a major north-south connection that was built by the former Soviet Union in 1961.

The Salang tunnel reaches an altitude of 3400 meters and is 2.5 km long. Around 1969 I heard rumors in Kabul that the Soviet Union was preparing to send military tanks rumbling down the Salang Pass. Ten years later in December 27th, 1979 that nightmarish rumor turned into reality .

In 1989, ten years after the Soviet invasion of Afghanistan, the Mujahideen (Jihadists, or Muslim warriors) with considerable backing from the US, forced the Soviet army to withdraw north through the same route. Ahmed Shah Mussoud is still revered by many for having protected the Panjiser Valley from the Soviet forces.

3) 庶民の乗り物
The mode of travel for the ordinary citizen

（ファイザーバードのバザール / The bazar in Faizabad）

(1) 特に地方ではロバも主な交通手段

(1) In the rural areas donkeys are the main mode of transport.

(2) 中世と現代が混在する

　タンク・ローリーも立派なバスだ。ロバは庶民の手軽なクルマだ。この状景は現在も40年前と同じだ。ロバは近距離用の乗用車には勿論、時々は長距離用の軽トラックにもなる。

(2) The Middle Age and the Modern Age coexist.

　　Tank lorries that double up as buses. The donkey is the modest means of transport for most people. The mode of transport has remained the same during the last 40 years. Donkeys are a major mode of transport for short distances, while sometimes they are used as if they were mini- trucks for long distance travel

(1971.6)

（ファイザーバード付近 / Near Faizabad）

4) 岩塩の交易は昔話
Rock salt trade is a relic of the past.

(1) ロバで運ばれる岩塩塊

(1) Blocks of rock salt carried on the back of donkey

（バラック/ Both fig.s, Baharak）

（バラック / Baharak）

(2) 岩塩店は粉塩包装店に衣替え

　往時バダフシャーンの首邑であった、"泉の多い地"を意味するこの地のかつての岩塩屋は、粉塩パックの販売店に変身。今は昔となったロバの背による岩塩塊の交易。2005年頃から岩塩塊の製粉化が普及し、ファイザーバードでは全く姿を消し、バラックでもこの状景を見かける事は極めて稀になった。

(2) The blocks of rock salt are grinded into powder at a salt shop.

Baharak was once the capital of Badakhshan. "Baharak" means a place with many springs.
Whereas in the past rock salt was sold, only powder salt is available now. The sight of donkey laden with rock salt for sale has disappeared. From around 2005, the practice of pulverizing rock salt into powder became popular and in Faizabad today you cannot find rock salt. Even in Baharak one can rarely encounter a donkey loaded with rock salt.

5) アフガーンは阿片王国
Afghanistan is the kingdom of opium

　アフガーンはビルマ（現ミャンマー）を抜いて阿片生産王国[5]だ。最近は、カルザイ政権の監視が厳重になって、その支配下地域では、栽培が減少してきている。栽培が盛んであった北部の、バラック北郊でも2004年には、路傍の至る所にケシ畑が見られたが、2007年以降には、殆ど姿を消していた。

　Afghanistan has overtaken Burma (Myanmar) as the largest opium producer of the world[5]. Recently however, in government-controlled regions, opium poppies have been almost totally eradicated. Whereas in 2004, it was common to see opium poppies on the roadside, by 2007 they had mostly disappeared in the northern parts of Afghanistan and around the northern outskirts of Baharak.

(1) 美しいケシの花

(1) Beautiful poppy flowers

(2) 採汁後のケシ畑

　成熟した花に器具で傷を付け、一晩かけて採汁して原料を集める。採汁後は簡単な工程で（粗製の）阿片 "Taryak" が造れる。

(2) An opium poppy field after the seed pods have been scored to extract the latex, an opiate.

　The seed pod of a mature, opium poppy is slit open vertically to extract the milky sap or latex inside. The sap is left to ooze out for one night before it is scraped off the pod. A simple process is used to make opium or "tariyak" from the sap.

（いずれもカズデイ / All fig.s, Kazday）

(3) ケシ畑

路傍から離れた畑に群生する採汁前のケシ

(3) Poppy fields

　An opium poppy field off the main road before the seed pods have been scored.

ワハーン
Wakhan

氷雪の山脈は東部ヒンドゥ クシュ山脈　　The snow - covered mountains are the Eastern Hindu Kush Range

　緑に囲まれたca2550mの河岸台地、250m北下で、西下して来たオクサス河（アーブ・イ・パンジ）が北へ大迂回する。対（右）岸は旧ロシア・旧ソ連・現タジキスターン。南には、氷雪のヒンドゥクシュ山脈が東に折れて続く。ほぼ東経71°40′から74°50′、北緯36°25′から37°30′の範囲に位置している。ワハーン全体は東西長約300km、南北幅15 〜 65kmの虫垂（いわゆる盲腸）のような形をしてる。その形状から回廊とも称ばれる。19世紀後半、特にその東部は英露のグレートゲーム（権益角遂の場）に捲き込まれ、1895年6 〜 8月の現地で催された両国のパミール国境画定委員会[6]により、アフガーン領となった。古いシナの資料では（どの範囲か明確でないが）休密（シュウミ）[7]、伽倍（ジヤペイ）[7]、護密（フーミ）[7]、胡密（フーミ）[8]、鉢和（ポーホー）[9]、達摩悉鐵帝（ダー・モ・シッティ・ティ）[10]として記されている。またイシュカーシェムを商彌（シャンミ）とする説[11]がある。なお商彌はチトラールかマストゥーヂとする説[12]もある。

　アフガーンでは一般に、サルハッドまでがワハーン、それ以東がパミールと称ばれている。ワハーンの人口は約1万。住民はワハーン人（ワヒ、ワハーニ）と称ばれ、金髪・緑眼の人も多い。ワハーン語（ワヒ）を話す。宗教は殆んどの人がイスラーム教のイスマーイーリ派である。

　イシュカーシ（ェ）ム（Ⓓ）は、小麦が多く収穫出来る地の意味。

　A river terrace covered by trees at an altitude of 2550 meters. 250 meters downstream to the north the Panj (Oxus) changes its westerly course and turns north. On the opposite bank is Tajikistan, a republic of the former Soviet Union. To the South, the snow-clad mountains of the Hindu Kush turn east. The Wakhan area lies between 71°40' and 74°50' east longitude, 36°25'and 37°30' north latitude.The total length of the Wakhan is about 300 km, and the width ranges from 15 km to 65 km at its widest. Because the valley is shaped like a human appendix, it is known as the Wakhan Corridor.

　In the latter half of the 19th century, Wakhan became the stage of the Great Game where the Russian Empire and the British Empire competed fiercely for supremacy in Central Asia. In the summer of 1895 (between June to August) the Pamir Boundary Commission[6], representing the two powers, reached an agreement to officially recognize the Wakhan as part of Afghanistan.

　Wakhan appears as Shu-mi[7], Jia-pei[7], Fu-mi[7], Hu-mi[8], Po-ho[9]and Ta-mo-his-t-ie-ti[10] in several historical Chinese annals. The Chinese annals also mention Shang-mi[11] which is believed to correspond to Ishkashim, Chitral or Mastuj[12].

　Generally speaking, in Afghanistan the term Wakhan applies to the area east of Ishkashim up to Sarhad. All the eastern regions beyond are known as the Pamir. The population of Wakhan is about 10,000. Most of the inhabitants are Wakhi, who are blue-eyed and fair in complexion. Most of them speak the Wakhi language and are followers of the Ismaili sect of Islam.

　"Ishkashim (Eskashem)" means the land where abundant wheat can be harvested.

（イシュカシェム　対岸（左端）にダジギスターンにも同名の町がある。
/ Ishkashim On the opposite side of the river to the left is Ishkashim, Tajikistan.）

7) 拝火教徒の城（?）趾
Ruins of Zoroastrian fort?

(1) 城（?）趾の遠望

ヒンドゥクシュ山脈の北麓、オクサス河に向かって延びる低い支根の基部に、カーカーと謂う名の拝火教徒の城趾[13)14)]と謂われる、スレート岩を数層積み重ねた外壁の正方形の遺趾がある。

実測すると2辺が、38m×40m、高さは3mほどであった。

(1) A distant view of the remains of a fort

Along the northern foothills of the Hindu Kush, at the foot of a low spur that juts out towards the Oxus, stands a square-shaped structure called Kakah. The outer wall is constructed with several layers of slate and it is believed to be the remains of a Zoroastrian fortress.[13),14)]

A measurement taken on site showed that the length of the two sides of the enclosure was 38m x 40m , and the height 3 meters.

(いずれもイストラーク/
Both fig.s, Istrakh)

[補注] 本遺構は参考文献13) 14) の城趾ではない。その城趾は当地から東約3kmの Kazideh のオクサス河を挟んだ、対岸（右岸）畔の Namadgut （Tazikistan 領）に在る。

[Supplementary annotation] The ancient structure mentioned here is different from the remains of the fortress mentioned in bibliography 13) and 14). That ancient fortress is located in Namadgut (in Tajikistan), about 3km east of this site, on the opposite bank（right bank）of the Oxus River, and lies right across Kazideh (in Afghanistan). The origin of this ancient structure is unknown.

(2) 仏教寺院の僧房を思わせる小部屋

岩の隙間は塗り固めもなく高さも低く、城廊の役を全くなしていない。内部は全体が小部屋に分かれ、そのすべてが低い通路で結ばれている。パーキスターン北部のタフティ・バイやタキシラに遺る仏教寺院の僧房跡の造りに似ている。字や他の遺趾は全く見あたらない。

(2) Small rooms that recall images of Buddhist monasteries

There are big gaps between the rocks that have not been filled in, and the structure is too low in height to have served as a fortification. There are more than 50 small rooms, which are connected by a low corridor. Though the structure looks similar to the ancient Buddhist monasteries of Takhti-i-Bahi and Taxila in northern Pakistan, no written inscriptions or other antiquarian relics have been discovered in the vicinity to date.

(タジキスターン：ダラシャイ / Tajikistan, Darshai)

(8) ワハーン渓谷のオクサス河　タジキスターン側を流れるオクサス河

　外国人には、古代ギリシャ語に由来するオクサス河として馴じまれているこの河は、現地では一般に上流のサルハッド（時には小パミールのボザイ グムバース）辺りから中流末のクンドゥーズ北方辺りまでを、アーブ・イ・パンジ（Ⓓ）（5つの水）あるいはダリアー・イ・パンジ（Ⓓ）（5つの河）、それより下流をアームー ダリアー（Ⓓ）と称んでいる。ワフジール路の源流域の呼び名はまちまちである。

　源[15]をワハーン回廊東南端のパミール・イ・ワハーンのワフジール峠の氷河（図34）、図35）参照）に発し、回廊を西に縦断し、西の基点イシュカシェムで北に大迂回し、次いで西に折れ、クンドゥーズ北方で西北に曲り、アラル海南縁に注ぐ2540km[16]の中央アジアの代表的な大河の一つである。流域には、シルク ロード時代の有名な地名が多い。古いシナの文献には嬀水（ウィースイ）[17]、烏滸河（ウーチュウホウ）[18]、縛芻河（フーチュウホウ）[19]などの名でみられる。殆んど一年中強い西風が吹き、ワハーンの風"ボーディ・ワハーン"[20]（Ⓓ）の名で有名だ。

(8) The Panj (Oxus) as it flows through the Wakhan valley on the Tajikistan side

　The river may be better known by its ancient Greek name, the Oxus, but midstream from Sarhad (or in some cases Bozai Gumbaz in the Little Pamir) the contemporary name of the river is the Ab-i-Panj (Ⓓ) (five waters) or the Darya-i-Panj (Ⓓ) (five rivers). Downstream beyond Kunduz, the river is called the Amu Darya (Ⓓ) from the point where it is joined with the Vakhsh River. Near the headwaters in the Wakhjir, the river is referred to by many different names.

　The source[15] of the majestic Oxus is the glacier that straddles the Wakhjir Pass, located at the southeastern edge of the Afghan Pamirs, or the Pamir-i-Wakhan. The river flows in a westerly direction until it reaches Ishkashim, where the river takes a sharp turn to the north. Further downstream, it turns west again. From beyond Kunduz, the river heads northwest till it reaches the Aral Sea, located 2540 km[16] from its source. Villages are scattered along its banks with names that have left their footprint on the history of the ancient Silk Road. In the ancient Chinese annals, the Oxus appears as Ui-sui[17],U-shu-hou[18], or Fu-chu-hou[19]. A strong, westerly wind known as the "Bad-i-Wakhan" [20] (Ⓓ) prevails throughout the year. It is one of the major rivers of Central Asia.

9) ワハーン渓谷の両岸
Both banks of the Wakhan valley

（1）右（北）岸・タジキスターン側の地形：ヤムグ

　谷喰は少なく、それも谷の奥行きは浅く、開口部も小さく、扇状地が発達しない。

(1) The terrain on the right-side (northern side) of the Panj in Tajikistan : Yamg

The valleys are less eroded and shallow, the entrance to them are narrow, and alluvial plains are undeveloped.

（ハンドゥードゥ / Khandud）

（タジキスターン：ダルシャイ東方 / Tajikistan : Upper Darshar）

（2）右（北）岸・タジキスターン側の地形：ウーゲント ポヨーン

　谷の奥行きは深く、開口部は広く、扇状地が発達する。"ポヨーン"（Ⓓ）は下（しも）手の意味。

　図11）（4））のように、夏季には谷奥の山の融雪で増水した激流のため、車が渡れなくなる扇状地も有る。

(2) Left (south) side The terrain on the Afghan side : Urgunt-i-Poyon)

The valleys are deep, the mouth of the valleys are wide, and alluvial plains are more prevalent. "Poyon" (Ⓓ) means downstream.

(Fig.11)(4)) shows several alluvial plains that can turn into dangerous, rapid streams during the summer.

（3）道端で談笑する若い女性

アフガーン側では道端で若い女性を見かけることはまずない。

(3) Young women chatting gaily by the roadside

（タジキスターン：ヤムグ / Tajikistan : Yamg）

（4）明るい子供たち

タジキスターンの子供は服装もさっぱりとしてきれいだ。タジキスターン側では服装もカラフルだ。

(4) Happy –looking children

The children living in Tajikistan look clean and are neatly dressed. In the Afghan Wakhan, young women can rarely be seen on the roadside. The women on the Tajikistan part of the Wakhan are colorfully dressed.

（タジキスターン：ヤムグ / Tajikistan : Yamg）

10) ハンドゥードゥの仏教遺趾
Buddhism ruins in Khandud

　玄奘は大唐西域記[21]（以下西域記）に、「達摩悉鐵帝国在兩山間、…臨縛芻河…。…。　　　…昏駄多域国之都也。中有伽藍。」と記している。達摩悉鐵帝国がワハーン[22]、昏駄多がワハーン最大の村ハンドゥードゥ[23]である事は、オーレルスタイン卿や他により周知の通りである。

　近年フランス隊により、ハンドゥードゥに仏教遺趾[24]の在ることが発見されている。

　In his detailed account, the Ta-tang Shi-ui-ji (henceforth Shi-ui-ji)[21], the piligrim Hsüang-tsang refers to "the Kingdom of T(D)a-mo-hsi-t'ie-ti which is situated between mountains and lies along the River Fu-chu (Oxus). The account also mentions that " Hun-t'o-to[23] is the capital of the kingdom. In the center of the town there rises a Buddhist temple. The identity of Wakhan[22] with the territory of the Ta-mo-his-t'ie-ti, has been recognized by Sir Aurel Stein and others. Recently a French archeological expedition discovered the ruins of a Buddhist monastery or temple[24] in Khandud.

(1)"アーシヤーブ・イ・ボードゥ"　(1)"Asyab-i-Bad"

----

(1)-A 仏龕　(1)-A　A hollow space in which the statue of a Buddha was place on the rock

（いずれも風車（?）の丘 / Both fig.s, The hill of Wind mill?)

(1)-B 石臼　(1)-B Stone mill

　ワヒでは"ナガーラ・イ・ボードゥ"と称ばれる。いずれも（屋根のある）風の水車（風車?）を意味する。場所は村の中央に架かる橋（2,011年夏、本格的な橋に再架中）の東南約700mに、ca 3,500m（高度差約600m）ばかりの山頂台地である。最初に直径数mの壊れた円型の石囲みの"監視哨"を意味するトゥープハーナ（Ⓓ）が目に入る。続いて東南背後の緩い起伏の頂上台地に、数多くの仏教遺趾が佇んでいる。遺された石垣は円型を偲ばせるものが多い。基壇と思われる30cmほどの高さで、5mぐらいの長さの泥煉瓦造りも在る。高さ2mぐらいの双耳岩の片側には、仏像が収っていたと思われる龕（がん＝厨子）（図（1）-A）が掘られている。凹んだ石臼（図（1）-B）も転がっている。周囲の多くの岩には、動物と狩人の線刻画が描かれている。

　In the Wakhi language it is also called the "Nagara-i-Bad", which means the mill of wind (wind mill(?). The place is located 700 meters southeast of the bridge in the center of the village. In the summer of 2011, a new bridge was being built on a plateau 600 meters above the village at an altitude of 3500 meters. The first structure to meet the eye is the Tup Hana (Ⓓ) (watch tower) which is a round enclosure made of stone with a diameter of several meters. To the southeast along the undulating slopes higher up, one can recognize several ruins of Buddhism temples or monasteries. Most of the stone enclosures are round in shape. On what must have been the foundation of the structure, one can see the remains of a wall five meters long and about thirty centimeters high made of dry bricks. A rock that has two peaks and is two meters high, has an alcove that has been cut out into one of its sides. Most probably, a statue of Buddha was placed in that hollow (fig. (1)-A). I also noticed a hollow stone hand mill (fig. (1)-B) lying on the ground. Many petroglyphs depicting animals and human hunters can be seen here as well.

（2）ハンドゥードゥ谷左（西）岸流域

　ハンドゥードゥ谷の左（西）岸を橋から南に約700mばかり進む。西側の高さ100mばかりの山の礫岩断崖には、バーミアンの大石仏（2001年3月ターリバーンにより破壊された）が並ぶ断崖に、数多く遺る僧崖のような小洞が祭ってある。ここから2km詰めると、長径10mぐらいの崩れた楕円型の積み石が遺っている。更に2kmほど大小の岩の間を縫いながら詰めて行くと、小円型や長径10m、高さ1mぐらいの楕円型の石垣（図（2）-A）が、断崖の岩の上や大きな岩を背にして遺っている。とある断崖の巨岩の上には、チベット仏教の祈祷の旗"タルボチェ"のような、多くの色とりどりの小旗が、細い木の柱（図（2）-B）に閃いていた。

　この一帯は"石垣"を意味する"ダルバンド"（Ⓓ）と称ばれている。谷の東側の礫岩崖面断崖には多くの僧崖（?）が掘削されている。

　この左岸一帯と右岸東南の丘の両遺趾とも、塑像や壁画などは遺っていない。

　なお文献[24]にある新しいモスク（1971年建立）の基部にある、仏教的装飾が彫られた石柱は、モスクの内外が塗り固められていて、窺う事ができなかった。モスクは1969年私達がシェール コーに登山（図11参照）した際、テントを張った橋の東側の石垣台地に、隣接して建立されている。

(2) The catchment area along the left (west) bank of the Khandud Valley

　On the left bank (western side) of the Khandud Valley, 700 meters south from the bridge, there is a conglomerate cliff that is 100 meters high, the surface of which is pock marked with numerous caves. The sight is evocative of the ancient Buddhist monastery in Bamiyan, Afghanistan, where two colossal Buddha statues carved out of the conglomerate cliffs were destroyed by the Taliban in March, 2001. Going two kilometers further, there is an oblong -shaped enclosure about 10 meters long made from many layers of stone. Proceeding two kilometers further and passing rocks of varying sizes, I came to a site with a small, cylindrical-shaped stone hedge (fig. (2)-A) that is oblong in shape, with a major axis of a few meters to 10 meters, and with a height of about one meter. What remains of the stone hedge can be seen leaning against large boulders (fig. (2)-A). On a huge boulder, I saw many small, colorful flags tied to a thin, wooden pillar that looked similar to the Tibetan prayer flags "Tarboche".

　The whole area is called the "Darband"(Ⓓ), meaning stone hedge. The caves dotting the conglomerate on the eastern side of the valley, may have been part of a Buddhist monastery or temple.

　Neither Buddhist statues nor murals have been discovered from the site. In 1971, when a new mosque was built in Khandud, some report[24] claimed that the stone pillars used for the foundation retained some decorations with Buddhist motifs. I could not confirm the accuracy of that claim, since the interior and exterior of the mosque had been painted over. The new mosque was built adjacent to the plateau, where I saw the remains of the stone hedges on the left side of the bridge. It was that same bridge where we had pitched our tent when I visited that area in 1969, to climb Ser Koh as a member of a mountain expedition (refer to fig. 11)).

（2）-A 伽藍の基台（?）　　(2) -A　The foundations of a Buddhist temple?

（2）-B 巨岩の上の祈祷旗（?）　　(2) -B　The Tibetan prayer flags? on the big rock

（いずれも谷 左岸 / Both fig.s,left bank of the valley)

11) Ser Koh（Ⓓ）6392m　ライオンの山
Peak The Lion 6392m

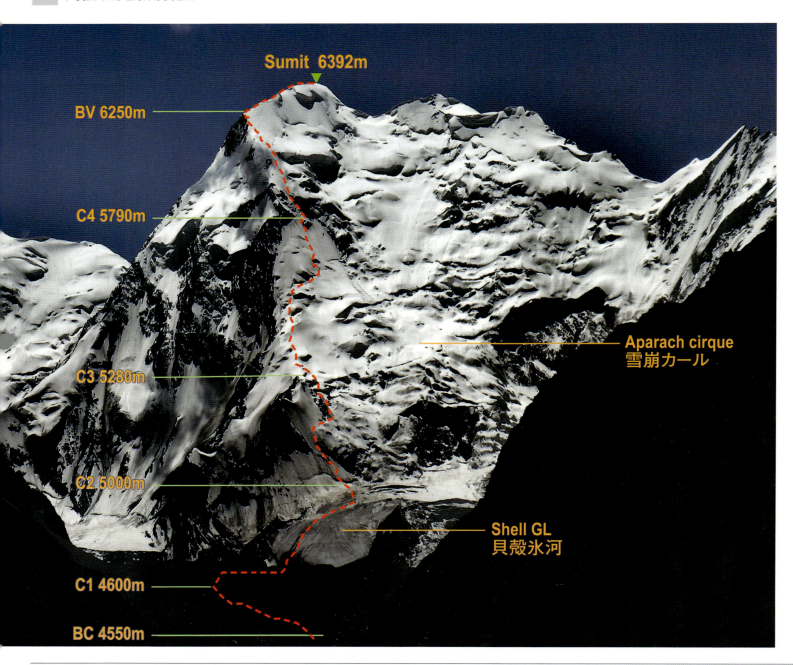

Sumit 6392m

BV 6250m

C4 5790m

C3 5280m

C2 5000m

C1 4600m

BC 4550m

Aparach cirque
雪崩カール

Shell GL
貝殻氷河

（1）シェール コー 北面と登頂ルート

　1969年8月5日、イシュムルグ谷を詰めた広島大学中部アフガニスタン学術調査隊北部支隊（広島大学医学部山岳会小パミール遠征隊1969）の平位剛、杉村功、土石川勝司、八幡浩、サーダート・サマード・ワルダックのうち、杉村とサマードを除く3名が、初登と違ったルートである北面からの新登頂（第2登）をした。以後、広島大学医学部山岳会は、MACHと略記。

(1) North Face of the Ser Koh and he route to its summit

　On August 5, after going on Ishmurgh Valley 1969 Go Hirai, Isao Sugimura, Katsushi Toishikawa, Hiroshi Yahata, and Sadat-Samad-Wardaq of the Medical Alpine Club of Hiroshima University (henceforth MACH) Expedition Little Pamir 1969 made an attempt to climb the summit of Ser Koh . Of the five- member team,three (excluding Sugimura and Sadat-Samad-Wardaq) successfully reached the summit via an unclimbed route of the north face.

（2）山頂より南西の展望

　　初登頂は、1968年のオーストリア・ユーゴー合同隊。彼等は北面麓を偵察後、西方のハンドゥードゥ谷を詰めて、街道から見えない反対（南）側から登頂した。私達は帰国後にこのことを知った。そのため、地域の人達は、私達がこの山を初登と思って命名した、シェール コー（ライオンの山）と称んでいる。ポーター達が、北面に頻発する大雪崩の情景を、ライオンの咆哮と称んだことから命名した。

(2) Panoramic view towards the southwest from the summit of Ser Koh

　　The Summit of Ser Koh was reached first by the Austrian-Yugoslav mountaineering expedition in 1968. After reconnoitering the north face, they traversed up the Khandud valley, and started climbing from the southern side, which is not visible from the road. We learned about their feat only after returning to Japan. We named the mountain Ser Koh after hearing the porters describe the sound made by the frequent avalanches of the north face as being similar to the roar of a lion. The local people still continue to call the mountain Ser Koh (the Lion Mountain), because they believe that we were the first to reach the summit.

Identity：T.Miyamori
1969.8.5

Saraghrar
7349m
S 7307m
Akher Chioh 7020m
E 7208m
Koh-i-tez 7015m
Datti Zom 6247m
Kotogaz Zom 6681m
Shayoz Zom 6855m
Udren Zom 7108m
Koh-i-Urgent 7038m
Koh-i-Shakaur 7084m
Keshni Khan 6745m
Nadir Shah 6814m
Koh-i-Hawar 6200m
Langar Zom 6750m
Koh-i-Naser Khosraw 6350m

H.Yahata

K.Toishigawa

Identified by J.Wala & T.Miyamori

（3）シェール コー北面遠望とイシュムルグ谷

イシュムルグ谷の幅は2kmを越える。夏期には10余りの激流枝がオクサス河に奔入する。

(3) Distant view of the north face of Ser Koh

The Ishumurg Valley is over two kilometers wide. During the summer, more than 10, torrential tributaries flow into the Oxus.

（対岸のタジキスターン / Tajikistan on the opposite bank of the Oxus River）
手前はオクサス河
The Oxus shown in the forefront of the figure

（4）イシュムルグ谷の渡り

渡河出来た前車のルートを外れるとこの態だ。

(4) Fording the Oxus at Ishumurg Valley

（谷の西北側 / Northeastern side of the Valley）
上方は、オクサス河
Above is the Oxus River

（5）待望の架橋が完成

2011年8月、3年を要して50〜100mの短橋を数個結んで、約800mの通過道が完成した。橋上の車はサフューラ君の乗用車

(5) The long-awaited bridge is finally completed

In August 2011, after three years of construction, several bridges ranging from 50 meters to 100 meters in length were completed and then joined together to form an 800 meter road. The car on the bridge belongs to Safiullah John.

（谷の西北側 / Northeastern side of the Valley）

12) かつてのワハーン潘王国の首邑カラ・イ・パンジャ（Ⓓ）
Qala-i -Panja（Ⓓ）, the former capital of the Kingdom of Wakhan

（[T・E・ゴートン中佐の著書25)]より（金子蔵書）/ [From Gordon's book]25) ,T. Kaneko's collection of books）

(1) 19世紀の城　西方より東方を望む

"カラ"は城、"パンジャ"は5の意味。往時、この地に5つの城（砦を含む）が在ったことから地名になったと謂う。

19世紀の報告書には、キラ パンジ26)、又はキラ　パンジャ27)としてある。1870年代前半は、オクサス河右岸・現タジキスターン、（大）パミール河右岸からゾル　クル（ビクトリア湖）、小パミール東端のネザ・タッシュ峠付近まで、ワハーン潘王国の版図であった。これらの地は、1880年前後にロシア帝国領となった。

1883年王国はアフガーンに併合され、バダフシャーンに編入された。

(1) A fort in the 19th century. Looking from west to east

"Qara" means fort, "Panja" is the number five. Qala-i -Panja owes its name to five forts that stood near this place in ancient times.

The place appears as Kila Panj26) or Kila Panja27) in the reports of the 19th century explorers. During the first half of the 1870's, the Kingdom of Wakhan encompassed the right bank of the Oxus, the right bank of the (Great) Pamir River in what is now Tajikistan, Zor Kul (Lake Victoria) and the area leading up to the Naiza Tash Pass on the eastern end of the Little Pamirs. In the 1880s, the territory of the Wakhan Kingdom was occupied by the Russian Empire.

In 1883, the Kingdom was annexed to Afghanistan and incorporated into Badakhshan.

(2) 現在の城趾

(2) The ruins of the fortress as it stands today

（上部と同じ位置から / The same location, as above）

(3) "聖者の指痕の石" が祀られている左河畔の城趾

(3) The ruins of a fort on tthe left bank of the Panj River which contains the "stone with the imprints of the five fingers of a saint"

(4) 聖者の5本の指痕が残る（？）石

(4) Imprints on a stone which the locals believe are the five fingers of a saint

（対岸はタジキスターン / Tajikistan on the opposite bank of the Oxus River）

　1838年2月、J.ウッド大尉[28]（英印海軍）や1874年5月のT.E.ゴードン中佐[29]（英陸軍）らは、ここからオクサス河を右岸に渉り、大パミールに進んでいる。今は昔の大パミール路とバクトリアを結ぶシルク ロード時代にも、ここが渡渉点であったのだろう。玄奘もマルコ ポーロもそうしたと思われる。

　なお、5つの城を語源とする説の他に、河畔の城に "その昔聖者が握ってできた5本の指痕が残る小石" が祀ってあることから、名付けられたと謂う説もある。どちらが正しいのかと、土地の古老に尋ねたところ、「教えて欲しい」という答えが返って来た。

　In February 1838, Lieutenant John Wood[28] of the British Indian Navy, and in May 1874, Lieutenant-Colonel T.E. Gordon[29] of the British Army forded the Oxus River to the right bank and proceeded to the Great Pamir. The ancient Silk Road must also have crossed the Oxus at this point, connecting the Great Pamir road with Bactria. Hsüang-tsang and Marco Polo must also have crossed the Oxus at this point.

　Qala-i -Panja in addition to having been named after five forts, owes its name to a stone that the local inhabitants believe carries "the imprints of the five fingers of a saint". When I asked an elderly inhabitant about the true origin of its name, he replied, "You tell me."

13) オクサス河本流と支流（大）パミール河の合流点
The confluence of the main Oxus River and its tributary, the (Great) Pamir River

（タジキスターン：ランガールまたはキフウン / Tajikistan : Langar or Kikhun）
中央広い河床が支流（大）パミール河。上方中央のやや狭い谷が本流。
The wide river bed shown in the middle of the figure is the (Great) Pamir River.
The slightly narrower valley seen on the top center of the figure is the main course of the Oxus River.

支流（大）パミール河口は、本流のそれよりもずっと広い。1838年2月、この情景を見たウッド[30]は、サルハッドからの流れ（パンジャ河・後に本流と判明）の方が大きいと看たが、（大）パミール河がオクサス河の本流とするワハーン人達の見解を容れ[30]、右岸沿いに3日間の騎行後の19日[31]にシル・イ・クル（ゾルクル）を再発見し、ビクトリア女王の即位のニュースを受け、これを祝しビクトリア湖と命名[31]した。そしてこの河を本流とした。

642年の玄奘も1274年頃のマルコ ポーロもウッドと同じ経路を辿ったに違いないと思われる。因みに玄奘[32]は西域記に「…至波謎羅川。…」と記しているが、この語句はパミールの名を最初に伝えた文献[33]である。

合流点のやや上流の（大）パミール河右岸畔のキフウン又はランガールより上流域を、両国の人達は大パミールとしている。玄奘の達摩悉鐵帝、マルコ ポーロのヴォカーンはこの辺りまでの範囲である。

ワハーン山脈は、（大）パミール河が本流に合流する直前の広い河口の東（左）岸際のガズ フウンすぐ背後から始まり、東に隆起している。（図左上）。

キフウンの辺りからゾルクル西端までは、直線距離で東北に約100km、路程（四駆車の距離計で）は約120kmと思われる。

The (Great) Pamir River is much wider than the Oxus at the confluence. John Wood[30] who arrived at this point in February 1838, observed that the river flowing from Sarhad was the bigger of the two, (subsequently the river flowing from Sarhad was determined to be the parent stream). However, Wood chose to heed the advice of the local inhabitants who believed that the (Great) Pamir River was the source of the Oxus. After riding for three days along the right bank of the Great Pamir River, Wood[31] became the first European to reach Zor Kul on February 19th, which he mistakenly decided was the source of the Oxus. In celebration of Queen Victoria's coronation, Wood[31] named it Lake, Victoria.

Hsüang-tsang in 642 and Marco Polo around 1274 most probably followed the same route. Hsüang-tsang became the first person[33] to record the name Po-mi-lo-Chuan, which corresponds phonetically to the Pamir in the Shi-ui-ji[32] (Records of the Western World).

The area above the confluence of the two rivers, above Langar or Kikhun on the Tajikistan side is known as the Great Pamir. Hsüang-tsang's Ta-mo-his-tie-ti and Marco Polo's Vokhan are identified with the Wakhan Valley up to this confluence.

The Wakhan Range rises up and then extends east from the left bank (east bank) of the (Great) Pamir River, shortly before the point where it joins the parent river. The river bed is wide at this point (left upper part of the figure). The distance from around kikhun to the western end of Zor Kul going northeast is about 100 kilometers as the crow flies, or 120km by a four-wheel drive car.

14) Koh-i-Baba Tangi (Ⓓ) 6507m バーバ タンギ峯 Mount Baba Tangi

"バーバ"は祖父、"タンギ"は谷の意味。1963年8月7日イタリア隊（C.A.ピネリ他）が初登。麓の集落は、1995年夏、同峰からの谷の氾濫で壊滅状態に陥り、現在に至っている。

"Baba" means grandfather , and "Tangi" means valley. On August 7, 1963 the Italian mountaineering expedition (led by C.A. Pinnelli) reached the summit first. In the summer of 1995, a massive landslide devastated the village on the foothills of this mountain. To this day, the area remains deserted.

（オクサス河右岸バーバ タンギ対面 / On the right bank of the Oxus right across Baba Tangi）

15) オクサス河本流（カラ・イ・パンジャ以東）の新旧の橋
The main course of the Oxus. (East of the Kalai Panj) The old and new bridges.

（パイナーブ / Pairab）

(1) 今はなき古い橋

1971年当時は、オクサス河にこの様な粗末な吊り橋が3カ所に架かっていた。

(1) The figure shows the old bridge which was replaced by the new bridge.

In 1971 there were three such flimsy , suspension bridges that crossed the Oxus.

（クレト / Kuret）

(2) 旧ソ連軍が架けた橋

この辺りの住民には、"旧ソ連軍は（自動車の通れる）道路と3ヶ所に橋を造ってくれた"と過去を懐かしんでいる人達がかなりいる。なお架かる橋にすべて吊橋である。

(2) The new bridge built by the Soviet army.

Some inhabitants of this area talked nostalgically about the past, crediting "the Soviet Union for building a road and three bridges that was negotiable by car". All the bridges spanning the river are suspension bridges.

Koh-i-Pamir
6286m

Koh-i-Khaen
6020m

Koh-i-Hilal
6281m

(連雲堡趾西方 ca 3700m /
Western side of Lien-yun-po
ca 3700m)

(1) ワハーン山脈の最高峰コーイ・パミール6286m、とコーイ・ハーン6020mと
　　コーイ・ヒラル6281m　　連峰の東南面を望む

ハーンはワハーン語で"最初"の意味。ワハーン山脈（セルセラ・コー・イ・ワハーン）Ⓓは古くはニコラスⅡ世山脈ともいわれた。オクサス河本流．・支流の合流点（図13）から始まり、小パミール東端のキジル　ラボート西背後に終わる、東西の長さ約165km。6000m級峰は10数座あるが、すべてサルハッド西方のイシック谷源頭周辺に集中している。この山脈に初めて入域・登山したのは、1971年7月のMACHパミール遠征隊1971（平位剛、藤井功、澤野邦彦、土石川勝司、八幡浩、山崎正数、サーダート・サマード・ワルダック）の七名であった。

(1) The highest mountain in the Wakhan Range, Koh-i-Pamir (6286m),
　　Koh-i-Khaen and Koh-i-Hilal(6281m)　　A view of the southeastern face

"Khaen" means first in Wakhi. The Wakhan Range (Selsela Koh-i- Wakhan) Ⓓ used to be known as the Nicholas Ⅱ Range. The Wakhan Range (Koh-i-Selsela-Wakhan) starts from the confluence of the Oxus River and the (Great) Pamir River, and ends near Kizil Rabot at the eastern end of the Little Pamir. It is 165 km long with an east-west orientation, with more than ten 6000- meters class peaks, all of which are concentrated to the west of Sarhad around the head waters of the Isshik Valley.

In July 1971, seven members (Go Hirai, Isao Fujii, Kunihiko Sawano, Katsushi Toishigawa, Hiroshi Yahata,Masakazu Yamasaki and Sadat -Samad-Wardaq) of the MACH were the first to set foot on the Wakhan Range.

Koh-i-Pamir
6286m

6101m

5989m

Koh-i-Hilal
6281m

6041m

5907m

5840m

5880m

Koh-i-Wood
5960m

Koh-i-Marco Polo
6174m

6040m

Identified by J.Wala

((コー・イ・ハーン頂上)手前の雪の隆起がコー・イ・ハーン / (Koh-i-Khaen Summit) The snow clad hump shown in the front of the figure is Koh-i-Khaen)

（2）頂上から北西の展望

　　1971年7月18日、MACHの澤野とサマードを除く5名が、6020m峰に初登し、コー・イ・ハーン（Ⓦ）初の山）と命名した。8月にはイタリア隊（C.A.ピネリ他）が、最高峰6286m、6174mと6281mの3峰に初登し、それぞれコー・イ・パミール（コー・イ・ベランドタラリン）、コー・イ・マルコ ポーロとコー・イ・ヒラルと命名した。なお、コー・イ・パミール、コー・イ・ハーンと北側のコー・イ・ヒラル、コー・イ・マルコ ポーロとの間の氷河は、ワハーン山脈に最初に入域したヒロシマ隊を記念して、J.ワラにより、ヒロシマ氷河と命名された。

(2) Looking from the summit towards the southwest

On July 18, 1971, five members of the MACH , exclusive of Sawano and Samad, made the first ascent to the summit at 6020 meters and named it Koh-i Khaen. Ⓦ (meaning the first mountain). In August of that year, an Italian expedition led by C.A. Pinnelli reached the three summits, one being the highest in the Wakhan Range at 6286 meters. The height of the second peak is 6281 meters and the third peak is 6174 meters. They subsequently named the highest peak Koh-i-Pamir (Koh-i-Belandtarin 6286m), the second Koh-i-Hilal (6281m) and the third Koh-i-Marco-Polo (6174m).

The glacier that lies between Koh-i-Pamir, /Koh-i-Khaen and the northern peaks of Koh-i-Hilal /Koh-i-Marco Polo, was named Hiroshima Glacier by J. Wala in honor of the Medical Alpine Club of Hiroshima University (MACH) expedition having first entered this region.

南の展望

ここはワハーン回廊の中央点、いわゆるワハーンの東界。オクサス河右岸に在る人口300人ほどの寒村である。

ワハーンの住民・ワヒが半農（小麦、大麦、粟、豆類、ジャガイモなど）・半牧を営み、定住できる東限地である。アフガーン最東端の行政府出張所と小学校がある。ワハーンの農業用水は雨水でなく、背後の東部ヒンドゥクシュ山脈とワハーン山脈の氷雪の融水の灌漑である。ここを過ぎると牛の姿は全く見られない。河床を網目状に流れるオクサス河は、ここの東はずれで険しいゴルジュとなり、小パミールへと遡って行く。

2km以上の幅の対（南）岸には、バロギール谷の開口部が望まれる。谷を詰めるとバロギールの最東端の峠・ドゥール ウィーン（Ⓦ）・ダルワーザ アン（Ⓒ）（門峠3880m）を越え、最短距離でヤルフーン河（パーキスターン：チトラール）に達する。

開口部西傍のオクサス河に臨んで、高度差が500mの急峻な岩山が望まれる。頂に747年唐の高仙芝軍が攻略したチベット軍の連雲堡趾が遺っている。

A Panorama view to the South from Sarhad

This is the midway point of the Wakhan Corridor, and the eastern edge of the Afghan Wakhan . Sarhad is a small hamlet situated on the right bank of the Oxus with a population of around 300 people. The Wakhis are the native inhabitants of the Wakhan.

Sarhad marks the eastern limit of human habitation in the Wakhan. The Wakhi are semi-nomads who cultivate wheat, barley, millet, beans and potatoes. The last government building in Eastern Afghanistan and an elementary school are located in Sarhad.

Instead of rainfall, the runoff from the glaciers that straddle the Wakhan Range or (East) Hindu Kush Range is used to irrigate the fields lying on its foothills. East beyond Sarhad, I have never seen cows.

The Oxus divides into many streams and meanders along the wide river bed , but if one were to go further upstream and eastwards towards the Little Pamir, the river contracts into a narrow gorge.

Beyond the gorge, on the opposite bank at a point where the river widens to more than two kilometers, one can view the mouth of the Baroghil Valley. At the end of this valley are the easternmost passes of the Baroghil Valley, the Dur Uween （Ⓦ） and the Darwaza An （Ⓒ） 3880m meaning the pass of the door, which are the shortest route to the Yarkhun River (Pakistan, Chitral).

Near the west side of the mouth of the Baroghil Valley, there is a conspicuous spur that rises steeply to a height of 500 meters. Here one can find the remains of the ancient Tibetan stronghold, Lien-yun-po, which was attacked by the Chinese general Kao Hsein-chih'tnoops of 10,000 in 747. A tributary flowing from the Baroghil debouches on to the Oxus right below this steep spur , as seen on the right side of the figure.

A way of gorge to Bozai Gumbaz

Baroghil velley to Baroghil Pass

連雲堡趾
Ruins of Lien-yun-po

Oxus River

Sarhad

(サルハッド北背後の丘ca 3300m / The hills that buttresses Sarhad to the north ca 3300 meters)

18) ワヒの生活
The lives of the Wakhi

(サルハッド / Sarad)

(シャーシュム 1971.7 / Shashm 1971.7)

（1）家屋の外観

　2mばかりの高さの泥土塀に囲まれ、窓が殆どない数室が狭い暗い通路で結ばれている。中央に在る居住室の天井には、煙出しと採光を兼ねた、"リッチェン"（Ⓦ）と称ばれる交互に菱形に木材を数層組み合わせた、三角隅持送り天井（菱形天井）・ラテルネン デッケ(Ｇ)が設えてある。塀の外には防風雪用に植樹されている。バーバ タンギ過ぎまでは杏が多くみられるが以東では姿を消し、柳や白楊に代わる。

　夏には、家族の誰かや数家族が一緒になって、山間部の牧草地で石造りの小屋を建て、近隣のヤク、羊や山羊を連れ、"アイラーク"（Ⓓ）（Ⓦ）と称ばれる放牧地を開く。その間に得た乳製品は、一部を家畜の持主に上納し、残りの全量を所得する。

（1）The exterior of a dwelling

　The houses in Sarhad are completely enclosed by a two-meter high mud wall . A narrow, dark corridor connects several windowless rooms. The skylight or " Richen " found in the main living area, is framed by four concentric, square wood layers known as laternen Decke (G). The skylight releases the smoke from the hearth and lets light in. Trees protect the house from the wind and snow. Until Baba Tangi, there are many apricot trees, but beyond only willows and white poplars can grow. .

　In the summer, families gather together to build stone shelters in the mountain pastures where the sheep and goats are taken to be grazed. These summer pastures are called " Yaylaq ". The dairy products that have been made during the summer time are divided between the owners of the animals and the shepherds.

（2）"リッチェン"からの陽光に浮かぶ母と子

　"リッチェン"の真下には"ガウフ"（Ⓦ）（竈）が築かれている。

（2）A mother holding her child under a skylight or " Richen "

　Right underneath the richen or skylight is a hearth called the " Ghauf " in Wakhi..

(3) 親しい間の挨拶　頬にキッスする

(3) A show of intimacy as two friends kiss each other's cheek

(4) 毛糸つむぎ　ワハーンでは男の仕事の一つ

(4) Spinning the thread is a man's job in the Wakhan

(5) "ガウフ"（竈（かまど））と"ヒュッエ"（パン）

竈の真上は主婦の定位置（シャーシュム）

(5) Baking bread in the hearth (1971 July)

The woman's place at home is right in front of the hearth.

（カルコット / Karkot）

（サルハッド / Sarhad）

（シャーシュム 1971.7 / Shashm1971.7）

（サルハッド / Sarhad）

(6) 人動式耕耘機

牛がいなければ人がする。

(6) Manually ploughing the soil

If there is no cow to plow, then the work must be done manually.

(7) 牛踏みによる小麦の脱穀と脱稃（脱皮）及び風選による脱稃した小麦の選別

(7) The wheat or barley is threshed and hulled with oxen feet, and then winnowed by throwing it up into the prevailing westerly wind.

（A）一連の進行風景

　ワハーンでは、牛を使って収穫した麦の廻し踏みをする一連の作業を、チャトウィ クサクウォンウェグと称び、"ワハーンの風"による風選で麦の選別作業をブン・ボードゥサルティシュと称ぶ。

(A) Proceeding scene

　Chatwi Kusakwonwek (Ⓦ) : The wheat or barley is threshed with the stamping feet of oxen.
　Bun-Badsartish (Ⓦ) : The mass which is a mixture of straw, husks and kernel are thrown up into the air. The prevailing westerly wind "Bad-i-Wakhan" then blows off the straw, husks and separates the grain or seed.

（B）脱糞予防

　脱糞による麦の汚れを防ぐため、牛の尻近くを鍋を持って追う

(B) Prevention for oxen's feces

　In order to prevent the cow's feces from dropping and soiling the grain, a person carrying a small pan follows the cattle from behind.

（いずれもイシュムルグ / Both fig.s, Ishmurg 1969.8)
ワハーンでは今でもこの風景が。
Scenes that can still be observed in Wakhan today.

(8) All dairy products are made in a " Forus " (Ⓦ) or barrel. Different types of barrels and agitators.

樽と撹拌棒のいろいろ

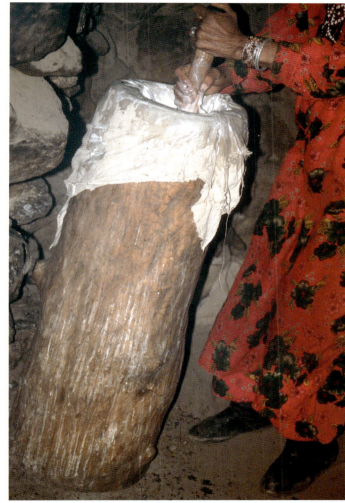

（サルハッド / Sarhad）
珍しい丸木の樽
A unique barrel made from a single log

（シャーシュム / Shashm）
一般的な貼合せ型樽と丸型の撹拌棒
A barrel in popular use, which is made from many wooden panels attached together, with a round agitator.

（サルハッド / Sarhad）
スクリュー型の撹拌棒
Screw -shaped agitator

（カジデー / Kajide）
珍しい金属製樽
A unique metal barrel

（ミルザ ムラート / Milza Murat）
効率の良い四翼式撹拌棒
An efficient agitator with four wings

ワヒはバター（"マスカ"）、濃いヨーグルト（"パイ"）や薄いヨーグルト（"ディーグ"）など、クリーム（マリック）を除いて、すべての乳製品を樽（"フォルス"）で造る。板材を貼り合わせたものが多く、最近ではプラスチック製品も見かける。撹拌棒を2〜3時間ついて造る。バターはキルギスと違ってオイル（"ルーグーン"）にして貯える

Except for cream, the Wakhi produce butter ("Maska") thick yoghurt ("Pai") and thin yoghurt ("Deeg") in the barrel ("Forus"). The barrels are made with wooden panels that have been joined together, but recently plastic barrels are also used.

The milk is mixed with an agitator for two to three hours. Unlike the Kyrgyz, the Wakhi's agitate the butter till it turns to butter oil rather than storing butter as it is ("Rogoon").

19) チベット軍の連雲堡趾
Lien-yun, the ruins of a Tibetan stronghold

(1) 岩山に聳える連雲堡趾　ca 3700m

(1) Lien-yun standing atop a rocky spur. 3700 meters in altitude

（連雲堡趾の南面）城壁直下約20mは70°〜80°の急斜面、その下から城麓までの約80mは約45°の急坂だ。
(The southern side of Lien-yun-po)
20 meters immediately below the stronghold, the gradient is 70 degrees to 80 degrees.
Further below for about 80 meters to the bottom of the fort the incline is steep at 45 degrees.

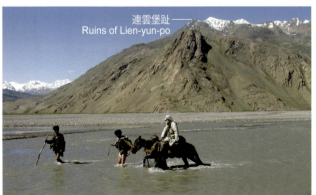

連雲堡趾 ———
Ruins of Lien-yun-po

(2) オクサス河を渉り連雲堡趾に向かう

(2) Crossing the Oxus towards ruins of Lien-yun-po

高仙芝の故事にならい早朝（減水期）にオクサス渡渉
Taking a cue from the records of Kao Hsien-chih, we crossed the Oxus early in the morning when the water level is still low..

旧唐書[34]によると、747年唐の高仙芝は玄宗皇帝の命を奉じ、1万の騎馬歩兵を率い、吐蕃（チベット）軍を討伐した。

舊唐書(?)を基にしたスタインの説明[35]によると、彼は3隊に分けてタシュクルガーンを発し、パミールに入った。高仙芝率いる主本隊はアリチュール・パミールを通りシュグナーンに至り、ワハーンを東進し、一隊はネザ・タッシュ峠かワフジール峠から"赤仏堂"を通り、3000人の隊は大パミールから"北谷"を辿り、7月13日（現代暦の8月中旬）に連雲堡に会するように定めた。同じく舊唐書[36]によると、牲を祭り城下の婆勒川を渉り、山を攀じ登り、陽のある内に、1000人の城兵が守る堡塁を陥落させた。

次いで南側の山に拠る8〜9000人の兵を駆逐、併せて5000人を斬殺し、1000人を捕虜にした。更に進んでバロギール峠と坦駒嶺（ダルコット峠）を越え、ヤシーンとギルギット(小勃律国)も陥落させた。

スタイン[37][38]は1906年5月21日、この史実に基づき、減水する早朝オクサス河を渉り、連雲堡趾に攀じ登った。その記録によると、南縁の東西長は約400フィート（122m）である。因みに2007・2009年の私の測量でも、約122mであった。

According to the T'ang Annals, or Chu-Tang-Su[34], in 747 AD, the Emperor Hsüang-Zong directed his deputy –protector Kao Hsien-chih to take charge of a military campaign against the Tibetans with a force of 10,000 cavalry and infantry. According to Stein' analysis[35] of the T'ang Annals, Kao Hsien-chih divided his forces into three columns when he started out from Tashkurgan and entered the Pamirs. The main column led by Kao Hsien-chih marched through the Alichur Pamirs into Shughran and then proceeded eastwards up the Wakhan Valley along the Ab-i- Panj. Another column might have descended from the headwaters of the Ab-i-Panj after crossing the Wakhjir Pass or the Naiza Tash Pass via the "Hall of the Red Buddha", and the third column of 3000 horsemen passed through the "Northern Valley". According to the T'ang Annals[36], the three columns having converged at Lien-yun-po on July 13 (mid-August according to the Gregorian calendar), commenced its attack on Lien-yun-po. Kao Hsien-chih after offering a sacrifice to the river, crossed the P'o-le river (current Ab-i-Panj or Oxus River), led his troops up the mountain side and defeated the 1000 Tibetans who were defending the stronghold, successfully capturing that fortification. He then pushed on and defeated 8000 to 9000 soldiers who were defending the mountains south of Lien-yun-po, killing 5000 and taking 1000 prisoners. He continued his attack, ascending the mountains until he crossed the Boroghil and Darkot passes and occupied Yasin and Gilgit (Little Po-lu).

On May 21, 1906, Stein[37][38] retraced Kao Hsein-chih's route as described in the historical documents, crossing the Oxus early in the morning when the water level was low, and scrambled up the spur till he reached the remains of Lien-yun-po. According to Stein's measurements, the length of the south side of the stronghold, which runs east to west, is about 400 feet (or about 122 meters). According to my own observations taken in 2007, and 2009, the length of the southern side of the stronghold is 122m.

（3）連雲堡趾の東南壁

　東面と南面の数カ所には、日干し煉瓦を積み重ねた、高さ数m、厚さ2mほどの防壘が設えてある。煉瓦層の間々には、ほぼ規則的に樹枝が組込まれ木舞の役割りをしている。スタイン[38)] はこの構造を詳しく記録している。

(3) Southeast wall of Lien-yun-po

In several places on the eastern and southern flanks, one can observe bastion walls made from bricks that are stacked to a height of a few meters and are two meters thick. The bastion walls have been reinforced by placing regular, thin layers of brushwood which separates the courses of sun-dried brick to ensure greater consistency. Stein[38)] has left us a detailed analysis of the construction of Lien-yun-po.

（4）チベット軍の監視塔趾

　連雲堡趾の麓からバロギール谷の左岸を3㎞ほど詰めると、西側の山から谷に延びる扇状形の斜面台地に、チベット軍の監視塔趾が遺っている。スタイン[39)] は同じくここも訪れている。

(4) Remains of a Tibetan watch tower

The ruins of a Tibetan watch tower can be seen three kilometers from the foot of Lien-yun-po, on an alluvial –shaped plateau that tapers off from the mountains to the west towards the valley below. Stein[39)] also visited this ancient watch tower.

（バロギール谷左岸 / Left bank of the Baroghil Valley）

20) バロギール峠はどれ？
Which is the Baroghil Pass?

東部ヒンドゥクシュ山脈の北と南の両麓に、ダシュト・イ・Baroghilと称ばれる地域が在る。"ダシュト"（Ⓓ）（Ⓦ）は、平原を意味する。両平原はそれぞれ東西に5〜7kmほど延び、幅1km前後の牧草に富む高原渓谷である。この間の山脈は高度が下がり、四つ在る峠も標高4000m未満と低く、峠路にも周辺にも氷河は見られない。因みに、ワハーン回廊に通じる同山脈越えの峠は10余数えられえるが、この地域（バロギール）以外では4600m台の一峠を除いて、すべて5000m前後と高く氷河を伴っている。

四つの峠には、東端の"門"を意味する"ダルワザ"（Ⓓ）・"ドゥール"（Ⓦ）3880m、西に続く3峠はバロギール峠と総称されている、東、西寄り、西端のそれぞれのca3900m、ca3920m、ca3810mの3峠にも、パーキスターンとアフガーン側で、それぞれ固有の名が付けられているが、何れにもBaroghilの名はない。史上有名な、バロギール峠3804mとはどれなのであろうか。なおBaroghilはパーキスターンではボロゴル、アフガーンではボロギールと称ばれている。

On the northern and southern foothills of the Eastern Hindu Kush Range lies the area known as the Dast-i-Baroghil. "Dast"（Ⓓ）means plains. Two foothills extend each about 5 to 7 kilometers from the east to the west,1 kilometer wide and grassy enough to graze cattle. In this Baroghil area the mountain range is low. There are four passes through which one can enter the valley, all of which are exceptly less than 4000 meters in on the sea level. No glaciers could be observed in and around these valleys. There are more than 10 passes that lead into the Wakhan Corridor. All the passes outside of this region are around 5000 meters above sea level and covered with glaciers, with the exception of one pass which is around 4600 meters above sea level.

The four passes are known by different names on the Afghan side and the Pakistan side. For example, the eastern most pass is called the "Darwaza"（Ⓓ）•Dur（Ⓦ）(meaning the gate)ca 3880m.

The remaining three passes lie somewhat west in succession and together are called the pass of Baroghil. Looking from east to west, the eastern pass is ca3900m high, the pass to its immediate west is ca3820m high and the pass to the furthest west is ca3810m high. None are called the Baroghil.

Which of the four passes corresponds to the historic Baroghil Pass at an elevation of 3804 meters? Baroghil is pronounced Borogol in Pakistan, and in Afghanistan Boroghil.

（1）アフガーン側バロギール草原から西端の峠とヒンドゥ ラージ
(1) A panaromic view of the Hindu Raj and the western edge of the pass from the Afghan Baroghil pastures

（2）国境標の石 上方（北）はワハーン
(2) A stone marking the boundary between Pakistan and Afghanistan.

Looking towards the Wakhan seen here at the top (north) of the photographThe view towards the Southwest Hindu Raj (Pakistan) from the middle of the Baroghil plains

Koyo Zom 6872m
Pechus Zom 6514m
C6200m
Identified by T.Miyamori

（アフガーン側のDasht-i-Baroghil / Dasht-i-Baroghil on the Afghanistan side）
下方の低い平野に国境線
The low ridge seen in the lower portion of the photograph is the boundary between Pakistan and Afghanistan.

（東の峠：ガリル峠 / Eastern Pass : Garhil Pass）

小パミールとワフジールへ
Proceeding to the Little Pamir and the Wakhjir

21) ゴルジュとなったオクサス河
The Oxus flows through a gorge.

バハラック上方から西を望む

サルハットの東で、広いオクサスの河床は突如ゴルジュとなり、小パミールの西端、オクサス河に架かる最東端の橋下まで続く。夏（増水期）の右岸沿いに造られている路は、500m前後の高捲きの断続となる。往時、夏のシルク ロード[40] は大パミール路であった。

A view towards the west from a site over Baharak

The Oxus divides into many streams and meanders along the wide river bed , but if one were to go further upstream and eastwards towards the Little Pamirs, the river contracts into a narrow gorge east of Sarhad. From this point we enter the western end of the Little Pamir where the last bridge on the eastern extremity of the Oxus lies. During the summer months when the water level of the river rises, the path traverses along the right bank of the river intermittently climbing to an elevation of 500 meters above sea level. In ancient times, during the summer, travelers of the Silk Road passed through the Great Pamir[40].

（バハラック上方 / A site over Baharak）
(East side of the Shaur Valley) The gorge continues until it reaches the western end of the Little Pamir.(fig.26)

22) 落ちないで渡れる?
Can we cross the bridge without falling into the side valley?

ワハーン山脈からオクサス河に流れ込む渡渉に困難な支谷は6本ある。うち2谷に橋が架けられているが、その1基は橋とは思えない代物だ。

There are six side valleys that descend to the Oxus which are extremely hard to ford. Bridges have been built across two of the six, but one is too dilapidated to be of use.

（アク ガウ / Ak Gau）

23) ラーマン クルの脱国
Rahman Qul flees Afghanistan.

1978年7月、4月のクーデターで樹立したタラキの共産革命政権を嫌った、ア・パミールの首領ハジ ラーマン クル ハーン（以下ラーマン クル）は、私兵にグルンディ谷口に在った最東部哨所を襲撃させ、予めバーイ カラに招聘・捕虜としていた残りの半数の数名と共に捕虜とした。

彼はア・パミール（殆んどは小パミールとワフジール路）居住の一族、郎党約3000人のキルギス人と共に、ホーラ バート峠（図28）を越え、パーキスターンのイミットに脱国した。途中峠手前で捕虜を着縄のまま釈放した。

襲撃時に、バラックの支谷と本流最東端に架かる2ケ所の橋を破壊、哨所に通じる電線を切断したため、サルハッドから救援隊が駆けつけたのは、1週間後であったと謂う。

ラーマン クルはその後、3000人の大多数と共にトルコに亡命したが、数年前に逝去した。これらの話は、2004年7月小パミールの代表者アブドラシード ハーンのユルトで、彼の息子の婚約式に招待されて、トルコから"帰郷"したラーマン クルの2人の息子から聞いた。

In July 1978 , Haji Rahman Qul fled. Afghanistan after a communist government led by Taraki was installed in April of that year. The Kyrgyz tribal leader of Wakhan, Rahman Qul , led a band of insurgents and attacked the eastern -most military garrison situated at the mouth of the Grundeh Valley. His forces also took as hostages soldiers that had been stationed at Bay Qara.

Rahman Qul fled to Immit in Pakistan via the Khora Bukhart Pass together with 3000 followers, most of whom lived in the Little Pamir and along the route to the Wakhjir (fig.28)). When Rahman Qul reached the Khora Bukhart Pass, he freed the hostages leaving them with ropes tied around their necks.

Rahman Qul's forces also destroyed two bridges, one that spanned a side valley of Baharak, and another that was the easternmost bridge spanning the main course of the river(fig.26). Because the insurgents also destroyed the only communication line with the local garrison, the government was unable to send reinforcements from Sarhad until one week after the attack.

Rahman Qul and most of the 3000 followers emigrated to Turkey. Just a few years ago, Rahman Qul died. I came to know of his death in July 2004 when I was visiting the Wakhan ,and happened to be invited to a wedding ceremony of the son of the present tribal leader of the Little Pamir, Abdullahseed Khan. Rahman Qul's two sons were present on that occasion, having returned from Turkey to attend the wedding.

(1) ラーマン クル

(1) Rahman Qul

[D.-Naumannの著書41)より]
[From D. Naumann's book41)]

(2) 襲撃された哨所趾

(2) The government military garrison that was attacked by Rahman Qul

(グルンディ /
Entrance of Grudeh)

(3) ミールザー ムラート東方から南を望む

中段左方がバーイ カラ、中段の河はオクサス河その上部がルプスーク谷

(3) Looking south from the east side of Miruza Murat

The Bai Kara is visible to the left of the center of this picture. The river shown in the middle of the picture is the Oxus. Further upstream lies the Lupsuk Valley

24) Karwan-Bala-Si (Ⓚ)

Karwan-Bala-Si (Ⓚ)

"カールワーン"はキャラバン、"バラ"は男の、"シィ"1人の意味。昔々、シナの隊商長の男の子供がここで死んだ。隊商は遺体をここに安置してインドに行き、帰りに収容して帰国したと謂う。

平な石を積重ね、泥土で隙間を塞いでいる。天井の一角に直径1m足らずの明かり採り、換気用(?)の兼用の短煙突がある。

スタインは、連雲堡趾を踏んだ後、ワフジール峠に向かう途上ここに立寄り、私と同様の話[42]を聞いている。また遺趾の造り[43]を調べ、高仙芝軍が通過した赤仏堂と同定[43]している。

"Karwan" means caravan , "Bara" means boy and "Si" means one. According to a local legend, in ancient times the young son of the leader of a caravan of Chinese merchants died here. The merchants erected a tomb for the boy before proceeding to India. On their return journey, the caravan revisited the site and took the remains of the boy back with them to China. The tomb is cylindrical in shape and is constructed with sun-dried bricks. There is a skylight in the ceiling with a diameter of less than one meter and a short chimney for ventilation.

After surveying Lien-yun-po, Stein visited this site on his way to the Wakhjir Pass and heard the same legend[42]. An archeological observation[43] led him to identify[43] the ruin with " the hall of the red Buddha" that the Chinese general Kao Hsien-Chi is believed to have passed through during his campaign against the Tibetans.

（小パミール西口西方 / Close to the western fringe of the Little Pamir）
一辺2m余、高さ約2.5m、スレート岩を積み重ねている。
The enclosure is 2 meters long on one side and 2.5 meters high, and is constructed by layering flat stones like slate slabs.

25) ラボート (Ⓚ)

Rabot

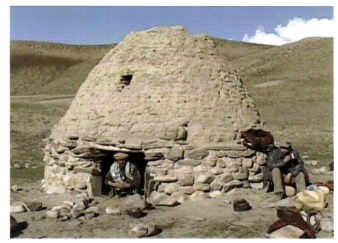

（1）外観

（1）The exterior

（2）内部

（2）The interior

（いずれも小パミール西口 / Both fig.s, Western entrance of the Little Pamir）
ラボートはキルギス人の旅人小屋
Rabot is the hut used by Kyrgyz travelers

小パミールとワフジール
The Little Pamir and the Wakhjir

26) 小パミールの西口とワフジールへの分岐点
東方に小パミールを望む
The junction from where the western entrance to the Little Pamir and the path to the Wakhjir diverge.
Looking east towards the Little Pamir.

（オクサス河に架かる最東端の橋 / The easternmost bridge over the Oxus River）
右方は東から蛇行する本流。左方は東から合流する小パミール河。
The right side of the picture shows the winding main course of the river.
In the left side of the photograph is the Little Pamir River flowing for east its confluence with the Oxus.

サルハッドから順調にいけば、3日目の夕方にここに着ける。東（左上）からの清澄な小パミール河と南（右方）からの濁ったオクサス本流の合流点の少し下流に、オクサス河最東端の小橋が架けられている。

東に進むとチャクマク・ティン湖を経て、アク‐スー沿いに小パミール東端に至る。

北（左方）に向かい、西に進んだ後に北に転じると、大パミール・ゾル クル西方に出る。

南に向かうと、ワフジール峠4907mかその南奥の峠ca5200mを越え中国に至る。

橋を渡り左岸沿いに西行し、夏の放牧地バーイ カラを経て南に転じると、ホーラ バート峠4630mやイルシャド峠4925mを越え、パーキスターンへ出る。それぞれ3日ほどの行程である。

橋はラーマン クルの脱国の際に破壊され、その後2回ほど新しく架橋し直された。

If all goes well, the site can be reached in the evening of the third day after leaving Sarhad . At the confluence, the Little Pamir flowing from the east is clear (top left of the figure), while the Oxus flowing from the south appears turbid. Slightly downstream from the confluence stands the small, easternmost bridge that spans the Oxus.

From this juncture, the valley (met the river) leads to Lake Chaqmak-tin and follows the Ak-Su (river) until it reaches the eastern edge of the Little Pamir.

If one was to turn north (to the left) from this point and then proceed to the west and then turn north again, the path would take you to the west of Zor Kul (Lake) in the Great Pamir.

The Wakhjir Pass 4907m and another pass ca5200m lying further south can be reached by proceeding south from the confluence, from where one can enter China.

Crossing the bridge and turning west along the left bank of the river, the summer pastures of Bay Qara can be reached. Due south from here lie the Khora Bukhart pass 4630m and Irshad pass 4925m that lead into Pakistan. Each of these passes can be reached in three days.

The bridge was destroyed by Rahman Qul and was subsequently rebuilt twice.

27) ルプスーク谷
Lupsuk Valley

(ルプスーク谷上流 / Upstream of Lupsuk Valley)

(1) ゴルジュを岩橋で跨ぐ

　ラーマン クル時代はキルギス人の夏の大放牧地、今はサルハッドのワヒのアイラークになっているバーイ カラ。その西縁に、南背後のカラコルム山脈西端のイルシャド峠4925mの氷河帯などを水源とする、ルプスーク谷が開口する。早朝出発し広い流れを渉り、ゴルジュを岩の橋で渡り、右岸の谷畔の台地で幕営。

　ゴルジュに落ちる斜面を高捲き、カランダール峠4600mに通じる氷河の舌端を対岸に見下ろした後、谷畔に下りる。対岸に、ホーラ バート（石臼）峠からの谷が注いでいる。現地の人ならその日の内にイルシャド峠を越え、パーキスターン側に着く。

(1) A rock bridge spans the gorge

　When Rahman Qul still reigned over the Afghan Pamirs, Bay Qara was a major grazing ground of the Kyrgyz. Today the Wakhi of Sarhad come here in the summer to graze their livestock or "yaylaq". On the western fringe one can find the mouth of the Lupsuk Valley. In the background to the south are the Karakorum Mountains, where the glaciers that straddle the Irshad Pass (which is the westernmost pass) 4925 meters, give rise to the headwaters of the Lupsuk Valley. I started out early one morning, forded the river where it was still wide, crossed a stone bridge over a gorge to reach the right banks of the river, and then set up camp on a plateau.

　I then traversed across a precipitous cliff that confined the gorge until I reached a slope from where I could look down at the snout of a glacier that leads to the Qalandar Pass. From there I descended down the banks of the valley. On the opposite side, I had a view over the valley descending from the "Khora Bukhart" Pass (the "stone grind mill"). It takes barely one day for the local people to cross the Irshad Pass into Pakistan.

(峠北下 / North below the pass)

(2) ホーラ・バート峠　北面

　幅20mほどのルプスーク谷の急流を左岸に渉ると、パーキスターンのチャプールサーンのワヒのアイラークが在る。5月から11月までの間、100頭ばかりのヤクを2人で管理している。1頭当たり500ルピー（約1000円）の報酬だと謂う。支谷左岸の山腹を高捲きながら登り、植生帯が終るca4200mの台地で幕営。

　翌日は峠まで約3時間、右側の山腹の岩・石礫の斜面に付けられたおぼつかない踏路を辿る。途中数ヶ所でモレーンを踏むが楽な登りだ。

(2) The southern slopes of the Khora Bukhart Pass

　After fording the torrents of the Lupsuk Valley and reaching the left bank, there is a summer pasture used by the Wakhi inhabitants living in Chapursan, (Pakistan). Between May and November, two herdsmen tend 100 yaks, who are paid 500 rupees per yak for their labor (equivalent to about 1000 yen). I scaled the left bank of a side valley and set camp on a plateau with an elevation of ca 4200 meters where the vegetation zone ends.

　The next day I walked three hours to reach the pass by following an unstable, narrow track that led over a rock-strewn slope. The ascent was not difficult, though I had to pass through several moraines en route.

Koh-i-Warght 6130m
5601m
Koh-i-Chateboi 6217m
C6009m
5945m
5324m
C5700m
5724m
5728m
5685m

Identifitied : T.Miyamori

（峠頂上 / Top of the pass）

（1）峠より南の展望

ワハーン側から峠を南に越えて、コロムバール河沿いに東南下するとパーキスターン：イミットに通じる。南面には氷河や急斜面は全くなく、3時間足らずの楽な下りだ。

峠の路傍に小岩が在り、上に二つに割れた直径40㎝ほどの古びた石臼が置かれている。その昔、飢饉に困ったフンザから助けを求めて、使者がイミットに送られた。土産を託された使者は、この峠まで辿り着いたが、余りにも荷が重過ぎるので、開くと石臼であった。彼は怒り、投げ捨てたところ二つに割れた。この地方に伝わる物語である。

ラーマン クル摩下3000人のキルギス人達は、数百頭のヤク、数千頭の羊や山羊を連れて、丸一日かけて峠を越したと謂う。

"ホーラ バート アン"（ⓒ）・"ホドログゥース ウィーン"（Ⓦ）・"ティゲルマン ビル"（Ⓚ）すべて（水車小屋の）石臼峠の意味。

（1）Panoramic view looking south from the pass

The pass connects the Wakhan with Immit in Pakistan after descending southeast along the Karmbar River. The southern slopes are devoid of glaciers and the gradient is not steep, so it was an easy, three hour descent.

On a small rock lying by the path, I saw a stone grinding mill, with a diameter of 40 cm that was split into two. According to a local legend, in ancient times when there was a famine, a messenger was sent over the pass to Immit to seek help from the inhabitants of Hunza. By the time the messenger had reached the pass, the weight of the gift had become so unbearable that he untied the package, only to find that he had been carrying a stone grind mill. The messenger became so infuriated that he threw the stone grind mill to the ground with such force that it split into two.

The three thousand Kyrgyz insurgents that followed Rahman Qul are believed to have fled to Pakistan from this pass, taking with a couple of hundred yaks and thousands of goats and sheep.

The names "Khora Bukhat An"（ⓒ）, "Hodurgwuth Uween"（Ⓦ）, "Tigerman Bel"（Ⓚ）all mean Stone of water Mill Pass.

（2）2つに割れた石臼と両国のワヒ

（2）The stone grind mill that is split in two, and the Wakhis of the two countries, Afghanistan and Pakistan

左はパーキスターン：チャプルサーン、右はサルハッドのワヒ
On the left is Pakistan: Charpursan, on the right the Wakhi people of Sarhad.

（ボザイ グムバーズ / Bozai Gumbaz ）
（Ⓚ）

オクサス河最東端の橋から小パミール河右岸沿いに約1km、低い河岸台地に13基ほどの"グムバーズ"が佇んでいる。

グムバーズは、日干し煉瓦を積み重ねた四角型の土台の上に、同様に円錐型に積み重ね、泥塗りをした塔屋式のキルギス人の墓。

周りには多くの地下埋葬所が見られる。1845年頃、カンジュートゥーからの侵入者と闘って戦死した、この地の首領ボザイの墓が在るとされている。それがどれか知る者はない。この周囲は無人の境である。夏期に数km北へ、ワフジール路のキルギス人が、放牧に移住してくるだけである。

1890年8月、ワフジール峠を越えて来たF.E.ヤングハズバンド大尉[44]（英印陸軍）は、ゾル クルから（誤った訓令を受領して）引き返して来たイオノフ大佐（ロシア帝国陸軍）から、丁重に"ロシア領"からシナ領に退去させられた。彼等はつい4日前には極めて友好的に晩餐を共にしたばかりであった。

1980年春には、小パミール東端から侵攻した、旧ソビエト軍がここに司令部を置いていた。辺りには朽ちた鉄条網や空罐が散乱している。因みにソビエトは1981年5月に、傀儡バブルク・カルマール大統領と、ワハーンを永久管理地とする協定[45]を結んだ。

One kilometer from the bridge furthest east, one can find thirteen "Gumbaz" standing along the right bank of the Little Pamir River on a low, terraced plateau. The "Gumbaz" are Kyrgyz graves made of sun- dried bricks that have been layered to form a square-shaped foundation, upon which rests a cylindrical structure that has been coated with mud. The graves are shaped like towers.

Many underground tombs have been discovered at this site. According to a local legend, Bozai was a local chieftain who was killed in combat in 1845, when the village was attacked by the Kanjuts, but none of the local residents could point out which one was Bozai's grave.

The areas arround Bozai Gumbaz are mostly uninhabited throughout the year, except for the summer months, when only a handful of Kyrgyz move further north towards the Wakhjir for grazing purposes.

In August, 1890, Captain F.E. Younghusband[44] crossed the Wakhjir Pass from China and entered the Wakhan where he was reprimanded by the Russian Colonel Yonoff, who had been sent back from Zor kul to check a false alarm. Younghusband was given a courteous reception before he was forced to return to Chinese territory. Just four days prior to the incident, the two had enjoyed an amicable dinner together.

In the spring of 1980, when the former Soviet Union invaded Afghanistan from the eastern edge of the Little Pamir, a Soviet garrison was stationed in Bozai Gumbaz. To this day the area remains littered with rusty, barbed wire and opened tin cans left by the Soviet soldiers. In May 1981, the former Soviet Union and its puppet regime in Afghanistan, headed by Babrak Karmal, signed a bilateral agreement[45] that transferred the administration of the Wakhan region to the Soviet Union for eternity.

ラーマン クル時代（1978年夏まで）のア・パミールのキルギス人の人口は、彼の息子達[23]参照）の話によると、3000余人、シャラーニ[46]によると1800人、当時の内務省の報告では5600人とされている。

トルコ・蒙古系と考えられ[47]、顔や体系とも日本人によく似ている[48]。黒と赤の2族に大別されている前者[47]）に属する。宗教はイスラム教でハナフィ派[49]である。

ラーマンクル時代のワフジール路（パミール・イ・ワハーン）には、オクサス河左（西）岸の数か所にもキルギスの放牧地が在ったが、彼の脱国後は消滅した。

現在はワフジール路で約150人（私の推定）、小パミールで約500人（在住の小パミール代表者アブドラシード ハーンの話：2007年）、大パミールで約250人（大パミールのアルバーブ（D）・"村長"に相当の話：2007年）と、計1000人足らずと思われる。最大の人口居住地は小パミールのアンデミン（図39）参照）の約60人であった。

冬期から夏期への季節別居住地の移動（一部は春の放牧地を圣て）は、[1]ワフジール路の住民は、殆んどがボサイ グムバース西北の山麓ハルガーズと北の山麓クルチンに [2]ボサイ グムバース東北のビルギット・ウヤーは、西北の山麓に [3]チャクマク・ティン湖北畔は南畔に [4]アク - スー北岸は南岸にとぼ一定している。いづれの放牧地にも（アク - スー北畔東端を除いて）きれいな渓流が在る。

なお冬の放牧地は"クシュトー"（K）、夏の放牧地は"ジャイロー"（K）と称んでいる。

備考：放牧地の季節別は 冬：○, 春：●, 夏：● で示した。①②③の数字は便宜上（冬の）ワフジール路南端から始め、チャクマク・ティン湖北畔、次いでアク - スー北畔の順に付し、各々に相対する春と夏居住地を冬放牧地の数字で示した。なお、同一地名内で居住地が1km以上離れている場合は、(a)(b) …の符号で示した。各放牧地の番号は、それらの冬放牧地の番号に従った。

During the reign of Rahman Qul, (in the summer of 1978) the population of the Afghan Kyrgyz was 3000 according to his sons (refer to 23), 1800 according to M.N.M. Sharani[46], and 6500 according to the Ministry of Interior Affairs of the Kingdom of Afghanistan.

It is widely believed that the Kyrgyz are descended from the Turks and the Mongols. Physically they resemble the Japanese[48]. The Kyrgyz are divided into the black and red tribes, of which those living in the Little Pamir belong to the former[47]. They belong to the Hanafi[49] sect of Islam.

During the Rahman Qul era there existed several Kyrgyz grazing camps even on the western side of the Wakhjir (Pamir-i-Wakhan) way, along the left bank of the upper Oxus River, but after he fled Afghanistan, these pastures were deserted and eventually became uninhabited.

According to my own estimate, currently there are about 150 Kyrgyz living in the Wakhjir Valley (Pamir-i-Wakhan) and 500 living in the Little Pamirs as of 2007 (according to Abdula Sheed Khan, who is the current tribal leader of the Little Pamir). And 250 Kyrgyz are living in the area of the Great Pamir as of 2007 (according to an "Arbab" (D) of the Great Pamir which corresponds to the head of a village). The total population of the Kyrgyz in the Wakhan is believed to be no more than 1000. The largest settlement in the Afghan Pamirs is at the Andemin in the Little Pamir where 60 Kyrgyz live. (Refer to fig.39)).

The Kyrgyz living in the Pamirs migrate from their winter settlements to their summer pastures (via the spring pastures in some cases) . In the summer [1] the inhabitants of the Wakhjir area migrate to the northwest of Bozai Gumbaz along the foothills of the Khargaz . They also migrate to the foothills of Qurchin, north of Bozai Gumbaz. [2] Those living around the Birguit Uya ,which is northeast of Bozai Gumbaz, move to the northwestern foothills.[3]Those on the north bank of Lake Chaqmak-tin move to the south bank of the lake. [4] Those on the north bank of the Ak-Su (River) move to the south bank of the river. Each of these grazing grounds are drained by a clear river (with the exception of the extreme east of the northern bank of the Ak-Su).

The winter pastures are called "Kushuto" (K) and the summer pastures are called Jailo (K).

Notes: The location of the grazing camps is indicated as follows:
Winter pasture:○ Spring pasture:● Summer pasture:●
As for the numbering scheme used here, the smaller numbers identify the grazing grounds on the southern edge of the Wakhjir (winter) area, and the numbers increase as the area they identify moves east towards Chaqmak-tin Lake up to the north bank of the Ak-Su.

The spring, summer and winter grazing grounds are identified with the same numbers. (a) (b)has been added to the numbers to distinguish two separate settlements that are more than 1 km apart but have same names. The number of each pasture is based on number of its winter pasture.

季節 Seasonal grazing	放牧地 Grazing area	ワフジールと小パミール ボザイ グムバーズ周辺	Wakhjir and Little Pamir arround Bozai Gumbaz	小パミール、チャクマクティン湖 あるいはアクスーの南北畔	Little Pamir, side of shore of Chaqm k-tin Lake or Ak-Su	
冬 Winter		ワフ ジール	Wakhjir	北 畔	Northern shore	
春 Spring		ワフ ジール	Wakhjir	北 畔	Northern shore	
夏 Summer		小パミール	Little Pamir	南 畔	Southren shore	

Except for Birguit Uya and Irumanutok
Their both grazings of the winter and summer are on the same side but their locations move Southren shore

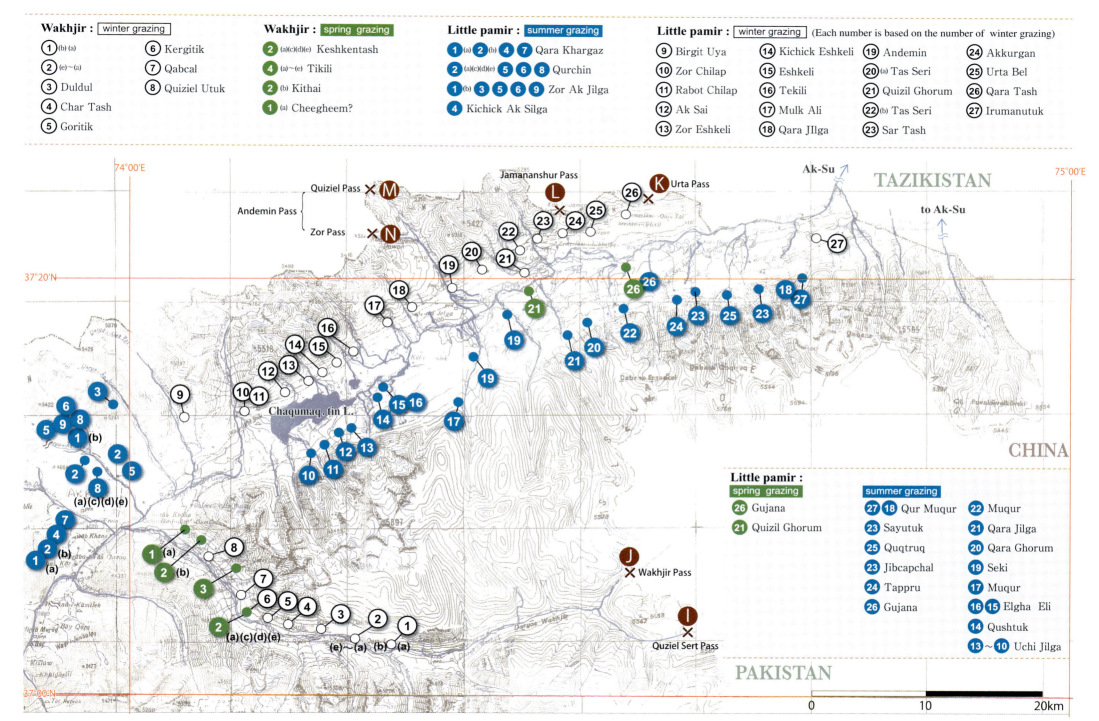

（キタイ・カタイ / Kithai·Kathai or Cathay（Ⓚ））

"キタイ・カタイ"はシナの意味。その昔シナ軍の女兵士がこの地に駐屯していたという伝説から、この地名になったと謂う。殆どのキルギス人は、冬と夏の２回放牧地を移動するが、春の放牧地を持つ者もいる。ここの住人の冬の放牧地はセキの一つだ。

"Kithai, Kathai" or "Cathay" means China . According to an ancient legend, "Kithai" owes its name to a Chinese garrison of women soldiers who were stationed in this place. Most of the Kyrgyz inhabitants move their settlement twice a year during the winter and summer, but there are others who also move during the spring time. The winter pasture of the inhabitants shown in this picture is called "Seki" (meaning garden in the local language). Individual groups of settlements are also called "Seki".

(カラ タッシュ / Qara Tash(Ⓚ))

"カラ"は黒い、"タッシュ"は石の意味。キルギス人の放牧地名は、その地の地形の特徴から付けられていることが多い。所変われど名は同じ、という場所があちこちに見られる。

ラーマン クル時代には、この先2ヶ所に冬放牧地が在った由。

"Qara" means black and "tash" means stone. The names that the Kyrgyz give to their grazing camps usually are derived from the unique topological attributes of the place. Though the location of the pastures may change, they retain their names, and many are similar.

During the reign of Rahman Qul, there were two winter pastures beyond this point.

（峠への分岐点北傍 / The juncture with the valley that leads to the pass）
東（左方）から西下する清澄な本流と、南（前）から北下する濁った支流が合流する。
The translucent waters of the parent river coming from the east (left side of the figure) flows west to join the turbid tributary, which comes from the south (front side of the figure) and flows north into the parent river.

支流（正面）の河床の方が、本流（左方）のそれよりずっと広い。本流沿いに東へ3時間余り遡ると中国国境のワフジール峠だ。支流に沿って南に4kmほど詰めると、南西奥に見える氷雪の山の麓で広い河床は閉じる。

初めてワフジール峠を訪れたのは、1999年7月2日、詰めたのは2001年7月1日。"支流"の河床を詰めた。西は、パーキスターンに通じるハポチャン氷河の舌端が落ちていた。東側からの氷河と北側の岩石帯で挟まれた急な谷が迫っていた。その谷の上方から一本の流れが落ちている。この流れの"奥の院"に、オクサスの"真の水源"が?と思ったが、ガレ場は容易に登れそうには思えなかった。

1891年10月ヤングハズバンド[50]は、シナ側からワフジール峠の南の峠を越えて、オクサス河上流に出ている。それはこの谷に間違いないが、どこを下りてきたのか?と思いを巡らせた。

The river bed of the tributary (shown in the front) is much wider than that of the main course of the river (shown on the left). The Wakhjir Pass, which forms the boundary with China, can be reached by following the river upstream for about three hours. Proceeding four kilometers further south along the tributary, the river bed ends at the foot of the terminal wall of a snow-clad mountain that stands at the far end of the valley to the southwest.

On July 2, 1999, I reached the Wakhjir Pass for the first time. On July 1, 2001, I trekked up the river bed of the tributary. On the west I could see the snout of the Hapochan Glacier that leads into Pakistan. I could also see a steep valley confined to the east by the glacier, and to the north by a zone of rocks and glacial debris. A stream originating from somewhere at the deepest end of the valley trickled down. "Could it be the true source of the Oxus?" I surmised. Unfortunately, however, the incline was too steep for me to reach the source of the stream.

In October, 1891, Younghusband[50] entered the upper drainage area of the Oxus from China via a pass situated to the south of the Wakhjir Pass. Without question Sir Francis Younghusband must have descended this valley to reach the region where the Oxus is still young. But over which part of the valley did the explorer actually descend? I mulled over this intriguing question.

34) ワフジール峠 (K) 4907m
Wakhjir Pass (K) 4907 m

(1) 峠から北を望む・オクサス河の源

カーゾン[15]は1894年秋、シナ側タ ーグドゥムバシュ・パミールからワフジール峠を越えた際、この氷河を実地検証し、オクサス河本流の水源とした。

(1) Looking north from the pass The source of the Oxus

In the fall of 1894, Curzon[15] crossed over to the Wakhjir pass from the Taghdumbash Pamir in China. Based on his first-hand observations, he concluded that the source of the Oxus was the glacier straddling the Wakhjir pass.

(峠頂上 / On the top of the pass)
北からの真っ白な氷河がオクサス河の水源。東が中国国境
The white glacier to the north is the source of the Oxus. To the east lies the border with China.

(2) 国境の2層の鉄柵

2001年にはなかったが、2010年には、1963年建立の国境塔から10mほど中国側に下がって、南北の分水嶺に2kmほどの遮断柵が張られていた。

(2) Looking towards the east from the boundary with China

In 2010, for the first time I saw a barbed-wire fence running for two kilometers that stood below the pass 10 meters inside Chinese territory. On my last visit to this site in 2001, a lone pillar, erected in 1963, had been the only structure to mark the border between Afghanistan and China.

柵の東側は中国　East side of the fence is China.

(国境の西側：アフガーニスタン / West side of the border : Afghanistan)
近年中国側には、湖南を通るジープ道路が造られていた。
Recently the Chinese have constructed a jeep road along the southern bank of the lake.

35) パミール最高位の湖　真のオクサス河の源（?）　ca 5099m
The highest lake in the Pamirs. Can it be the true source of the Oxus? ca 5099m

（1）湖南西端から東・北を展望

「Dr.これは湖だ!」通訳のサフューーラが上ずった声で叫んだ。モレーンの間に佇む私達の直ぐ眼下には、谷間に楕円形の平らな雪原が拡がっていた。これが湖であった。湖は一年の大半が凍結している。訪れたのは2010年8月19日。やっと湖西端（右下）が僅かに融氷し、2mほどの幅で湖水が石磔の河床に流出していた。ガイドのワフジール路の若いキルギス人が、2年前に2人の外人を"この湖"に案内にしたと云った場所は、約500m下方のモレーンの間に在る残雪の窪地であった。

そこからはグーグル アースの衛星写真を手に、それと余りにも違う風景に戸惑いながら、幾つかのモレーンを越えて登ってきたところだった。

谷の入り口の手前から巨岩が群在し馬では進めず、支流右岸の45°ぐらいの斜面をヤクの背で斜登しながら谷筋に入った。急斜面を暫く登ると、蝶が全く姿を見せない緩やかな傾斜のお花畑帯に出る。過ぎるとモレーンの波となる。一年前の6月中旬に、湖を知っているというこのガイドの父親トルソン ボイと、騎馬で谷の入口近くの巨岩帯まできたのだが、吹雪のため引き返した。

ヤングハズバンド[50]は、1891年10月初旬にこの小湖と（オクサス河に）流出する小流を確認している。残念ながらオクサス河の源に関しては何も述べていない。

その3年後、北に隣接するワフジール峠をシナ側から越えたカーゾン[51]はこの事を知っていたが、ワフジール峠北奥から南下する氷河の舌端(図34(1))をオクサス河の源[15]とした。もし彼がここを踏んでいたならば、どちらを源と考えたであろうか?

(1) A panoramic view towards the east and north from the southwestern end of the lake

"Doctor this is a lake." Safiullah, my guide, shouted with excitement. We were standing on a moraine looking down at an oval-shaped, flat snow field hemmed in by the sides of the valley. This was no doubt a lake. I visited the lake on August 21th , 2010. Though the lake is frozen for most of the year, the western edge of the lake had thawed slightly, and was draining over the debris –strewn bed. Two years prior to my visit, a young, local Kyrgyz guide said that he had guided two Westerners to a snow-filled depression located 500 meters below this lake. Though the visitors had apparently mistook the depression to be a lake, on visiting the site, I was able to confirm that this hollow in the moraine only contained residual winter snow . After passing through this depression, we had climbed up several moraines to reach this lake. I had taken along some copies of satellite pictures of the area, but the actual scenery was quite different .

Near the entrance to this valley, riding on yaks, we traversed a slope to the right hand side of the tributary with a steep incline of 45 degrees, in a bid to penetrate the deeper ends of the valley. After climbing the rock-strewn, difficult slope for some distance, we came to a meadow with a gentle gradient filled with flowers, but I could not see any butterflies. Beyond that meadow we had to cross a series of undulating moraines. Two years ago in mid –June, I had ridden a horse up to the boulder-strewn, mouth of the valley with the father of my local guide Mr. Torsun Boi ,only to be turned back by a blizzard.

In the beginning of October, 1891, Younghusband[50] reached this small lake where he had observed a small stream that debouched into the Oxus River. Unfortunately, Younghusband did not mention anything about the source of the Oxus.

Three years later, Curzon[15] crossed the Wakhjir Pass which lay to the north of the lake from the Chinese side .

Though Curzon[51] knew about Younghusband's report [51] he concluded that the true source of the Oxus was the river that issued from the tongue of the glacier[15] (fig. 34 (1)). If Curzon had set foot on the banks of the lake, what would his conclusion have been regarding the true source of the Oxus?

（2）湖を見つけたサフューラ君（右）

(2) Safiullah John who discovered the lake (shown on the right side of the picture.)

（湖南西畔 / The southwestern end of the lake）
湖の東北端上部に中国との国境をなす、赤い石が多い庭峠を意味する氷河 "クィジール セルト ビル"（Ⓚ）ca5200m が望まれる。
The Chinese border is in the middle of the shore on the northeastern end of the lake and is called the Quiziel Sert Bel Ⓚ (meaning the pass of a narrow garden with red stones) ca 5200 meters.

小パミール
The Little Pamir

36) 塩性の温泉岩小屋
A stone cottage that encloses a salty, hot spring bath

(ボザイ クムバーズの東方 6km / Six kilometers east of Bozai Gumbaz)

(1) 岩小屋と周辺

　内と外の2ヶ所に塩分0.2％の温泉"ウスブログ" (Ⓚ) がある。湯温は約37℃と低い。付近の渓流の塩分は0.02％であった。

　30mほど下の窪地には、キルギス人が家畜に食塩として与えている、白色の結晶状の堆積帯が在る。分析では主成分はNa2CO3（重炭酸ナトリウム）であった（表83 (5) 参照）。

(1) The stone cottage and the surrounding area

　The "Usublok" (Ⓚ)(meaning hot spring) with a salinity of 0.2% has an indoor and outdoor bath. The bath water is lukewarm at 37 degrees. The salinity of the river stream nearby is 0.02%.
　In a basin 30 meters below the hot spring, there is a belt of white, crystallized salt that the Kyrgyz nomads feed to their livestock. An analysis showed that the main properties were Na_2CO_3 (sodium bicarbonate)(refer to tab.83) (5)).

(2) 内湯の内部

(2) Inside the hot-spring bath

（Chaqmak-tin Kul（Ⓚ）西北畔 / The northwestern bank of Lake Flint）

"ラボート"は孤独または極めて小さいの意味。チラップは、チャクマク・ティン湖の両畔地帯の名称。ここは阿片吸引常習の中高年夫婦が住む一軒だけの冬の放牧地だ（図81）（2）参照）。湖の北畔からアク-スー左岸一帯には、12ケ所に放牧地が在る。すべて冬のそれである。

"Rabot" means lonely or very small. Chilap is the name given to the area along the banks of the Chaqmak-tin lake. This is the winter grazing camp of just one family comprised of a middle-aged man and his wife, who are both addicted to smoking opium (refer to fig 81)(2)).
There are twelve grazing camps along the northern banks of Lake Chaqmak-tin and the Ak-Su (River) that flows from the lake. All of them are winter grazing camps.

38) Chaqmak-tin kul (Ⓚ) 火打ち石湖の西端 ca4013m
The Western end of the Lake Flint stone ca 4013m

(1) 西端北畔より南を望む

　小パミール河が源を求めて北に曲がり、河床の窪地帯は約200m東で閉じる。50mばかり高い両側のなだらかな台地はつながり、草の疎らな荒れた平原台地が3kmほど東の湖西端まで続く。分水嶺がどこか解らない。湖端近くは湿地帯が多い。"Chaqmak"は、火打石（火打ち道具）の金属の部分、"tin"は、"石"の部分の意味。

(1) The view to the south from the west end of the north shore

　The Little Pamir River turns north towards the headwaters. Only 200 meters further east, the depressed river bed is buttressed by a cliff which rises 50 meters above the river. The gently sloping plateau on both sides of the river joins together at this point. The plateau is almost completely devoid of grass, and continues eastwards for about three kilometers until it reaches the western end of the lake. The watershed cannot be confirmed. The ends of the lake are marshy.
　"Chaqmak" means the metal tool of the an apparatus to make fire, while "tin", is the flint itself.

（オクサス河右岸バーバ タンギ対面 / On the right bank of the Oxus right across Baba Tangi)

(2) 湖東端　ca4010m

"アク"は白、"スー"は流れの意味。出入りのある西端と違って東端は単純で、アク・スーの出口は一ケ所。湖端近くは夏の増水期でも常時渡渉できる。西端よりも豊草帯が拡がり、絶好の牧草帯だ。清澄な流れは、約200m下流で、南から流入する白濁のイルガイ谷と合流してから、白い流れに変わる。

河は40余km東方の小パミール最東地（タジキスターン）で北折する。その間多くの場所で分岐し、時には河幅は1kmにも拡がる。夏期には増水のため、この場所を除いて渡渉地点とされている場所で渡渉できなくなる年もある。

(2) The eastern edge of the lake ca 4010 m

"Ak" means white, and "Su" means flow, or river. Unlike the western end of the lake, where the river flow is more complex, the Ak-Su drains from the eastern end of the lake at one point only. Even during the summer when the water level is high, the edges of the lake can be forded. The eastern end of the lake is endowed with rich pasture as well. A white stream coming from the south joins the main course of the Ak-Su about 200 meters downstream from the edge of the lake. After it joins with the white-colored flow of the Eligha Eli valley, the waters of the Ak-Su River turn white.

The river turns north 40 kilometers east from this point (in Tajikistan). The river branches off frequently until in some places it widens to about one kilometer. The river swells during the summer, and in some years the water level is too high to ford.

（湖東端・アク-スー（Ⓚ）の流出口 / The eastern edge of the lake from where the Ak-Su（Ⓚ）starting）

（3）チャクマク・"ティン"

東端近くの北畔傍に火打ち石の"石"を意味するチャクマク・"ティン"と称ばれる小島がある。湖名の由来になっている。（中央右端）

(3)（Chaqmak）-"tin"

On the northeastern end of the lake, there is a small island called (Chaqmak)- "tin" which means "flint stone". The entire lake has been named after the island (shown in the center of the figure to the right).

ラーマン クル時代（1978年夏まで）のア・パミールには、トム（Ⓚ）と称ばれる樽木の屋根と窓の付いた土壁の家屋は、数軒しかなかった由である。

それらはすべてラーマン クル一族の所有家屋であった。なかには、日干し煉瓦造りで、西欧風の構造物としての煙突も設えているものもある。

Until the summer of 1978, the few houses that had earthen walls with windows and oak roofs were all owned by Rahman Qul, the chief of the Afghan Pamirs at that time. Called "tom" in the local language, there were even a few brick houses with chimneys that looked quite European.

(1) ラーマン クルの親族の旧住居

"カラ"は黒い、"ジルガ"は谷の意味。西傍を流れている大きな谷だが、それほど濁っていない。

(1) The house where Rahman Qul's relatives used to live

"Qara" means black and "Jilga" means valley. The stream coming from the wide, spacious side-valley flowing west is not that turbid.

（カラ ジルガ / Qara Jilga）

(2) ラーマン クルの旧住居

現在では殆どの冬の放牧地に、1〜2軒のトム（固定式家屋）が造られているが、1989年に旧ソ連軍が撤退した際に、残していった廃材を利用して建てたものか、最近になって造られたものである。ラーマン クル時代には、一族以外はすべて、ユルト住まいでペチカ（Ⓚ）（ストーブ）もなかったと聞く。

(2) The house where Rahman Qul lived with his family

Today, at most winter grazing grounds, one or two doms (non-portable houses) are built. In 1989, after the Soviet military left, the construction material that they left behind was perhaps used to build these houses. Or they may have been recently built. During Rahman Qul's reign, except for his family, all the inhabitants lived in yurts and did not have a stove or pechika.

（ムルク アリ / Mulk Ali）
中央がラーマン クルの旧居宅
Rahman Qul's former residence is shown in the middle of the picture.

40) Andemin Bel ⓚ 4536m　アンデミン峠
Andemin Pass 4536m

(1) Zor Bel ⓚ ca 4530m　東側の台地から西北を展望

　ア・パミールで最大の人口を有する、冬の居住地アンデミンの北背後で、タジキスターンと境する峠である。アンデミンはこの峠を発見したとされる人の名前。"ビル"は峠、"ゾル"は大きいの意味。大パミール・タジキスターン側からは、ジープで乗り越せる険しくない登りと聞く。峠手前にジープの軌跡があった。小パミール・アフガーン側も峠入口の岩石帯を除くと大変緩やかだ。国境である分水嶺に小湖（池?）がある。北縁と南縁からそれぞれ大パミールと小パミールの両側に流れ出る小流が見られる。非常に珍しい現象[52]だ。

　約4km東北に"赤い岩"を意味するクィジール峠ca4762mがある。両峠への登り口は、大パミール側では約2km離れているが、小パミール側では冬の放牧地アンデミン1ヶ所で、両峠への分岐点はゾル峠から東へ3km、クィジール峠から南へ1kmの広い谷間である。当地では共にアンデミン峠と称んでいる。4536mの峠はどちらなのか?。

　1890年8月にリトルデール夫妻[53]がClimbingしてアクスーに出た峠はどちらなのか?

(1) Large Pass ca 4530m
A panoramic view looking towards the northwest from the plateau on the eastern side of the valley.

　Andemin is most populous in the Afghan Pamirs during the every season. Immediately north is a pass that forms the boundary with Tajikistan. Andemin is the person who is said to have discovered the pass. "Bel" means pass and "Zor" means large. I was told that the pass is so easy that it could be crossed with a jeep from the Tajikistan-side (Great Pamir side). Right before the pass crests, the deep ruts of a jeep track could be seen. Coming from the Little Pamir on the Afghan side the slope is very gentle except for the rock-strewn slope at the entrance to the pass. There is a little lake (pond) at the top of the pass that marks the boundary between Tajikistan and Afghanistan. A stream flows out at either end of the lake, one to the Great Pamir and the other to the Little Pamir, a rare sight [52] indeed.

　The Quiziel Pass ca 4762m lies four kilometers to the northeast of the Zor Pass. "Quiziel" means red. The entrance to the Zor and Quiziel passes are 2 kilometers apart on the Great Pamir side, whereas the only entrance to the two passes from the Little Pamirs is the winter grazing camp at Andemin. The watershed is located 3 km east of the Zor Pass and 1km from the Quizil Pass. On the south side, right below the ridge that forms the watershed lies a wide valley from where the path bifurcates, one leading to the Zor Pass and the other leading to the Quiziel Pass. Here the valley is extremely broad. The locals call both passes the Andemin. Which pass is 4536m above the sea level?

　In 1890, the Littledales[53] reached the Ak-Su via one of these two passes. Which pass did they choice and climb?

（ゾル ビル / Zor Bel）
中央にタジキスターン側標柱。分水嶺に両国へ流れる小湖（池）が在る。
In the middle of the picture is the pillar marking the national boundary with Tajikistan. There is a small lake at the watershed, from where a stream drains into Tajikistan and Afghanistan.

（クィジール峠 / Quiziel Pass）

(2) Quiziel Bel ⓚ ca 4762m

　峠の東側は赤い岩石が多いので、"赤い峠"と称ばれている。タジキスターン側から麓よりヤクで3時間の登高。谷は狭くやゝ険しい。クィジールは"赤い"意味。

　玄奘が大竜湖（大湖・ビクトリア湖・ゾル クル）を過ぎ「谷の途中から東南に向かって山を登り…」と西域記[54]に記した峠はどちらであろうか?

(2) Looking towards the north into Tajikistan

　True to its namesake, there are many red rocks on the east side of the Quiziel Pass. From the Tajikistan side, it is a three-hour climb on the back of a yak. The valley is slightly narrow.

　Hsüang-tsang[54] in the Shi-ui-ji writes that after passing the Great Dragon Lake or Zor Kul, he proceeded along the valley, and then turned southeast to climb a mountain. Which pass has he climb?

41）ユルトの移動はヤクで
The yurts are transferred on the back of yaks.

（アンデミン近く / Near Andemin）
一部の地区を除いて、6月中旬は夏の放牧地への移動の最盛期だ。8頭前後のヤクで1軒のユルトの移動が出来る。
Except for some areas, mid-June is the peak season when nomads migrate from winter to the summer pastures. It takes eight yaks to transport one yurt and all of the houshold belongings.

42) アク-スー左岸東端　冬の放牧地　北背後の稜線はタジキスターン国境であるウルタ峠　4295m

The winter grazing camp by the Ak-su River on the eastern end of the left bank
The mountains ridge shown in the background (towards the north) is the Urta Pass which forms the boundary with Tajikistan. 4295m

"カラ ターシュ"（黒い岩石）の名は、ワフジール路にも同じ地形に由来する同名の地がある。東端に在るこれら3ヶ所の冬の放牧地には、充分な生活用水を得る渓流がない。積雪が消える4月初めにはアク‐スーを渉り、渓流の在る右岸の夏放牧地に移住する。背後の稜線は、中間の峠の意味する"ウルタ ビル"（Ⓚ）。麓との高度差は400m未満と低い。同様に低い東4kmのワハーン山脈東端のグンジ ボイ峠と西4kmの粗悪な塩を意味する"ジャマナンシュル"（Ⓚ）峠ca4388mの中間に在る。後者はジープで越せる。

"Qara Tash" means black stone. There is a valley with similar terrain in the Wakhjir, that is also named Qara Tash. Three grazing camps occupy the eastern end of the Afghan Pamirs, but there is insufficient water to support them. At the beginning of April when the snow has melted, the nomads ford the Ak-Su, and move to their summer pasture on the right bank of the river where there are many clear streams.

The mountain ridge in the background is called the "Urta Bel", or the Urta pass in the middle. It is only a 400 meter climb from the foothills to the pass. The Urta Bel (Pass) lies between two passes: the Gunji Boi Bel on the eastern edge of the Wakhan Range, and the "Jamananshur Bel" which means the pass of the bad quality salt. The Jamananshur Bel ca4388m is located 4 kilometers to the west of the Urta Bel and can be crossed on a jeep.

（"カラ タッシュ"（Ⓚ）/ "Qara Tash"（Ⓚ））
背後の山の黒い岩が地名になっている。
The place was named for the black boulders that can be seen in the background of the picture.

アク - スー右岸は夏の放牧地　　アク - スーを挟んで北にタジキスターンを望む
The right bank of the Ak-Su is the grazing camp during the summer.　　This figure shows the view across the Ak-Su looking towards Tajikistan in the north.

（サユトゥック / Sayutuk）（Ⓚ）

　中央手前でワハーン山脈は終わる。左方の低い鞍部はウルタ峠。タジキスターンから毎夏やってくるヤク泥棒には、低い国境は逃走に都合が良い御用達峠だ。

The end of the Wakhan Range appears shortly before the middle section of the figure. The Urta Bel appears as a low depression on the left.
Every summer yak thieves from Tajikistan cross this pass and enter Afghanistan illegally. It is easy to raid the summer camps when the pass is so low.

（イルマヌトック / Irmanutuk）（Ⓚ）

"イルマヌトック"は窪地の意味。アク‐スー右岸の東端に、アフガーン最東端の放牧地が在る。右岸は夏の放牧地だが、ここだけが例外で冬のそれである。遥か東方にタールグドゥムバシュ パミール（中国）の氷雪の高い山脈が望まれる。

"Irmanutuk" means a depression, or dip. The grazing grounds located at the eastern end of the right bank of the Ak-Su (River) is the farthest east you can reach within Afghanistan. The right bank of the Ak-Su are the summer grazing grounds, but this area is the only pasture that is used during the winter. The lofty, snow-covered peaks of the Taghdumbash Pamir (in China) appears far away to the east.

45) ワハーン回廊の東玄関
タジキスターン最東南端とタークドゥムバシュ パミールを展望
The eastern gateway to the Wakhan Corridor
A panaromic view of the eastern end of Tajikistan and the Taghdumbash Pamir

　正面の連山の左端を東進すると、ネザ ターシュ峠4548m、右方（南）に進むとベイク峠4596mを越え、いずれもタークドゥムバシュ パミール（中国）に通じる、シルク ロード時代の有名な峠だ。しかし現在はどちらの峠も閉鎖されている。

The Naiza Tash Pass 4548m can be reached by proceeding east (to the front) along the left edge of the mountain ridge shown on this figure. The Beyik or Peyik Pass 4596 meters can be reached by proceeding to the right side of the same mountain range towards the south. Both passes lead into the Taghdumbash Pamir (in China) and were historically important junctures on the Silk (or Ancient) Road. Today both passes are closed to travelers.

（アフガーン小パミール最東端：ティゲルマン-スー左岸台地 / The far eastern edge of the Afghan Little Pamir: the plateau on the left bank of the Tigruman-Su.）
中景の山脈はタジキスターン・中国国境。遠景はタークドゥムバシュ パミールの連山
The mountains shown in the center of the figure form the boundary between Tajikistan and China. The lofty ranges of the Taghdumbash Pamir appear further beyond.

46) マルコ ポーロ羊
Marco Polo Sheep

　13世紀の中頃、元に向かうマルコ ポーロが、大湖（ゾル クル）周辺で見かけた、巨大な・大きいものでは6パーム（1パームは、一杯に開いた母指と小指の間の長さ・約23㎝）にも及ぶ角を持つ大きな野生羊のことを、"東方見聞録"[55]に記載している。このことからオビス・ポリ（ポーロ羊）と称ばれるようになった。

　マルコ ポーロ羊又はマルコ ポーロ アルガリ学名Ovis ammon polii は、ウシ科Bovidae Varの野生羊アルガリの一種で、主としてパミール結節部（高原）やアルタイ山脈などの高所山岳地帯に棲息する。他の一種の天山アルガリ学名Ovis ammon karelini は、主としてヒマラヤ山系の少し低い山岳地帯に棲み、ポーロ羊よりやや小型である。

　アフガーンでもタジキスターンでも、マルコ ポーロと俗称され禁猟になっている。アフガーンでは、小パミール東端ティゲルマン - スー源流域（図45)）、アンデミン峠（図40)）とワフジール峠（図33、34）が3大棲息地として有名である。

....

　Around the 13th century, Marco Polo saw a herd of big wild sheep near the area around Zor Kul (Lake) on his way to the capital of the Yuan Empire in China. The sheep are large and can be distinguished by their long, spiraled horns, the longest of which can be six palms long . The *Ovis polii* (Marco Polo sheep) are so called because they were first to have been mentioned in "The Travels of Marco Polo"[55].

　The Marco Polo sheep live in the high mountains of Central Asia such as the Pamir Knot and the Altai Mountains, belong to the bovi family (scientific name *Bovidae*) and are a subspecies of the wild sheep (argali). They are named *Ovis ammon polii*. There are another kind of wild sheep named *Ovis ammon karelini*. The habitat of the *Ovis ammon karelini* are mainly the lower-lying hills of the Himalayas and they are smaller than the *Ovis ammon polii*.

　The habitat of the Marco Polo sheep span both Afganistan and Tajikistan where hunting them is forbidden. In Afghanistan the three main habitats are the headwaters of the Tigerman-Su (fig. 45)) at the eastern edge of the Little Pamir, Andemin Pass (fig. 40)) and the Wakhjir Pass (fig, 33), 34)).

（カラ・ジルガ / Kara Jilga）

（1）天日干し
....

(1) Being dried in the sun

（2）マルコ ポーロ羊の角と頭蓋骨
....

(2) The horns and cranial bone (skull) of the Marco Polo Sheep

（Tigeraman-Su（Ⓚ）源流域 / Tigerman-Su（Ⓚ）near the headwaters）

（3）マルコ ポーロ羊の群
....

(3) A herd of Marco Polo Sheep

（ティゲルマンースー源流域 / Tigerman-Su near the headwaters）
"ティゲルマン"は（水車小屋の）石臼の意味
"Tigerman" means the stone grind at the water mill

47）小パミール最東南 端
The southeastern rim of the Little Pamir

（1）南に中国国境を展望

(1) A panaromic view of the border with China looking south

Beyik Pass

（いずれもシャイマック / Both fig.s, Shaymak）
中央に玄奘が越した?ベイク峠4482mが望まれる
The Beyik Pass 4482m is shown slightly to the left side of the center of the figure.
Hsüang-tsang may have crossed this pass.

（2）西方にアフガーン国境を展望

(2) The border with Afghanistan can be seen to the west

（シャイマック / Shaymak）
右端はタジキスターン
The area shown on the far right of the figure is in Tajikistan.

48) 夏の放牧地は燃料造りに忙しい
During the summer, the inhabitants are busy preparing fuel.

(1) 天日干しされるカック
(1) Qack being dried in the sun

(2) カックの掘り起こし
(2) Digging up the Qack

(いずれもクルチン / Both fig.s,Qurchin)(Ⓚ)
石垣の上に天日干しされる"カック"。手前の袋の中は刈り取った羊毛
The "qack" is hung over the stone hedge to dry in the sun.
The bag shown in front of the stone hedge is filled with woolen fleece.

　"クルチン"はユルトの吊し戸の横の支柱桟を造る小灌木の名。ここはワフジール路の夏の主な放牧地で、クルチンが多く生えている地なので、その名で称ばれている。
　日暮れ近く帰って来た羊、山羊は"クルガーン"と称ばれる石垣の囲いの内側クルンチに集められる。数ヶ月間で糞と尿は踏み馴らされ粘泥状になっている。スコップで縦・横・高さそれぞれ20×30×10cmほどのブロックに掘り出し、10日ほど日干しすると、"カック"あるいは"オーテ(ト)"と称ばれる絶好の燃料ができる。因みにチベット界隈では、アルガリと称ぶ乾燥させた羊、山羊の糞粒を用いている。

　" Qurchin" means a small bush that is used to build the door frame of the yurt. This place is the main grazing ground in the Wakhjir area during the summer.
　The place is named after the bush that is particularly abundant here. Shortly before nightfall, the sheep and goats return to their "Qurgan" which means inside the stone pen. which is a rectangular enclosure made with stones.
　After months of having been trodden on, the dung and urine of the sheep and goats become as hard as clay. The clay-like substance is then shoveled out and cut into blocks with a dimension of 20cm × 30cm × 10 cm, and then sun-baked. This natural fuel is called either "qack" or "ote". In Tibet the dung of the sheep or goats are dried for use as fuel, which is called argali.

49) 真夏の降雪で消えた峠
The road leading up to the pass is buried under a blanket of snow in mid-summer.

（グルンディ ビル / Grundeh Bel）(Ⓚ) ca 4660m

（2）岩の間を"適当に"登る

(2) Threading between huge boulders as we climb the pass

（峠東直下 / Right below the eastern side of the pass）
"グルン"は大きな岩が多い、"ディ"は所の意味。
"grun" meens many boulders and "de" meens place.

（1）白一色の峠から西を望む

　クルチンから北西に向かう2つ目の峠。巨岩の間を縫うような難路は時ならぬ積雪で見当がつかなくなる。運良く路馴れたキルギス人がヤクで先導してくれた。

(1) Looking west from the snow-covered pass

　Proceeding northwest, this is the second pass after Qurchin. The difficult, boulder-strewn path has disappeared under the unseasonable snow. Fortunately, a group of Kyrgyz who just happened to pass by offered to guide us on their yaks.

（カラ ビル / Qara Bel）（Ⓚ）
ca 4943m、黒い峠
The black pass ca 4943m

クルチンを出発した翌々朝、スパット・キシュ谷が東から南に大きく曲る右岸に在る、サルハッドのアイラークca 4290mを後にする。ここには子供を含む20余人が、ほぼ 100頭のヤク、300頭の羊と山羊を放牧している。

南北の山嶺を見上げながら、山腹の間を西に石礫を踏んで登行する。3時間ほどで、7月初めなら残雪が一面に見られるカラ ビル ca 4943mに着く。大・小パミールを結ぶ峠のうち最も高い。西眼前にワハーン山脈核心部の東部が拡がる。

周りの稜線やその直下の至る所から、黒い帯状が山腹を流れ落ちている。恰かも冷えた溶岩流のように映る。近づくと、浅い溝に黒色の大小様々の流紋岩が、溢れるばかり詰まっている。それで"カラ"黒い峠と称ばれている。

・・・・・・・・・・・・・・・・・・・・・・・・・・・・・・・・・・・・・・

Two mornings after leaving Qurchin, we left the yaylaq (Wakhi's summer grazing camp) of Sarhad ca 4290m. which is located on the right side bank of the Spat Kish Valley. From this point the orientation of the Spat Kish Valley turns abruptly from the east to the south. About 20 inhabitants including children, 100 yaks, and 300 goats and sheep spend the summer season here.

Heading westward, we climbed the stony foothills of the mountains which rise steeply above the summer camp. In three hours we reached Qara Bel ca 4943m which was still covered with snow in early July. This is the highest pass that connects the Great and Little Pamirs. The eastern side of the heart of the Wakhan Mountain Range opened its vista to us.

The ridgeline and the mountainside are streaked in black, recalling flows of lava that have cooled. On closer inspection, these streaks were found to be thick layers of rhyolite of varying sizes. That is the reason why the pass is called "Qara" (Black) Bel (Pass).

51）（南の）シャウル谷：オクサス河側と大パミール側（ゾル グル西方）を結ぶ谷（高仙芝軍の "北谷"）
The south side of the Shaor Valley：The valley that connects the Oxus River side with the (Great) Pamir River side (west of Zor Kul) The "north valley" of Kao Hsien-chih.

（1）谷上流の西南面
(1) The southwestern slopes of the valley upstream

（カラ ビルからの下降地 / Downstream from Qara Bel）

（2）谷の源流地は西方に氷河が多い
(2) The headwaters of the valley is saddled with many glaciers particularly on its western side

（谷の源流地 /
The headwaters of the valley）

　カラ ビルを西に越える。石礫、巨岩の間と草混じりの斜面の順に2時間ほど下ると、（南）のシャウル ジルガ（Ⓚ）左岸に出る。

　遡ると、点在する牧草地や葱叢（そうそう）林を過ぎ、2時間ほどで流れは消え氷河帯に入る。その日は近くのワヒが建てた旅人小屋を意味するスワーブ ハーナ（Ⓦ）に泊る。低い入口を除き、キルギス人のラボートの造りと異なり、石積みの平屋で上部（天井）に窓はない。

　南（左方）に下ると30分でサルハッド西方のシャーシュム周辺のアイラークを過ぎる。更に一時間足らずで、西方からサルハッドに通じる路筋となる谷が合流する地点（図57）に達する。合流した谷は10kmほど下流で、東北から流下するスパット・キシュ谷を併せ、バラック谷となり、同名の地でオクサス河に注ぐ。

　1894年シナ側からワフジール峠を越え、オクサス河右岸を西下してきたカーゾン[56]はこの谷を渉る時に、供のキルギス人から、「この谷を北に遡るとゾル湖と大パミールに出られる」という報告を受け、"まだ踏査されていない（大パミールへ出る）峠がありうる"と記している。

　Passing over the Qara Bel and heading west. It was a two -hour descent down a somewhat grassy slope that was strewn with stones and huge boulders till we reached the left banks of the Shaor Jilga （Ⓚ）(situated to the north).

　After ascending the valley for about two hours, and after passing several pastures and grasslands, the stream disappears under glaciers. That night we stayed at Musaher Khana, which is a small cottage built by the Wakhis for temporary shelter. Similar to the "Rabot" built by the Kyrgyz, the cottage is made with stones, but it does not have a skylight in the ceiling. Both types of shelters have a low entrance.

　By descending south (left side of figure) in 30 minutes we reached the "yaylaq"(summer camp) around Shashum, west of Sarhad. From there after a two- hour ride, a valley leading to Sarhad converges with the path. (fig. 57)). Ten kilometers further downstream from that point, the Spat Kish valley joins from the northeast direction to form the Baharak valley, which drains into the Oxus River at Baharak. In 1894, Lord Curzon crossed the Wakhjir Pass from China and descended in a westerly direction along the right bank of the Oxus.

　A Kyrgyz guide told Curzon that Zor Kul and the Great Pamir could be reached by ascending this valley. Upon hearing this news, Curzon[56] wrote that "It is possible therefore that there may still be unexplored passes in this part of the range that lead to the Great Pamir. "

（シャウル ビル / Shaor Bel）
ca 4850m
峠南直下10mに広がる南北幅が
数百mある大氷河。
A view of the glacier that is
several 100 meters in width,
taken from a vantage point
10 meters below the south of
the pass

　ムサヘル ハーナを出発し45°ぐらいの斜面を巨岩の間を縫いながら暫らく登ると、西からの氷河の南側面舌端に出る。年により異なるが、南面か東面の舌端部と東側の不安定なモレーン帯との裂け目のどちらかが、氷河の上に出る通路になる。氷河の南北幅は数100m。表面にペニテンテス（S）（小さな尖った氷雪塔）が見られる。

　峠が開くのは例年7月中旬。舌端の昇り降りには馬は困難でヤクを雇うのが楽だ。あるキルギス人は"シャウル"は非常に寒いの意味だと呟いた。

After starting from the Musaher Khana, I ascended a steep 45 degree slope. Carefully choosing my path between huge boulders, I reached the southern tip of the snout of a glacier descending from the west. The crest of the glacier can be reached by traversing the chasm that lies between the southern or eastern side of the snout of the glacier, and the unstable moraine on the east side. The route may vary yearly, depending on weather conditions. The width of the glacier north-south is a couple of 100 meters, and it is covered with penitentese (s) or sharp, small icicles.

The pass is usually open from mid-July. Horses have difficulty negotiating the jagged terrain of the snout, so it is best travelled with yaks. A Kyrgyz who accompanied me explained that "Shaor" means very cold.

大パミール
The Great Pamir

53) ゾル クル（大龍池・大湖・ビクトリア湖）西端 ca4111m

Zor Kul (Variously called Great Dragon Lake, Large Lake or Lake Victoria) The western end ca 4111 m

(1)（大）パミール河源流左岸より東方に湖を望む

(1) From the left shore of the (Great) Pamir River looking east towards Zor Kul

（大）パミール河源流左岸 /
The left shore of the foreground of the starting point of the (Great) Pamir River)

(2) 東方の展望

(2) A panoramic view looking towards the east

オクサス河本流と支流（大）パミール河の合流点（図13））から、後者の右岸沿いに、東北へ約120km、4駆車を8時間ほど走らせるとゾル クル西端に至る。ウッド[31]は1838年2月19日午後5時、騎行3日で到着し、約600年前のマルコ ポーロ[55]の記述が正確なことを実証した。

西端は南北に弧状に拡がり、東方は遥か煙霞として青い湖面が広がるのみである。南側は緩やかな斜面で、数km退いてワハーン山脈の氷雪の山嶺が1000mも高く東西に続く。北側はそれよりも低く近く、アリチュール山脈の前衛の稜線が連なる。湖は両山脈に包まれるように位置している。西端からは50mほどの幅で（大）パミール河が西方に流出している。

大きさは年や季節により変化する[57]が、旧ソ連参謀本部の地図[58]では東西長は約18㎞で、南北幅は最大の場所で4㎞足らずと示されている。アフガーンとタジギスターン両国では現在はゾル クル、外国人にはビクトリア湖と称ぶのが一般的である。

642年湖北畔を辿った（と思われる）玄奘は、西域記[32]に「波謎羅川（ポーミーローツアン・パミール渓谷）中に大龍池が有る。東西三百里、南北五十余里。（我が国の里程と規準が異なり、数値も形容的だが）…その地で最も高い。…味は甚だ甘味。…池の西から一大流が出て、達磨悉鐵帝国（ワハーン）の東方で縛芻（オクサス）河に合流し西流する。」と記している。玄奘の地理的記載は頗る正確[59]である。因みに湖水のpHは6.4、塩分は0%であった。

1274年頃のマルコ ポーロはいわゆる東方見聞録[55]に次のように述べている。「ヴォカーン（ワハーン）から東北に、山また山の路を3日間進むと、世界の最高地と思われる峯々に囲まれた所に至る。ここは2筋の山脈の間に一大湖があり、清澄な一条の河が流出している。…。食物を煮焚きしても低地のようにうまくできない」。玄奘の記述よりも描写がより具体的である。

By following the right bank of the Great Pamir River upstream for 120km towards the northeast, from the point where it joins (fig.13)) its parent, the Oxus River, one can reach the west end of Zor Kul. Wood[31] reached the lake on February 19th, 1838 at 5:00 in the evening. Whereas the trip took him three days on horseback, today that distance can be covered in eight hours on a four-wheel drive car. Wood vindicated the accuracy of Marco Polo[55] description of this place 600 years ago in his travelogue "Travels of Marco Polo".

The west end of Zor Kul is shaped like an arc with a north-south orientation. The view to the east is hazy but the expansive, blue lake stands out nonetheless. The southern shore rises gently till it reaches the foot of the snow-covered Wakhan Range that runs east-west and rises abruptly for 1000 meters. The mountains that buttress the valley to the north are lower and closer to the lake, and are the front hills of the Alichur Range. The lake is hemmed in by the two mountain ranges, and the Great Pamir River, 50 meters wide, debouches from the lake and heads west.

The size of the lake varies[57] according to the season , and from year to year. According to the military maps of the former Soviet Union[58], the lake is 18 kilometers long east-west, while the maximum width in the north-south direction is only four kilometers. The lake is called Zor Kul in Tajikistan and Afghanistan, while it is commonly known as Lake Victoria in other countries.

Hsüang-tsang who is believed to have reached the shores of Zor Kul in 642 AD, reports in the Shi-ui-ji[32] that "there is the Great Dragon Lake in the Po-mi-lo-chuan (Pamir Valley). It is 300 li east-west, and 50 li north-south and it is the highest point in elevation. The water of the lake tastes extremely sweet. There is a large river that drains out of the western end which flows into the Fu-chu (Oxus) east of the Ta-mo-his-tie-ti (Wakhan) and proceeds further west. "

The length of one li differs from Japan and China, and the distance may be exaggerated, but Hsüang-tsang 's geographical observations[59] are exceedingly accurate.

The water sample I took from the lake measured 6.4 for pH and 0 % for salt content.

Marco Polo who passed here around 1274, described the area in his "Travels of Marco Polo "[55] as follows:

"Upon leaving this country (Wakhan), and proceeding for three days still in an east-north course, ascending mountains after mountain, you at length arrive at a point of the road, where you might suppose the surrounding summits to be the highest lands in the world. Here, between two ranges, you perceive a large lake, from which flows a handsome river….It was affirmed that from the keenness of the air, fires when lighted do not give the same heat as in lower situations. " Marco Polo's descriptions are more detailed than that of Hsüang-tsang.

（ゾル クル西端南畔（大）パミール河流出口 /
The south bank of the starting place of the (Great) Pamir River
or left bank of the west end of Zor Kul)

(ゾル クル南畔のムックール / Muqur ,great Pamir)
背景は南背後のワハーン山脈東部
In the background of the figure looking southwards, are the mountains of the east Wakhan Range.

(1) 真夏の積雪は馴れっこ

夜半の積雪は強い日照で平地では昼過ぎに消える。"ムックール"(Ⓚ)は高いを意味する。湖畔の夏の放牧地の中で、最も高地ca4400mに在る。夏の放牧地は一般に冬のそれより山麓よりに移る。

(1) The inhabitants are used to snowfalls during the summer.

The snow that has fallen during the night melts away by noon because of the strong sunlight. "Muqur" means high. This is the highest summer grazing camp at ca 4400 meters. Generally speaking, the Kyrgyz move up their summer grazing camps closer to the foot of the mountains than their winter grazing camps.

(2) 東方の展望

(2) A panoramic view looking towards the east

（スティク / Steq）
湖対岸4kmほどの北はタジキスターン
Tajikistan lies four kilometers from this location, across the lake.

(3) 南畔最東端の冬放牧地

(3) The winter grazing camp located on the east end of the south bank

（コックブルク / Kokbulq）
夏と同じく湖畔に在る。
The winter camp is located in the same side
as the summer camp near the shores of the lake.

他の夏の放牧地は湖畔を離れ、南背後のワハーン山脈の麓近くに開かれるが、ここだけは湖畔に在る。数ヶ所に開かれる夏の放牧地で最も東に在る。冬の放牧地コックブルクは更に東方に移り、ゾル クル東端の3km手前でやはり湖畔に位置している。そこには数軒のトムと西背後の低い丘に数基のグムバーズが見られる。

Most grazing camps relocate in the summer to the foothills of the Wakhan Range to the south and away from the shore of the lake. This camp, located further east than the others, remains near the shore. The winter grazing camp known as Kokbulq moves even further east to within 3 km of the easternmost end of Zor Kul, and remains near its shore. There are several toms here and a number of low gumbaz (tombs) lying atop some small hills on the west.

55) ゾル クル東端
Eastern end of Zor Kul

(1) 南畔　アフガーンより北にタジキスターンを展望

(1) South shore　A panoramic view from the south shore of Zor Kul in Afghanistan looking northwards at Tajikistan

アフガーン側標柱
A pillar marking the border
with Tajikistan on the Afghan side

国境標台
The foundation of the pillar

タジキスターン側標柱
he pillar marking the border
on theTajikistan side

（南畔　高度差５０ｍの台地 / The south shore　A plateau that rises ca 50 meters in height）

(2) 北畔　タジキスターンより南にアフガニスターンを展望

(2) North shore　A panoramic view from the northern shore of Zor Kul looking southwards at Afghanistan

（北畔 ca 4114m / North shore ca 4114m)

湖畔の裾野は、アフガーン側がタジキスターン側よりも、傾斜帯が深く緩やかで、起伏も少なく牧草地も多く、ユルト群が点在する。タジキスターン側は冬期には、東端に在る国境監視隊を除けば無人の境となる。夏期でもタジキスターン・イシュカシェムのワヒの小さなアイラックが、2ヶ所に見られるだけである。アフアガーン側は夏・冬を通じて、数ヶ所にキルギス人の放牧地が在り、優に100を超える人々が常住している。

On the Afghan side, the slope along the lake leading to the foothills of the mountains is gentler and wider with better pasture than the Tajikistan side. There are many groups of yurts here. In the winter time the shores of Zor Kul in Tajikistan are totally devoid of people, except for Tajik soldiers manning the military post at the eastern end of the lake. Even during the summer, I could only observe two yaylaqs (summer camps) belonging to the Wakhis that move here from Ishkashim in Tajikistan. On the Afghan side, however, throughout the year there are several grazing camps populated by at least 100 Kyrgyz.

（湖東北端 / East northern end of the Lake)
南方の展望
A view towards south

　湖東端北畔に、東から幅20mぐらいの一条の極めて緩りとした流れが注いでいる。玄奘が西域記[32]に「池東派一大流」と記した流れと思われる。

　湖東端を過ぎ東へ暫く進むと、どこが分水界なのか解らない曠野に至る。そこに一本の流れで結ばれている、コクジギトゥと称ばれる双子の娘湖が在る。西側の湖の西縁から一条の流れが母湖に流れ出ている。流れは母湖南東からの複数の谷水を併せ、入江状の流入口直前で蛇行して母湖に入る。極めて緩りとした流れは、絶え間なく吹きつける西風のボーディ・ワハーンが立てる漣で、恰も緩りと東流しているように見える。

　玄奘が池の東から一本の河が"東に流出している"と観たのも無理ないと思われる。私が撮ったビデオでも漣は東に流れている。この様子を見れば地形的知識がなければ、誰の目にもそのように映るであろう。玄奘の地理的記述の的確さには驚かされる。

　因みに、この流れの源である双子の東側の東縁の僅か東方に、分水界が在ると思われ、1874年5月ゴードン一行のトロッター大尉[60]（英陸軍）は、14,300フィート（約4333m）と測量している。そこを越えほゞ同緯度で、少し東南方に在る小湖カラドゥンギ湖からは、イスティク河の源流が東流し、間もなくアンデミン峠の北麓で東北に流れを変え、後にアク‐スーに注ぐ。

　A slow-flowing river, only about 20 meters wide, meanders slowly into the eastern end of the north shore of Zor Kul. This must be the river that Hsüang-tsang mistakenly described as flowing east in his travelogue, the Shi-ui-ji.[32]

　From the eastern end of Zor Kul, as one proceeds further east, the plain widens. But the undulation is so gentle that it is difficult to discern the location of the watershed. In the area, there are two lakes called Kokjigit (meaning twin girls) that are connected by a single river. From the west end of the first lake (of the twin lakes, the lake on the west side) a stream debouches towards Zor Kul. The stream is joined by several rivulets that drain from the valleys to the southeast, before it meanders into the marshes that appear like an islet at the eastern end of Zor Kul. The river flows slowly, but the prevailing westerly winds called the "Bad-i-Wakhan"whip up waves that leave an impression that the river is actually flowing east.

　Therefore, one cannot blame Hsüang-tsang for concluding that "the river flowed eastwards" from where it debouches from the east end of the lake. The video that I took would also leave the same impression. Without any topographical knowledge about the area, anybody would think that the river flowed east. I am always astonished by how accurate Hsüang-tsang 's geographical descriptions are.

　The actual watershed which is this area of this river, can be found some further east than the pair of lakes. In May, 1874, Captain Trotter[60] of the British Army, who accompanied Gordon on his mission to the Pamirs, measured the altitude of this place at 14,300 feet (about 4333 meters). Beyond the watershed, there is another small lake called Karadungi situated slightly to the southeast and at almost at the same latitude as Kokjigit Lake. The lake is the source of the Istyk River, which flows east. Near the northern foothills of the Andemin Pass, the Istyk river turns northeast before it joins the Ak-Su (River).

2人は①ワハーンのオクサス河左岸沿い・アフガーン側を通り、②パミール渓谷を辿り大龍池・大湖（ビクトリア湖・ゾル クル）に至り、③ここからは別々の路筋でシナに入った。これらはほぼ定説であるが、オクサス河をどの辺りで渉ったのか?、パミール渓谷を辿るのに(大)パミール河の左・右どちらの岸側を辿ったのか?などのついては、言及がされていない。これらの点について、2人の記述と現地踏査の印象とを併せて、次のような推察を試みた。

因みに私はこれらの地域を、①では右岸沿いに2往復と左岸沿いに6往復、②では両岸沿いにそれぞれ2往復および湖北畔を一往復と南畔を3往復し、③では湖の少し東方で大パミールから小パミールの主部に抜けるアンデミン峠（赤い峠）（図40(2)）に一往復しまた小パミール側からは、冬放牧地アンデミン北背後で、赤い峠に一往復、大峠（図40(1)）に2往復した。さらにその東方に位置するジャマナンシュル峠およびウルタ峠（図43)）にそれぞれ一往復している。期間としては1999年〜2011年の6月〜9月である。

(1) ワハーンから大龍池・大湖 (ゾル クル) へ

玄奘：西域記[21]に「達摩悉鐵帝国。在兩山間。…狹則不踰一里。臨縛蒭河。…。眼多碧緑異於諸国。…昏駄多域国之都也。中有伽藍。」とある。ワハーンの地形とワハーン人に多く見られる、金髪緑眼の外見の特徴を適格に伝えている。達摩悉鐵帝がワハーン、昏駄多がワハーン回廊最大の集落ハンドゥードゥであることは、スタイン[22]他[23]により同定されている。これはほぼ定説である。近年には複数ヶ所に仏教遺趾[24]（図10)）が発見されている。因みにオクサス河右岸には、該当する地名はない。

20kmほど東のカラ・イ・パンジャで、オクサス河を右岸に渉った。シルク ロード時代の夏の路[41]は、大パミール路であった。1874年4月末にゴートンら[29]もここで河を渉り、(大)パミール河右岸を辿り、ゾル クル北畔を通りシナに入っている。オクサス河を渡渉すると少し東進し、本流と支流（大）パミール河の合流点から、後者の右岸沿いに東北へ一日と半日ほど進む。始めは河畔を離れ山中を、次いで河畔の絶壁に近い山腹（図59)(4)）を辿る。河畔に下り（図59)(2)）同じ日程でゾル クル西端（図53)(1)、57)(1)）に達する。左岸（アフガーン側）沿いの路は、所要日数が長くなる（図59)(2)）。西域記[32]には、「至波謎羅川。…狹隘之處不踰十里。據兩雪山間故、寒風凄勁。春夏飛雪昼夜飄風。…草木稀少、…絶無人止。波謎羅川中在大龍池。…池西派一大流。西至達摩悉鐵帝国東界、與縛蒭河合而西流。」と記されている。

Based upon my speculation, I propose that Hsüang-tsang and Marco Polo in the Wakhan Corridor :
It is generally believed that Hsüang-tsang and Marco Polo took the following routes through Wakhan.
①The left bank of the Oxus River of what is now Afghanistan.
②Along the(Great)Pamir River until reaching the Great Dragon Lake or Large Lake (Lake Victoria, Zor Kul), which today is in Tajikistan
③The two chose different passes to cross over to China.

But at what point did they ford the Oxus River? Which side of the (Great) Pamir River did they traverse, the right side, or the left when they passed through the Pamir Valley? Such details are not mentioned in their travelogues. Having traveled several times in this area, I will make an attempt to retrace the route that Hsüang-tsang and Marco Polo took, based on the records they left, and drawing upon the impression I gained of the area.

As for my own travels in the region :
For ①, I traveled along the right bank of the Oxus River (Ab-i-Panj) making two round trips. I made six round trips along the left bank .
For ②, I traveled along both banks of the (Great) Pamir River making two round trips each. I also made one round trip along the north shore of Lake Zor Kul. On another occasion, I traveled along the north shore of Zorkul in the same direction once. And yet another time I made three round trips along the south shore of Zorkul.
For ③, I made one round trip to the Quiziel Bel or Red Pass (one of the Andemin Pass) (fig.40)(2)) which is located somewhat to the southeast of Lake Zor Kul and connects the Great Pamir with the main area of the Little Pamir. From the Little Pamir side I made one round trip to the Red Pass , and two round trips to the Zor Bel or Large Pass (another one of the Andemin Pass)(fig.40)(1)), from the northern hinterland of the winter pasture Andemin. I made one round trip each to the Jamananshuru Pass and the Urta Pass (fig.42),43)) which are located somewhat further east. I visited the area three times between 2006 to 2010, during the summer season from June to September.

(1)From the Wakhan to the Great Dragon Lake ・the Large Lake (Zor Kul)

Hsüang-tsang ：Hsüang-tsang tells us in his Shi-ui-ji[32] that "The Kingdom of Ta-mo-his-tie-ti (Wakhan) is situated between two mountains. At the narrowest point it is less than 1 Li. It lies along the River Fu-chu (Oxus), and is populated by people who for the most part have greenish-blue eyes that distinguish them from other people. Hun-to-to is the capital of the kingdom. In the center of the town there rises a convent"((Buddhism temple or monastery?)). ("English"translation,from bibliography 22 and double parenthesis, author's note). Stein[22] and others[23] have identified the Kingdom of Ta-mo-his-tie-ti with Wakhan and Hun-to-to with the present day Khandud, the largest settlement in the Wakhan. In recent years the remains of structures that are believed to be Buddhist temples or monasteries[24] (fig.10)) have been discovered. On the right bank of the Oxus, none of the settlements have names that would correspond to Khandud.

20 km further east, Hsüang-tsang crossed the Oxus at Qala-i -Panja to reach the right bank. The summer route[41] during the age of the Silk Road followed the (Great) Pamir River. At the end of April, 1874, Gordon[29] also forded the Oxus at Qala-i -Panja, and followed the right bank of the (Great) Pamir River till he reached the northern shore of Lake Zor Kul before he crossed into China. After fording the Oxus, further east, and after passing the confluence of the (Great) Pamir River and the main course of the Oxus, the track proceeds along the right bank of the (Great) Pamir River for one and a half days. From this point one must traverse a track that meanders high up along the mountain side. The track on the mountain side becomes precipitous (fig. 59)(4)) before it descends to the banks of the river (fig. 59) (2)). From this point it takes another day and a half to reach the western end of Zor Kul (fig.53)). It would take even longer to reach Zor Kul if one should follow the left bank (Afghanistan-side) (fig. 59) (2)).

According to the Shi-ui-ji,[32] "The Pamir Valley is 10 Li at its narrowest point. It winds between two snowy mountain ranges. The snow falls even during spring and summer. The cold winds and icy storms rage.

渓谷右岸沿いの地形、風景や7月初旬を想わせる気象を如実に述べている。現在でもハルグーシにタジキスターン軍の駐屯地と2軒のキルギス人家屋が在るのと、道傍から遠く離れた山中に、小規模のワヒのアイラークが2〜3ヶ所開かれているのみで、他には住む人を見ない。

湖の西端から流出した（大）パミール河（図53）(1)）は西南下し、オクサス河に合流する（図13））。大龍池の位置の記述はゾル クルの現状そのものである。更に西域記[32]には「…浮遊乃鴛鴦…諸鳥大卵遺殻荒野或沙渚上。」とある。北畔は南畔よりも出入りが多く、岸辺には茸のような草叢が見られる所も在る。鳥が卵を産みやすい。事実水鳥は北畔の湖面に多い。6月の湖[57]は半ばが氷雪に覆われている。南畔のキルギス人からも6月下旬でも氷塊が漂っている年があると聞いている。記述には氷塊のことなどはないことからみると、上記「春夏飛雪…」を併せて、夏期の早期7月上旬が考えられる。西域記[32]の記述は右岸（図59(4)）を彷彿させる。大龍池は北畔を過ぎた。

大龍池をチャクマク・ティン湖とする説もあるが、「至波謎羅川。…西派一大流。…與縛芻河合而西流。」の記述からみて、この説は諒とできない。

マルコ ポーロ：東方見聞録[61]によると、「バダフシャーンを後にして3日後にボカーンと謂う小じんまりした地方に着く。どの方向に旅しても3日で済む。…。住民はイスラーム教徒で、固有の言語を持ち…。」とある。大きな河を渉るような記述はなく、オクサス河左岸を進んでいることが分かる。

同録には続けて[55]「2つの山脈の間に大湖が在る。そこより一本の美事な河が流れ出し、その流域は新緑で覆われ、どんなに痩せた家畜でも10日間も放牧すると、きっと肥えるに違いない。…なかでも大型の野生羊が非常に多く棲息している。その角は大きいものでは6パームにも達し…。」とある。7月上・中旬の(大)パミール河の右岸畔は流出口から10余kmの間は、新緑の草地帯で美しい。この草地帯は8月中旬には黄色くなっている。左岸は草が乏しい。東方見聞録の記述からすると右岸を辿り、ゾル クル北畔を進んだと思える。

行く路の周囲の雪については記述がない。それで彼は玄奘より少し遅れて、この地域を通ったものと思われる。なお彼はパミールの名を初めて記録したヨーロッパ人[62]である。東方見聞録の和訳本は20冊前後あり、"大湖"をラン湖あるいは(小?)カラ湖と注釈しているものが複数みられるが、地理的にも地形的にもゾル クル以外には考えられない。

玄奘のような湖畔の記述がないが、そのまま湖北畔を通ったと考えられる。

There are no trees . Scarcely have travelers entered this region. In the middle of the Pa-mi-lo Valley lies the Great Dragon Lake. A large river drains from the western end of the lake, and joins the Fu-Chu River (Oxus) at the eastern end of the Kingdom of the Ta-mo-his-tie-ti." ("English"translation,from bibliography [66]).

Hsüang-tsang' description of the topography and scenery along the great Pamir valley are accurate as they match my own observations and the climate I have experienced in that region in early July. Even today in Khargoush, Tajikistan, the area is uninhabited with the exception of a military garrison, two Kyrgyz houses and two or three Wakhi summer grazing camps, known as yaylaq.

The (Great) Pamir River (fig. 53) (1)) which drains from the west end of Zor Kul flows downstream in a northwesterly direction until it joins the Oxus (fig. 13)). Hsüang-tsang 's description regarding the location of the Great Dragon Lake stands true today. The Shi-ui-ji [32] provides us with additional descriptions.

"Floating on its surface are ducks, wild geese , cranes and so on. Many other types of water-fowl are resting on its sandy shore." ("English"translation,from bibliography 66.There is much more inflow and outflow of rivulets on the northern bank of the lake when compared to the south, and the banks are covered with reeds in some places. The shores of the lake offer good shelter for nesting birds. As Hsüang-tsang so accurately describes, more birds can be observed along the north shore. Zor Kul in June[57] is still partially covered with ice and snow, and I was told by a Kyrgyz nomad when I visited the south shore of the lake, that in some years even at the end of June blocks of ice can still be seen floating on its waters. Since Hsüang-tsang did not mention seeing any blocks of ice, we can assume that he visited the lake around the beginning of July. The description of the area given by the Shi-ui-ji[32] evokes images of the right bank (fig.59)(4)) of the (Great) Pamir River (fig.59)(4)), and suggests that the pilgrim must have passed the north shore of the Great Dragon Lake.

Some suggest that Chaqmak-tin Lake corresponds to the Great Dragon Lake described by Hsüang-tsang. I would refute that view, based on the description given in the following text of the Shi-ui-ji[32]: " To the west of the lake there is a large stream which, going west, reaches so far as the eastern borders of Ta-mo-hsi-t'ie-ti (Wakhan) and there joins the river Po-ch'u (Oxus), and flows still to the west." ("English"translation,from bibliography[66]).

Marco Polo: The following description that can be found in the " Travels of Marco Polo[61] " does not mention a big river that has to be forded." Upon leaving this country (Badakhshan) and proceeding three days, I entered a small country by the name of Vokhan. It takes three days from any direction to reach this place. The inhabitants are Muslims, and have a distinct language". From this description, one can assume that Marco Polo traveled along the left bank of the Oxus River.

The "Travels[55]" continues as follows: "Here between two ranges, you perceive a large lake, from which flows a handsome river, that pursues its course along an extensive plain, covered with the richest verdure. Such indeed is its quality that the leanest cattle turned upon it would become fat in the course of ten days…In this plain there are wild animals in great numbers, particularly sheep of a large size, having horns six palms in length ". The verdure of the grassy plains along the right bank of the (Great) Pamir River stretching for a distance of 10 kilometers is green and beautiful during July, but by mid-August, the grass turns yellow. The left bank is nearly devoid of grass. Judging from the description of the place in the "Travels", we can assume that Marco Polo followed the right bank of the river and the north shore of Zor Kul.

There is no mention of snow in the Travels. Therefore Marco Polo must have passed by this area at a later time of year than Hsüang-tsang . Marco Polo is the first European[62] to have recorded the name, Pamir. There are about 20 different Japanese translations of " The Travels of Marco Polo", some of which claim that the Large Lake corresponds to Ran Kul or the (small?) Kara Kul (Lake). However, I would refute those claims, based on the geographical and topographical details given by Marco Polo about the Large Lake. The only lake that would fit the description is Zor Kul.

Unlike Hsüang-tsang , though Marco Polo does not provide us with a description of the area around Zor Kul, we can safely assume that he must have passed through the north shore of Zor Kul.

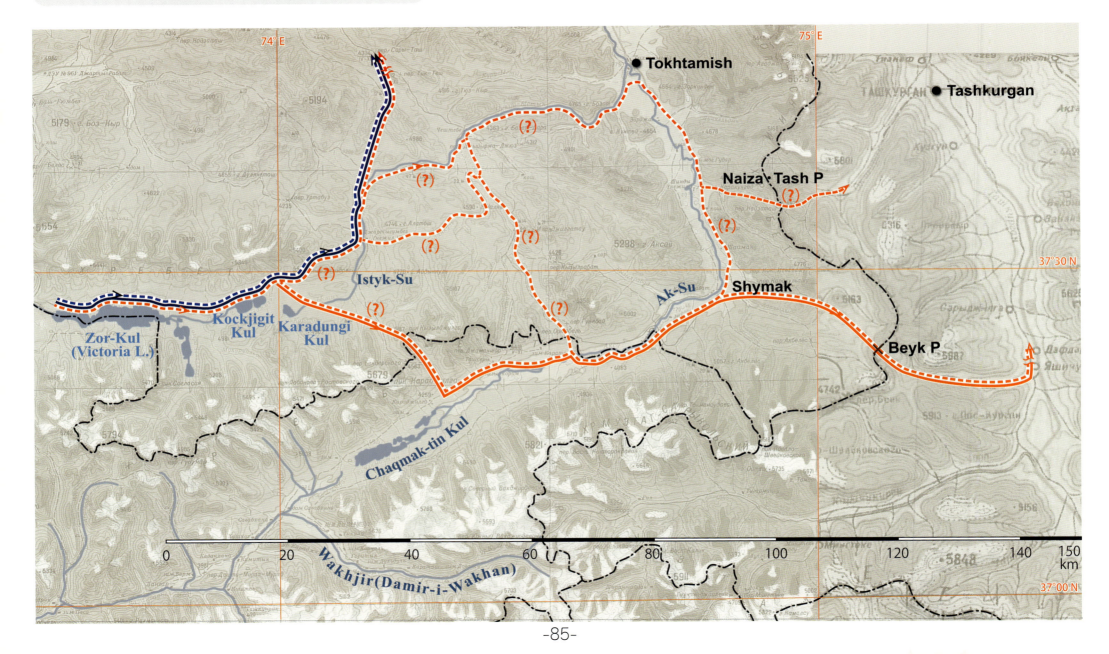

(2) 湖東端からタ一グドゥムバシュ パミールへ

玄奘：西域記[32)][54)]には、「池東派一大流。東北至…。…。自此此川中東南登山覆険。路無人里唯多氷雪。行五百余里至掲盤陁国。」とある。

湖東端から掲盤陁国（タシュクルガーン）への進路について、スタイン[63)]は二つの経路とそれの可能性の大きい路筋を述べている。「東へ進んで（北下するアク・スーを渉り：以下（ ）は筆者注）ネザ タ一シュ峠（4548m 換算約14,961ft.）を越える。考えやすい他の経路は、（東下する）アク・スー沿いに進み、（河が北曲する辺りから南折して）小パミールから越えやすいベイク峠（4482m 換算約14,743ft.）かその近辺の峠を越え、タ一グドゥムバシュ パミールに至る。

アク・スー側に出るには、いわゆるニコラス（ワハーン）山脈をベンデルスキ（アンデミン）峠 14,705ft.(換算約4470m）か（少し東の）ウルタ峠 14,090ft.(換算約4283m）か最東端の最も低いキジル ラボート峠を越える」。酒井[64)]も「川中（渓谷）より東南に向かって山を登り」に一致する、としてこの仮説を支持している。因みに、後記2峠への路は、眞東へ進んだ後、眞南に向きを変えねばならない。

湖の東端からタ一グドゥムバシュ パミールへは、次のように考えられる。

東端からすぐ"東流する"流れは土手に隠れて見えなくなる。湖東端で3kmほどに狭まった渓間は、東へ行くにつれ徐々に展け、路筋は流れから北に離れていく。約12km東方の双子のコクジギイトゥ湖の西側の湖は、玄奘のいう"東流する"流れの源であるが、その状景は路筋からは見えない。ゾル クル東端からほぼ18km離れた東側のコクジギイトゥ湖の辺りでは、渓間は10km前後にも展ける。200～300m東でどこと解らない南北の分水界を越えた辺りから、東南に向きを変える。暫く進み緩りと東に下り、浅い流れを渉る。コクジギイトゥ湖とほぼ同緯度で、やや東南に位置するカラドゥンギ湖から東下する流れである。

地図のない時代、玄奘が"東流する河"と見誤ったとしても当然であろう。

間もなくアンデミン峠（クィジール峠）（図39）(2)）の登り口に着く。北を振りかえると、さきほどの流れは、数本の谷水を併せ東北に向かい、イステイク河となっていくのが眺められる。登路の谷間周囲の4000m級の山腹には氷河や雪が付いている。峠を越えアク・スー左岸沿いに東に進む。当時は無人の境であったのかも知れない。現在でも7月上旬にはキルギス人達は、右岸に移っていて姿が見られない。小パミ一ル東端で河が北曲する辺りから、南に向きを変え、まだ氷雪に埋ったベイク峠を越える。玄奘の記述[54)]を素直に解釋するとこの推察が浮かんでくる。

マルコ ポーロ：ゾル クルから先の路筋については、カシュガルに出たものと思われるが、東北あるいは東という方向と日数が記されているが、経路を推察するのは困難である。氷雪についての記録が見られない事からワハーン山脈を越えず、イステイク河沿い東北に向かったことは推察できる。

(2) From the eastern end of Zorkul to the Taghdumbash Pamir

Hsüang-tsang : According to Hsüang-tsang's Shi-ui-ji.[32)][54)] " On leaving the midst of this (Pa-mi-lo) valley and going south-east, along the route, there is there are neither men nor villages. Ascending the mountains, traversing the side of precipices, encountering nothing but ice and snow, and thus going 500 li, we arrive at the kingdom of Chieh-pan-to."

In speculating about the route that Hsüang-tsang must have taken between the eastern end of Zor Kul and the Kingdom of Chieh-pan-to (Tashkurgan), Stein[63)] gives us a detailed analysis regarding two possible routes. " He can either make his way in a generally eastern direction to the Naize-Tash Pass ((about 14,961ft)), the descent from which would bring him straight to Tashkurgan ((by crossing the Ak-Su which flows north)) . (Double palenthesis are author's notes). Or he may direct his route first into the valley of the Ak-Su (River), and thence reach the upper portion of the Taghdumbash Pamir by going southwards ((turning south where the river makes a bend to the north)) the watershed range being crossed here by a series of passes of which the Peyik or Beyik Pass ((about 14,743ft.)) is the most frequented and easiest." ("English" translation, from bibliography[63)] .

To reach the Ak-Su side, one must cross the Nicholas Range ((Wakhan Range)) by going over the Benderski ((Andemin)) Pass 14,705 ft., or by crossing over the Urta Pass 14,090ft. which lies further east. Or one can cross the Kizil Rabot Pass which is situated even further east and is the lowest pass of the three. Sakai[64)] also supports Stein's analysis that Hsüang-tsang must have first headed southeast in the midst of the Pamir and then climbed over a mountain. To reach the latter two passes, one must go due east first and turn to proceed due south.

Therefore we can assum that Hsüang-tsang proceeded along the following route from the eastern end of Zor Kul to the Taghdumbash Pamir. The river that was mistakenly described as flowing east from Zor Kul becomes hidden behind the undulating shore that form a natural embankment. The valley that lies to the east of Zor Kul which initially has a width of only 3 km, becomes wider the further east you go, while the track deviates northward away from the river. About 12 km to the east, there are two lakes called the Kokjigit Lake. Of these two lakes, the one which is located to the west is the source of "the river that flows east" as Hsüang-tsang mistakenly described. However, this flow cannot be seen from the path. Eighteen kilometers from the eastern end of Zor Kul near where the Kokjigit Lake is located, the valley widens to about ten kilometers. The north-south watershed is located about 200 to 300 meters further east of this lake but it is hardly discernible. From here the route turns southeast and descends a mild slope towards the east and then crosses a small shallow stream. This stream drains from a small lake called the Karadungi that lies at almost the same latitude and is slightly southeast of the Kokjigit Lake. The stream is the headwater of the Istyk River. At an age where there were no maps, it is no wonder that Hsüang-tsang mistook the direction of the river flow and concluded that "it flowed east".

The entrance to the Andemin Pass (Quiziel Pass) (fig. 39) (2)) is near this point. Looking towards the north, one can see that the stream we crossed a short time ago has gathered some tributaries and is now heading northeast to become the Istyk River. The valley that the track leads into is surrounded by mountains covered with glaciers and snow that include 4000 meter-class peaks. Hsüang-tsang must have crossed this pass and followed the left bank of the Ak-Su to proceed east. Perhaps the area in those days was completed uninhabited. Even today, by early July, the Kyrgyz have moved to the right bank of the Ak-Su, leaving the left bank devoid of people. At the eastern end of the Little Pamir where the Ak-Su turns north, Hsüang-tsang must have turned south, and crossed the snow-covered, Bayik Pass. A straightforward interpretation of Hsüang-tsang's record[54)] should allow this speculation to hold.

Marco Polo: Marco Polo is believed to have arrived in Kashgar after leaving Zor Kul. Yet though "The Travels" tells us that Marco proceeded either northeast or east, and yet though the general itinerary is explained, it is difficult to speculate on the course that he took beyond Zor Kul. It can be assumed, however, that he proceeded northeast along the Istyk River.

大パミール側からオクサス河側へ
From the area drained by the Great Pamir to the Oxus River side

(1) 展望
(1) Panorama

Shaor Pass

(2) 峠への入口
(2) The entrance of the pass

Shaor Pass

(ゾル クル西方ca 2,5km / West of Zor Kul ca 2.5km)
右端の小湖東端上方がシャウル谷
On the right, above the eastern end of the small lake
is the Shaor Valley.

　ゾル クル西端から（大）パミール河右岸沿いに、少し西下したやや高みの道路端から、南にシャウル谷入口を望む。ここ[65]は1915年8月27日アフガーンに入る許可を得られなかったスタインが、供のキルギス人から、大パミール側よりオクサス河側に越える峠が在る、ことを訊き出した地点と思われる。スタイン[66]は次のように記している。「旧唐書よると、高仙芝は軍を東・西・北の3方向から、現在のサルハッドに集合させた。…。しかし北からの進軍路については、大パミール側から入ったに違いないが、地図や文献からは情報を得ることができなかった。供の大変旅馴れた2人のキルギス人から、ワハーンのタジク族の羊飼いが、現在も使用している古くからの路が、大パミール湖の南の高い山脈を越えて、サルハッドに通じていると謂う、決定的な証檬を訊き出すことができた。」

　The mouth of the Shaor Valley is clearly visible at a point beyond the western end of Zor Kul, towards the south from a slightly elevated path on the right bank of the Great Pamir River. On August 27, 1915, Stein[66] who did not have the permission to enter Afghanistan, heard from two Kyrgyz who were accompanying his party about a pass that connected the Great Pamirs with the Oxus River side. I believe that it was at this place[65] that Stein learned about this pass from the two Kyrgyz. To quote to Stein's record[66], "in describing Kao Hsien-chih's expedition of A.D.747 across the Pamir, the T'ang Annals mention that he concentrated his forces at a point on the uppermost Oxus corresponding to the present Sarhad by three routes, from the east, west and north. But of the northern route, which must have led from the side of the Great Pamir, no information could be gained by me from maps and books. Now, inquiries from two much-traveled Kirghiz in my party elicited definite evidence as to an old track still used by Tajik herdsmen of Wakhan leading across the high range south of the Great Pamir lake to Sarhad".

58) "北谷" は古代からの路
The ancient track passes through the "North Valley"

(1) 仏舎利塔と梵語 (?) の岩絵
(1) A petroglyph of a stupa and Sanskrit writing

（合流点　西背後の斜面/ A slope on the west of the confluence ）

　シャウル ビル南直下の大きな氷河を横切り、(南の) シャウル ジルガ (谷) の左岸沿いに南下し、左手にカラ ビルへの分かれ路を過ぎ、大パミール側から8時間ばかりでワヒのアイラークに着く。

　翌朝出発後30分ほどで、サルハッドに出る路筋となる西からの支谷が合流する。その北傍で渡渉し、西からの支谷の左岸に出る。数ヶの岩に描かれた絵を意味する "サンギ・ナウィスタ" (Ⓓ) が目に入る。弓を射る人と動物が描かれている。西背後100mばかりの斜面台地の巨岩には、仏舎利塔と梵語らしい字が遺されている。いずれもこの路が古代から用いられていたことを物語っている。

　スタイン[66] は (南の) シャウル ジルガはアブ・イ・パンジャに注ぐが、その途中で草付きの緩やかな斜面を辿って、サルハッドに至る路が分かれる、とゾル クル西方でシャウル峠を望んだ際に推論した。

(2) 弓を射る人と動物
(2) A petroglyph of a human with a bow and arrow, and an animal

（合流点西畔 / North shore of the confluence ）

　Crossing the big glacier immediately below the Shaor Bel(Pass) (on the southern face), and proceeding southwards along the left bank of the   sorthern Shor-Jilga (Valley), one reaches a point where the route bifurcates. One route leads to the Qara Bel, while the second route leads to a Wakhi yaylaq (summer encampment) which I reached within eight hours from the Great Pamir side.

　Thirty minutes after we started next morning, we reached a side valley coming from the west which leads to Sarhad. At the confluence, I crossed over to the left bank of the side valley. My attention was drawn to a few boulders engraved with petroglyphs , or "Sangi nauista" (Ⓓ) in the local language. These petroglyphs depicted hunters holding bows and arrows, and animals. In the background towards the west, on a 100 -meter sloping plateau, the petroglyphs of a Buddhist stupa and Sanskrit writings were clearly visible on the surface of a big rock These petroglyphs prove that this was an ancient track that was traveled frequently in the past.

　As Stein[66] stood west of Zor Kul looking towards the Shaor Pass, he noted that the "Shor-jilga leads up to the Ab-i-Panj, while the other track was said to cross in succession the heads of the grazing valleys over easy slopes and thus to reach Sarhad ".

(3) Chap Darah (Ⓓ) Uween (Ⓦ) 左股谷峠より南にヒンドゥ ラージ山脈を展望

(3) A panoramic view of the Hindu Raj looking south from Chap Darah (Ⓓ) Uween (Ⓦ)・the pass in the valley on the left side

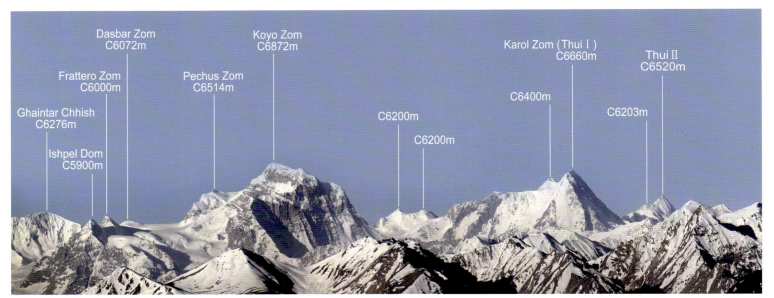

Identified by T.Miyamori

(峠頂上 ca 4734m / Top of the pass ca 4734m)

(4) 峠直北下の小湖

(4) A small lake mmediately below the north face of the pass

(5) "北谷" のサルハッド

(5) The " North Valley" from its mouth facing Sarhad

(サルハッド西北端 / Northernwest end of Sarhad)

　（南の）シャウル谷に注ぐ西からの支谷沿いに緩やかに3時間ほど進み、南に向きを変え2時間もすると、サルハッド直北背後のチャプ ダラ峠に達する。峠直北下に7月初旬だとまだ氷雪に埋れている小湖が在る。峠からは南に4000m台と低いバロギール地域のヒンドゥ クシュ山脈越しに、6000m級のヒンドゥ ラージの氷雪の屏風が展望される。

　峠を越え石屑の狭い谷間を3時間ほど降りる。下方で断崖状の高捲きをしながら、3時間も降りると突然眼前が展ける。広いオクサスの河床を挟み、急峻な岩山の頂に小さく連雲堡趾が目に入る。30分ほどでサルハッド西端に降り立つ図58（5））。スタインはこの行程と思われる路筋を"北谷"と推察し、1906年5月に連雲堡趾から、サルハッド東端の谷間を北谷路出口辺りとして写真[67]を残している。

　"チャプ"は左、"ダラ"は谷の意味。

Proceeding three hours along the gentle, undulating side valley that joins the Shaor Valley from the west, and then turning south and pressing forward for another two hours, the track reaches the Chap Darah Pass located immediately north of Sarhad. There is a small lake right below the crest on the north face that is covered with ice and snow, even in the beginning of July. Looking south from the pass, in the forefront of the panaromic view lie the relatively low 4000m-class peaks of the Hindu Kush mountains around the Baroghil Pass, beyond which the sheer, ice walls of the Hindu Raj stand majestically among 6000m-class peaks.

After climbing over the pass, it takes three hours to descend the rock-strewn, narrow defile. Proceeding for an additional three hours along a precipitous cliff, suddenly the view opens up across the wide river bed of the Oxus to show a steep spur on top of which the Tibetan stronghold, Lien-yun-po is perched high. From here in 30 minutes one can reach the western fringe of Sarhad(fig. 58)(5)). Stein speculated that this track was the "north valley", and in 1906 May, from the Tibetan stronghold, Lien-yun-po , he took a photograph[67] of the valley to the east of Sarhad , convinced that this was the outlet of the "north valley" route.

"Chap" means left, and "Dara " means valley.

（大）パミール河の両岸
The Great Pamir

（1）上流域の両岸

　右岸（タジキスターン側）河畔は湖西端から10余kmの間、夏には緑草帯が続く。

　左岸畔は流出口より10kmも西下すると、爪先上りの10kmにも及ぶワハーン山脈北麓が、西方に20余kmも続く。その間には数本の清澄な渓流が（大）パミール河に注ぐ。それらに沿って牧草地が点在し、その10数ヶ所に小規模のキルギス人のユルトが見られる。

(1) Both banks of upper stream

　The right bank (on the Tajikistan side) of the (Great) Pamir , is covered with verdure during the summer months for about 10 kilometers.

　Ten kilometers west after starting point of the (Great) Pamir on the left bank, the northern flank of the Wakhan Range rises abruptly and stretches westward for another 20 kilometers. Several clear streams flow out from the mountain range and join the (Great) Pamir River. The summer grazing camps are dotted along these streams. In more than a dozen of such summer encampments, the Kyrgyz have set up groups of two or three yurts.

Koh-i-Pamir 6286m
Koh-i-Khan 6020m
Koh-i-Malco Polo 6174m
Koh-i-Hilal 6281m

（アフガーン側：ワハーン山脈核心部北麓 /
On the Afghanistan side： the northern side of the quintessential stretch of the Wakhan Range)

（アフガーン側より：ハルグーシ西方左岸 /
View from the Afghan side :
The left bank on the west side of Khargoush.)

（2）中流域の両岸

　右岸は、タジキスターン側のワハーンのキフゥン（ランガール）に至る間、湖東北端及びハルグーシに在る軍の小さな駐屯地と2軒の民間人住居を除くと、玄奘が通過した1400年昔の時代と同じく、常住する人影を見ない。河畔の狭い平坦地にトラック道路が続く。

　左岸のアフガーン側ハルグーシには、キルギスの西端の冬の放牧地が在る。10km程緩やかに南上したワハーン山脈北麓のマザール タッシュには西端の夏放牧地が在る。ここから10km西下すると、ワヒの東端のアイラークであるバイ ティバートに至る。更に20km近く西下すると、アリ スー上流に在るアイラークが望まれる。

　同谷が（大）パミール河に流入する付近から下方は、右岸と同じ様に山肌が河峯に迫って来る。また数本の支谷が注ぎ、渡渉点を求めて迂回したり、上り下りにも時間を多くとられる。

(2) Both banks of the mid-stream

　Until one reaches Kikhun or Langar on the right bank (Tajikistan side), the area is devoid of human habitation, with the exception of a small garrison of Tajik soldiers in northeastern end of the lake, Khargush, and two houses. The scenery is probably not much different from what it was 1400 years ago when Hsüang Tsang passed through. There is a truck road along the flat, river bank.

　The westernmost winter pasture of the Kyrgyz is located on the Afghan side of Khargush (on the left bank). From here if one were to proceed for about 10 kilometers along the gentle slopes that lead to the northern foothhills of the Wakhan Range, one would come upon the summer grazing Mazar Tash. From here if one were to descend for about 10 kilometers in a westerly direction, you can reach Bay Tibat which is the Yaylaq located on the eastern edge of the Wahi. By descending further for about another 20 kilometers towards the west, one can gain a view of yet another Yaylaq that is lcoated on the upper stream of the Ali-Su (valley), which eventually flows into the (Great) Pamir river.

　From the point of confluence, the river passes through a gorge with steep cliffs. The left bank becomes difficult to negotiate from this point because there are several side valleys that flow into the river. The route because cumbersome because the traveler is forced to climb up and down each side valley, and is often forced to deviate in order to find a suitable ford.

(3) 左岸の支谷に架かる唯一の橋

(3) The only bridge that spans the side valley on the left bank

（アリ‐スー開口部近く / Near the mouth of the Ali-Su to the Great Pamir River）
左岸のアリ‐スー（アリ谷）は深い激流のため、ここには左岸の支谷で唯一の橋が架けられている。
The river of the Ali-Su (Ali Valley on the left bank) cannot be forded due to its deep, swift current, and therefore a bridge was built here.

　アリスーを過ぎ（大）パミール河の下流にかかると、両岸とも険しい山が80°ぐらいの傾斜で河に迫り、路は傾斜が少し緩い河面から数200〜300m高い山腹に移る。

　右岸には旧ロシア・旧ソ連時代に、河沿いの河面から少し高い所で垂直な崖を削り、トラック道が造られたが、玄奘も辿った（?）と思われる。シルクロード時代の頼りない昔の路が、左岸の路と同じ高さの山腹に望見できる。旧路は高い山肌に加えて単調なので、見通しが良く、路を踏みながら急斜面の遙か下方の急流が嫌でも目に入り、下からは強い風が吹き上げ、恐怖と難渋の路であったであろう。

　左岸は山腹が出入りし、路もそれに沿うので、見通しが悪く怖さは覚えない。

Beyond Ali-Su, as the (Great) Pamir River continues downstream, on both banks, the flanks of the mountains drop down almost perpendicularly into the river at a slope gradient of 80 degrees. The track contours about 100 meter higher than the river level where the slope is less steep.

On the right bank, one can see a truck road at a higher elevation than the river level, which was cut out from the perpendicular cliff during the Soviet times. Above it, one can see the remains of an old single-track used since the times of the Silk Road Hsüang-tang followed?, that contours at the same elevation as the track on the Afghan side. Not only is the track exposed to the steep incline of the mountain , but it is battered by the strong gusts that blow upward from the river . The sight of the torrential river far below the steep slope must have made this a terrifying and difficult track for all travelers.

The left bank of the river and the track follow a continuous succession of spurs that limit the visibility of the traveler, and helps reduce the fear.

(4) 玄奘も辿った (?) シルクロード時代の路と現代の道路

(4) The difficult path that Hsüang-tsang followed during the age of the Silk Road, and the road today

（大パミールのプリシェール：左岸 / Priser, Great Pamir : left bank）
上が古代の路
The above is ancient path

キルギス人の生活
The Life of the Kyrgyz

(1) 帽子、服装と衣服

　屋内は勿論、かたときも帽子を離さない。型は5種類ある。ヮァールパクはキルギス人特有だ。上下着は洋服で、長靴を就寝時を除いて一日中履いている。

　必携品は胸元に付けるお守り"クマール"（Ⓚ）と"カシュクール"（Ⓚ）と称ばれる、自家製の毛編みベルトの左側に差している大型ナイフ"ピーチャク"である。2001年頃までは火打ち石"チャクマク・ティン"もその一つであった。

　右端は小パミールを代表とするアブドラシードハーン（冬はクィジールゴラム、夏はカラジルガに在住、2010年初旬没）で、ワハーン回廊で見かけた唯一のネクタイ着用者であった。

(1) Hat, clothing and attirergyz

The Kyrgyz always wear their hats even when they are indoors. There are five different styles of hats. The "kalpak" is unique to the Kyrgyz. The Kyrgyz attire consists of a blouse and trousers, and boots are always worn throughout the day, except when sleeping.

The "Kumar" (Ⓚ) or amulet is always worn on the neck, along with the"Kashukuru"(Ⓚ), a hand-woven woolen belt, and the "Pichaku" (Ⓚ), which is a big knife that is inserted into the left side of the belt. Up until 2001, Kyrgyz men always carried a chaqmak-tin (flint stone) .

To the right end of the figure is Abdulla Sheed Khan , an influential Kyrgyz in the Little Pamir. He lived in Quiziel Ghorum during the winter, and Qara Jilga during the summer. He passed away in 2010. He was the only person I saw in the Wakhan Corridor wearing a necktie.

（小パミールのカラ ジルカ / Qara Jilga, Liitle Pamir)
左より"トマーク"、"クァールパク"、"シャプルダク"（2人）と"パコール"（Ⓚ）
From the left "Tomak", "Kalpak", "Shapurdak", (two people) and "Pakol" (all Ⓚ)

（2）キルギス人の靴

　男女ともヤク皮製の長靴 "マシイ"（Ⓚ）の上に、ゴム製の短靴 "カルーシュ"（Ⓚ）を履いている。長靴はキルギスの自家製、短靴は購入品である。以前は屋内の敷物域に入る時は、必ず短靴を脱いでいたが、2007年頃より安価な中国製の強い合成皮長靴が出廻り、短靴の必要性が無くなり、それに履き替える男が徐々に増加している。外から入ってきてそのまま上り込み、時には床敷 "チューチェ"（Ⓚ）の上に拡げた食事用敷物 "ダスハル　ハーン"（Ⓓ）（Ⓚ）の上を、ずかずかと歩く者も見られるようになった。

　チャクマク・ティンは、2001年頃までは男の外出時には必携品であり、火花を乾燥させた羊・山羊毛に移し、それを火付けにしていたが、マッチ "クックルト"（Ⓚ）の普及により、持たない者の方が多くなった。

(2) The shoes worn by the Kyrgyz

　Both men and women wear the "Mashi"（Ⓚ）which are long boots made from yak hide, on top of which they wear short, rubber shoes called the "Karush"（Ⓚ）. The long boots are hand-made by the Kyrgyz, while the rubber boots are bought. In the past, it was the custom to take the short rubber shoes off when one entered a yurt and stepped on the carpeted floor. But around 2007, strong and cheap synthetic rubber boots made in China, became quite popular , and the need for these short rubber shoes disappeared. Today, an increasing number of Kyrgyz men have replaced their rubber shoes made in China. These days, some of the Kyrgyz men do not hesitate to enter the yurt and step on the carpets when they are still wearing their synthetic rubber boots. Some are even insolent enough to keep their boots on and walk over the cloth that has been laid out to place food, called the "Tasuharuhan"（Ⓓ）（Ⓚ）which is laid atop the "Chuche"（Ⓚ）meaning carpet.

　Until 2001, the Kyrgyz men carried the "chaqmak-tin"(flint stones) when leaving their homes. They would use the flint stone to set fire to sheep or goat wool that would be used like matches. Since "Kukurt"（Ⓚ）(matches) have become popular these days, most Kyrgyz men do not carry the "chaqmak-tin"(flint stone) any more.

（A）長靴と短靴
(A) Long boots and short boots

（B）長靴は自家製
(B) The long boots are hand-woven.

（C）火打ち石を打つ男
(C) Using the flint

（D）火打ち石
(D) Flint and stone

（（A）・（B）は大パミールのムックール / (A)・(B), Muqur, Great Pamir）

（（C）・（D）は、小パミールのカラ ジルガ / (C)・(D), Qara Jilga, Little Pamir）

（大パミールのサル ムックール/ Sar Muqur, Great Pamir）

（1）ショールの色で未婚・既婚は一目瞭然

　ア・パミールの女性の被り布は伝統的特有で、キルギスターン、タジキスターンや中国のキルギス人には見られない。赤色の布地"クィジール"は未婚、白色の布地"ショロック"は既婚を示している。高さ5〜20cmの多くはラシャ製の赤いココット型の帽子"シャルパック"の上から被る。最近では帽子を被らず、丈も腰上までの短いジョロック姿の主婦を見掛けることもある。

（1）The color of the shawl betrays the marital status of the woman.

　The traditional shawl that is worn by the women in Afghan Pamirs has such a distinct style that I have never seen a similar one the Republic of Kyrgyz, Tajikistan or in China. The red -colored shawl known as the "Quiziel" (K) is worn by single women, while the white shawl known as the "Jolock" (K) is worn by the married women. The hats are 5 centimeters to 20 centimeters high, made from thick woolen fabric, dyed red and shaped like a cup. The women wear their white shawls over their hat-like, "shapurdak". Recently many hatless women can be seen, and one can sometimes encounter married women today who wear Jolosks that do not reach below the hip.

（小パミールのセキ / Seki, little Pamir）

（2）髪型

　老若を問わず3つ編みにしている。ワヒも同様である。後髪は長いのが美人とされ、赤色の毛糸を編んで延ばしている者も見られる。

（2）Hair style

　Both young and old women braid their hair. The Wakhi also braid their hair. Women with long hair are considered beautiful. There are some women who braid red, woolen threads into their hair.

62) キルギスの家畜
The livestock of the Kyrgyz

羊・山羊とヤクは必需家畜である。　Sheep and goats are indispensable livestock for the Kyrgyz.

（小パミールのカラジルガ / Qara Jilga, Little Pamir）

（小パミールのクィジール ゴラム / Quiziel Ghorum, Little Pamir）

（小パミールのイルガ イル / Elgha Eli, Lttle Pamir）

(1) ヤク

ワハーンでは夏期の暑い間は、涼しい山間部のアイラックで過ごすが、涼しい（寒い?）パミールでは夏でも人と共住の家畜である。重荷や人でも乗せられる全季の万能車役である。雌ヤク "マーダ コシガウ" Ⓚの妊娠期間は9ヶ月足らずで、出産は5月前後が最も多く、授乳期は約6ヶ月である。発情期はほぼ2年に1回だと謂う。乳汁は最高の乳製品の主役である。乳牛を "イネック" Ⓚ、雌と去勢後の雄を併せて "カタス" Ⓚと称ぶ。北部のパーキスターンの人達との有力な交易品だ。

(1) Yaks

The Wakhi spend the hot, summer months in Wakhan in the mountain grazing camps called "yaylaq" ⒹⓌ. But in the Pamirs where the temperature is much cooler or should we say cold, the people live with their livestock in the same encampments year round. Though it is laborious to look after animals, they are the ideal mode of transportation for carrying humans and cargo throughout the year. The term of pregnancy of a female yak called "Mada koshigau" Ⓚ is only nine months. Most baby yaks are born around May, and are suckled for six months. The yaks are in heat every two years. The yak milk makes the best dairy products. The female yaks and castrated yaks are both called "Kotos" Ⓚ. The yaks are traded between the Kyrgyz and the communities in northern Pakistan.

(2) 羊と山羊

羊はアフガーンの他の地区のものと同じく、脂臀羊　学名 *Ovis aries steatopygo* (オビス アリエス ステアトピジア) であるが耳が少しばかり短い。脂臀部は頭部と共に最高のご馳走である。山羊と共に乳汁は乳製品の源として、ヤクのそれの不足分を補っている。アフガーン内部やワハーン或いは北部パーキスターンからの商人との最も大きな交易品である。脂臀羊は括めて "コイ" Ⓚと称ぶ。

その他に富裕なボイは、駱駝も飼育している。主として冬季の貨・人運搬用である。

(2) Sheep and goats

Pamiri sheep are fat-rumped (*Ovis aries stetopygia*) and have slightly shorter ears than those of the same kind found in other areas of Afghanistan. The fat in the rump and the head of the sheep are particularly favored as delicacies. The Kyrgyz use goat and sheep milk to supplement dairy products made from yak milk. The dairy products are mainly sold to buyers who come from other parts of Afghanistan and the northern parts of Pakistan. The fat-rumped sheep are known as "koi" Ⓚ.

The wealthy Kyrgyz , (who are called "Boi") also own and breed camels, which are loaned out during the winter months for transporting cargo and humans.

(3) 去勢器を見せる若者

雄性のヤクと羊・山羊は生後半年までに種付け用を残して去勢される。手前の太いのがヤク用である。男は目を見開き、歯を咬みしめ、力いっぱい睾丸を圧砕するのだと説明してくれた。左手は羊・山羊用、右はヤク用。

（イルガ イル）

(3) A young man is showing off a castrator.

The male yaks, sheep and goats are castrated except for those that are spared for breeding. The thick castrator is used on yaks. Demonstrating the process, the man opened his eyes wide, gritted his teeth and made a clamping motion to show how the testicles are crushed.

(Elgha Eli)

(小パミールのアンデミン近く / Near Andemin, Little Pamir)

(大パミールのズラガーン / Zuragan, Great Pamir)

(ワフジール / Wakhjir)

(1) ヤクは通年万能車

　去勢後の雄ヤクが使われる。岩場に強く、激流も恐れず泳ぎも達者で、氷河を踏み進むのも慎重である。積載量は150kg前後（図41）とされ、寒さにも強く四季用の貨客車の役を担っている。歩行速度は3km/時ぐらいで馬より少し遅く、制御にやや難点があるが、乗っていて安定感がある。

(1) The yak can be ridden year round, and is the most versatile mode of transport.

　Castrated yaks are used for transport. Yaks can nimbly pick their way across stony terrain, can swim in a torrential river without fear, and are very cautious when they must traverse a glacier. The yak can carry loads of up to 150 kilograms; they are resistant to cold weather, and are useful year-round both for carryinhumans and cargo. The yaks walk slightly slower than a horse at three kilometers per hour. Though they can be skittish, and more difficult to control, the ride feels more stable.

(2) 駱駝は冬期万能車

　冬期専用で積載量は200kgにも及ぶ。2つ瘤のバクトリア駱駝で乗用にもなる。放牧地を遠く離れても行方不明にならない。富裕なボイは10頭以上も飼育している。雄雌併せて"トゥース"（Ⓚ）と謂う。

(2) The camel is a versatile, mode of transport during the winter months.

　The camel can carry 200 kilograms of load during the winter. The Bactrian camel has two humps so it can be ridden. Even though the camel may stray away from the encampment, they will never get lost. The rich "bois" may own more than ten camels. The locals call both male and female camels "Toos" (Ⓚ) .

(3) 馬は乗用専用車

　貧しいユルト群では見られないが、殆んどのボイは複数頭の馬を所有している。キルギス人は少し離れた所でも馬かヤクに乗る。冬期を除いた3期の乗用専用である。ウッドが記している馬乳酒"クミズ"は、どの放牧地でも答えがなかった。ロバの姿はない。

(3) The horse is only used for riding.

　Though it is rare to see horses at impoverished Kyrgyz camps, a wealthy Kyrgyz (known as boi) will own several horses. The Kyrgyz will ride horses or yaks everywhere, even if it is just around the corner. They ride horses throughout the year, except during the winter season. Though Wood saw "Kumis" (Ⓚ), an alchol beverage made from horse milk that the Kyrgyz make, I never came across that drink at any of the summer grazing camps. Nor did I see any donkeys either.

64) 毛糸
Preparing wool

羊・山羊とヤクは夏の放牧地で5・6月に、大型の鋏で刈り取りされる。ユルト内で、女性が粗毛を30cmばかりの細い棒に紡錘型の膨らみが付けられた、糸紡ぎ器"ドク"（Ⓚ）を廻しながら紡ぐ。手では把持しないで、天井から毛編みロープで吊るしてもいる。

ワハーンでは、上部に十字型の把手が付いている器具"チャールク"（Ⓦ）（図18）（4）を使う

The Kyrgyz use huge scissors to shear their sheep, goats and yaks in May and June at the summer grazing camp. Inside the yurt, some women spin the woolen fiber by manually rotating the spinning wheel , called "Dok", which is a thin rod that is thirty centimeters long and is slightly thick around the middle section. I have seem others who do not hold the spinning wheel with their hand, but let it hang from the ceiling where it is tied with a hand-knitted, woolen rope .

A cross-shaped spinning wheel is used in the Wakhan and it is called "Chark" Ⓦ (fig. 18) (4).

（いずれも大パミールのスティック / Both fig.s, Steq,Great Pamir）

(1) 毛糸を紡ぐ

(1) Spinning the woolen fiber

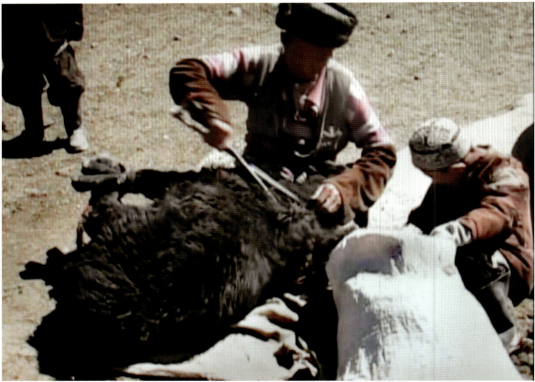

ビデオより / From the Video.

(2) 羊毛狩り

(2) Shearing wool from sheep

65) 機織り
Weaving

　女性の夏仕事の一つで、1m余の柳か樺の樹で組んだ三脚"ウッチ・バカーン"（Ⓚ）と刃渡り10余cmの刀型の織り板"グァリッヂ"（Ⓚ）を使って、長さ十数m　幅20～30cmの帯を織る。1日30cmぐらいの出来だ。毛糸の色は素地や購入した染色剤でいろいろあり、ユルトの支柱の固定や室内装飾（図65）(2)）に用いられる。

Weaving is one of the many tasks that women are responsible for during the summer. The "Uchi-bakan" (Ⓚ) is made by connecting a one-meter long branch of a willow or white birch tree into a tripod. A spinning board shaped like a blade known as a "Guariji" that is over 10 centimeters long is used to weave a long belt with a width of 20 centimeters to 30 centimeters, and a length of 10 meters. The women take one day to weave 30 centimeters of wool. The color of the fabric varies, depending on the quality of the wool and the dye that has been purchased. The woven belt is used to hold the pillars of the yurt frame in place, and to decorate the interior of the yurt (fig.65)(2)).

(1) 屋内

(1) Interior

(2) ユルトの支柱の固定や装飾に使う

(2) The belt is used to hold the pillars of the yurt frame in place, and for decorating the interior of the yurt.

（いずれも大パミールのサル ムックール /
Both fig.s, Sar Muqur, Great Pamir）

（大パミールのスティック / Steq, Great Pamir）

66) フェルト造り
Felt making

　夏の男・女共同の仕事で、箕の上に羊・山羊の毛を10cmばかりの高さに積み拡げ、散水しながら箕を捲き込む。箕の材料は秋にワハーンのサルハド周辺に採りに行く。素材にヤク毛を用いることもある。

　Mainly during the summer season, both men and women work together to make felt. The sheep and goat wool is laid out, flattened, layered to a height of 10 centimeters, and then evenly spread over a reed mat. The wool is then sprinkled with boiling soap-water and rolled with the reed mat. The reed used to make the mat is collected in the autumn near Sarhad in the Wakhan. Yak hair is used sometimes to make these mats.

(1) 羊毛を広げる
(1) Spreading the woolen fleece evenly over the reed mat

(2) 箕の子で巻く
(2) Rolling the wet fleece with the mat

（いずれも大パミールのサル ムックール / Both fig.s, Sar Muqur, Great Pamir)

居住地近くに広場があり、馬を所有している放牧地では、馬に挽かせて終日回転を続ける。馬がいない放牧地では、男が2人掛けでこれ又一日中捲き戻しを繰り返してフェルトを造る。この作業で目の詰まった防水性のあるフェルトが出来る。天候不順で季節移動が遅れると、冬放牧地でも行われる。フェルトはユルトの外壁や天井部分に用いられるが、交易品になることもある。馬動式を"ケースタード"、人力式を"ケースバス"と区別している。

Men and women roll the wet fleece together mainly during the summer months. If horses are available at the grazing camp, a horse will drag the rolled, reed mat in a circle the whole day long in an open square near the yurts. Where there are no horses, two men will roll and unroll the mat the whole day long. As a result, the felt will become tightly packed and waterproof. If the weather is irregular and the Kyrgyz migrate to their summer pastures later than would be normal, then the felt is made even during the winter time. Though most of the felt is used to cover the frame and the ceiling of the yurt, it is also sometimes traded. If horses are used, the process is called "Kestart" and when the felt is compressed by men, it is called "Kesbas".

（小パミールのアクソイ / Aksoi, Little Pamir）

(3) 馬引きで均らす（馬動式）

(3) Horses dragging the reed mat (horse-driven)

(4) 人力で均らす（人力式）

(4) Manual felt-making (manual)

（ワフジールのキタイ / Kithai, Wakhjir）

67) ユルト建設
Erecting a yurt

　キルギス人はユルトを"ビイイド"(Ⓚ)と称び、蒙古のゲルと同じく移動式家屋である。日本では中国語のパオが一般的である。組建てには男3～4人で4時間前後、解体には同じく2時間ほどで出来る。移動はヤクでする（図41）。

　入口はボディ・ワハーンを避けて、東か東南向きに設えてある。小パミールでは2004年以後、多くが吊し幕戸から木板を張り合わせた外向き木戸に変わって来た。

　The Kyrgyz call their yurts, "Beyit". Similar to the Gel of Mongolia, these are portable shelters. The Japanese follow the Chinese custom of calling these dwellings "Pao." It takes about four hours for a group of three to four men to erect a yurt, and two hours to dismantle it. The yaks are used to transport the yurt. (fig.41)). The entrance to the yurt usually faces the east or southeast in order to avoid the Bad-i-Wakhan (the wind of Wakhan). Since 2004, many of the yurts seen on the Little Pamir side have replaced the hanging felt covers with doors made of wooden panels, which open outward.

(1) 外壁柱の組立て
(1) Erecting the pillars for the outer walls

(2) 天井を支える
(2) Supporting the roof rib

(5) フェルトを張り完成
(5) The construction is finished when the wooden frame is covered with felt.

(3) 外壁の基礎造り
(3) Putting up the foundation of the lattice wall section

(4) 天井
(4) Ceiling

（小パミールのビルギット ウヤー / Birguit Uya, Little Pamir)

((4)(5)を除きすべて小パミールの東部のムックール / Except for fig.(4)(5) all fig.s, Muqur, eastern Little Pamir)

（小パミールのクシュトック / Qushtuk, Little Pamir)

2004年初夏太陽光発電による電燈の普及が小パミールに始まった。7月に小パミールのサュトゥックに在る一軒のユルトで見かけた。パネルは25cm四方の小さいもので、随分暗い光だった。

2009年の7月には小パミールで半数近くのユルトに大型化したパネルが見られ、2010年には小パミールとワフジール路では殆どのユルトにパネルが取り付けられていた。明るさは読書は難しいが以前より明るくなっている。

テレビは2004年頃にアパンディ ボイのユルトで見た。電源は発電機でビデオ専用であった。2009年には4軒のユルトで、しかもパラボラアンテナ付きで海外放送も受像できた。大パミールでは電気もテレビも極めて稀にしか見られなかった。

From early summer of 2004, the use of solar generated electricity became popular among the Kyrgyz in the Afghan the Little Pamir. In July of that year, I saw electricity used in just one yurt at the Little Pamir in Saytok. The solar panel was small, measuring 25 centimeters square, and could only generate very dim light.

In July, 2009, the use of large solar panels had spread to nearly half of all the yurts that I came across, and when I returned the following year, in 2010 most of the yurts that I saw in the Little Pamir, and in the valleys leading to the Wakhjir Pass had solar panels. The light was too dim to read a book by, but brighter than the first electric lights I saw in use.

Around 2004 I saw a television in the yurt owned by Apandy Boi. It was generated by an electricity generator and was only used for watching videos. In 2009, I saw four yurts with parabolic antennas, that could receive satellite transmission of foreign TV programs. In the Great Pamir I only saw a few yurts that had electricity and television.

（小パミールのカラ ゴラム / Qara Ghorum）

69) ユルト内部
The Interior of a yurt

(1) 天井の下

　ユルトの外壁の支柱は削った柳の樹を菱形矢来Ｘ型に組んだ木枠"ディルギィ"（(Ⓚ) 図69)）を、10組余り直径4〜5mの円型に結んで繋ぐ。

　その上端に、30cmほど上で70°ぐらいに曲げた、直径3mばかりの柳の樹"カール"を縛り付ける。その先端を矢張り柳の樹のドーム型天井枠"トゥンドゥック"(Ⓚ)にあけられた小孔に嵌め込んで支える。その数はユルトの大きさにより50〜60余本を数える。

　殆んどのユルトでは、直径数cmの樺の樹の"ビイト・バカーン"で補強している。この吹き抜け丸天井は"ウチュック・ディグダーン"(Ⓚ)（図67(4), 69(1)）と称ばれ、ユルトの中央真上を占める。これがユルトの唯一の明り採りと煙出口となる。

　この真下が火場・台所で、左側は一家団欒の場となる。この辺りから敷物が拡げられ、入って来た者は脱靴する。キルギス人は外側の短靴を脱すのが普通である。

　後の簾は"アシュハナ"と称ばれ、食品室"アシュカナ イーチェ"との隔壁。

(1) Below the ceiling

　The wooden frame that forms the outer wall of a yurt consists of 10 latticed pieces called "Dilgi", which are made from willow, that have been polished smooth and then pinned to form a circle with a diameter of 4 meters to 5 meters (fig.69)).

　30 centimeters from the top , the lattice wall is bent at a 70 degree angle, so that there will be a 3 meter diameter opening. The dome or conical roof of the yurt has a circle at the crown called the "Tuunduk" (fig.s, 67, 69)). The cupola beams are inserted into the small holes of the tuunduk (Ⓚ), radiating down to meet the lattice walls. 50 or 60 such beams are used depending on the size of the yurt.

　All of this is tied together with the "Beyit bakan" which is a stick made from the birch tree that is a couple of centimeters wide to reinforce the structure. It functions as a tension band. Usually there is a skylight called "Uchek digudan" (Ⓚ) (fig.s, 67(4), 69)(1)) in the middle at the apex of the roof. This is the only opening in the yurt for letting in light and releasing smoke.

　The hearth and kitchen are located directly underneath the skylight where the family gathers together. A carpet is placed near the hearth, where the visitors are expected to take their shoes off. The Kyrgyz usually take off their short boots. The screen partition called "Ashukhana" is used to divide the pantry "aschukhana eeche" from the rest of the yurt.

（小パミールのグジャナ/ Gujana, Little Pamir）

(2) 食品室

"アシュハナ"（食品室の隔簾）の裏は乳製品の保存室"アシュハナ イーチェ"で、煮沸後乳"シュウト"がいろいろな容器に貯えてある。少量のヨーグルトを入れ一夜或いは2〜3日静置すると、上部にクリーム"カィマック"と下部にヨーグルト"アイラーン"がどことなく分離する。

(1) The pantry

Behind the "ashukana" (the screen partition) dairy products are stored in many different containers in the pantry (called "ashkhana eeche"). After the milk or "sut" has been boiled, it is stored in many different containers. A small portion of yoghurt is added to the boiling milk and left to stand for 2 to 3 days. The liquid then separates into two layers: the top layer becomes the cream called "Kaimak" (Ⓚ), and the lower layer, yoghurt or "Ailan" (Ⓚ).

"お母さん　これだけ溜れば、クルト（乾燥ヨーグルト）が造れるね"

"Mother, we have enough milk to make kurt, don't we"?

（大パミールのムックール /
Muqur, Great Pamir）

（3）正面内部

　　正面にはトランク "サンドク"（Ⓚ）、その上にはカラフルな布団 "トゥシャク"（Ⓚ）などの家財置き場になっている。左手に手動ミシンが備わっているユルトもある。

(1) Inside a yurt facing its front

　　Looking from the front side, the view shows the trunk, or "Sandok"（Ⓚ）, on top of which one can see several layers of colorful blankets or "Tushak"（Ⓚ）. This is the place where the household goods are stored. In some yurts one may find a manually operated sewing machine.

お母さんお菓子をもらったよ！

"Mother, someone gave me sweets."

（小パミールのセキ / Seki, Little Pamir ）

70) ユルト内の1コマ
A common scene inside the yurt

(1) キルギス人は敬虔なイスラーム教徒

ア・パミールにはモスクがない。家屋内で西方マッカに向け、1日5回の"礼拝"をする。女性にはしない者もいる。

(1) The Kyrgyz are devoted Muslims

There are no mosques on the Afghan Pamirs side. The Kyrgyz pray five times a day inside their yurts facing west towards Mecca. There are some women who do not pray.

(2) 揺り籠

嬰児は揺り籠"ゴーヴァ"に寝かされる。寒さを防ぐために上部に薄団が掛けられている。母乳が出ない時は、授乳中の羊・山羊の乳房を切り取り、木製の乳首を付けた哺乳袋"カールーン"(K)に、軽く煮沸したヤク或いは羊・山羊乳を入れて飲ませる。子守りにはゴーヴァを激しく左右に揺する。

(2) The baby cradle

New born infants are place on baby cradles called "Gova" (K). The baby is wrapped in a blanket to keep it warm. The cradle is rocked quite hard to keep the baby from crying.

(3) 哺乳袋

(3) A baby bottle

When the mother does not have enough breast milk, the Kyrgyz cut off the breasts of either a sheep or goat during milking, attach a wooden nipple to it, and use it like a baby bottle (called "Karun" (K)). Yak, sheep or goat milk is first boiled before it is fed to the baby. The bottle(bag) is made of the brest of goats or sheep in lactation.

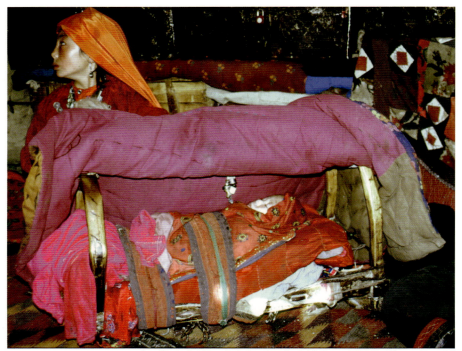

(いずれも大パミールのムックール / All fig.s, Muqur, Great Pamir)

71）簾造りは冬仕事
The screen partition ("ashukhana") is made during the winter months.

(小パミールのアンデミン /
Andemi, Liitle Pamir)

"アシュハナ"の簾造りは6ヶ月近くかかり、冬の遊牧地の屋内作業である。色とりどりに染められた、300〜400本の秋にサルハッドで刈り取った葦のような中空の草を編んで造る。

The ashukhana, or screen that divides the pantry from the rest of the yurt takes 6 months to make. It is prepared during the winter months indoors. The screen is made from 300 to 400 reeds were cut around Sar had that have been dyed into many different colors.

色鮮やかな結婚衣装を手に慶びの母と娘。結婚を2日後に控えたこのユルトでは、祝いのご馳走をしてくれた。花婿は再婚の30才、花嫁は初婚の16才と聞いた。キルギス人の結婚適齢期、男性16〜20才、女性14〜16才とも耳にした。

In the yurt a mother is proudly showing off the colorful wedding dress of her daughter, who will be marrying in just two days. I was treated to a feast in this yurt. This will be the first marriage for her daughter, aged sixteen. For her future husband, age 30, this will be his second marriage. Most Kyrgyz men marry between the ages of 16 to 20 years old, and women between 14 and 16 years old.

(小パミール、東のムックール / Eastern Muqur, Little Pamir)

ナーン焼き　Baking nan

（小パミールのセキ / seki, Little Pamir）

小麦粉"ブーダイ・ウンヌ"をヤク（或いは羊・山羊）の原乳"スートゥ"で捏ね、僅かな岩塩"トゥーズ"（Ⓚ）を加え、少量のイースト液"コープト・ヒク"（Ⓚ）を入れ、1時間ほど放置し、"タワー"（Ⓚ）と称ばれる、浅い鍋かドラム缶の蓋に丸く伸ばして並べ、鉄製の高さ20cmばかりの三脚台"トルガー"に載せる。燃料の"シュワック"（図79（1））が多い地域ではこの火勢と余熱で焼く。少ない地域で乾燥ヤク糞"ティーゼック"（図79（2））や、糞尿混合の乾燥した羊・山羊糞"カック"（図79（3））を使う所では、浅い蓋付きの鉄鍋"コマチドーン"（Ⓚ ⓌⒹ）と称ぶ鉄或いは鋳物製の蓋付き浅鍋を用いる。

ワヒは捏ねるのに水を使う。またワヒもタジキスターンのキルギス人も形は違うが、タンドールで焼く。

キルギス人のユルトに立寄ると、いつでもナーンと岩塩入り紅茶"カタック・チャイ"（Ⓚ）を提供されるのが常である。クリーム"カイマック"（Ⓚ）とヨーグルト"アイラーン"（Ⓚ）が添えられていることも多い。カタック・チャイの塩分は0.2～0.3%前後で、一度に2～3杯（200～300ml）を一日数回常用している。

ワヒはアフガーン内部と同様に、小麦粉を水で捏ね、竈"ガウフ"・タンドールでパン"ヒュッエ"を焼く。チョイ（チャイ）には通常砂糖"ブラー"（Ⓓ）を使い、乳を入れない事が多い。アフガーン内部ではナーンでなくノーンと発音する。

The flour, called "Buday un" (Ⓚ), is kneaded with boiled milk of a yak, sheep or goat, called "sut" (Ⓚ), after which a pinch of salt or "Tuz", (Ⓚ) and a small amount of liquid yeast, called "Koputopik" (Ⓚ) is added. The dough is left for one hour and then placed on a steel plate ("Tawa") which is cooked over a tripod called "Toruga", that has three legs that are 20 centimeters high. In places where there is plenty of fuel or "shuwakku" (fig.79 (1)), it is placed under the tripod to cook the nan. When fuel is scarce, it is substituted with dried yak dung called "Teezek" (fig.79 (2)), or the dung of the sheep and goats called "qack"(fig.79(3)) which contains some urine. Where there is poor of fuel, a shallow, steel or metal-casted pan with a lid called"Komachidon" (Ⓚ,Ⓦ,Ⓓ) is used.

The Wakhi use water to knead the dough. Both the Wakhi as well as the Kyrgyz living in Tajikistan use the tandoor(different type each) to bake nan.

Whenever we visited a Kyrgyz yurt, we were treated to nan, and salted tea, called "Kataku chai"(Ⓚ). Many times, we were also offered "kaimak"(Ⓚ) (cream) and ("ailan")(Ⓚ)(yoghurt). The salt content in the tea is usually around 0.2% to 0.3%. The Kyrgyz drink 2 to 3 cups (200ml-300ml) per break, several times a day.

The Wakhi follow the custom of the interior Afghan and knead their dough with water .They bake their nan in tandoors. They usually drink their tea (choi, or chay) with sugar (bra) and do not add milk. The Afghans except for Pamirs call their bread "non" instead of "nan".

原乳にヨーグルトを加えながら煮沸　分離した脂肪分を揉んでバターを造る

Yoghurt is added in stages to the boiling milk, and then the cream that has separated is agitated to produce butter.

いずれも小パミールのグジャナ /
All fig.s,Gujana,Little Pamir

(1) 原乳の煮沸

　原乳（ヤクと羊・山羊の乳を混ぜることはない）を深鍋 "コゾーン" (Ⓚ) に入れ、少量のヨーグルトを加えながら2時間ほど煮沸する。その間少量のヨーグルト "アイラーン" を加え、大型のお玉 "チャモーヂ" (Ⓚ) でたびたび撹拌する。

(1) Boiling milk

　Yak, sheep or goat milk ("sut" (Ⓚ)) which is never mixed, is poured into a deep pan called the "Kozon" (Ⓚ), and a small amount of yoghurt or "ailan" (Ⓚ) is added in several stages as the milk is boiled for two hours. During this time a big, round ladle or "Chamoji" (Ⓚ) is used to agitate the boiling milk.

(2) 脂肪塊を揉む

　浮遊してきた半凝固状の水分を含んだ脂肪塊を大きな洗面器に移し、石鹸 "サボン" (Ⓚ) で充分手洗いした後、時々冷水を掛けながら一時間余り揉み脱水するとバター "メシケ" (Ⓚ) ができる。

(2) The blocks of fat are kneaded.

　The milk fat (cream) that has coagulated and which still contains water is transferred to a huge wash basin. After washing the hands thoroughly with soap or "Zabon" (Ⓚ), the cream is hand-kneaded for one hour to squeeze the water out until it becomes butter or "Mesike". All the while, a small quantity of cold water is sprinkled over the cream.

(3) 一山にしたバター

(3) A heap of butter

(4) 羊・山羊の胃袋に保存

　羊・山羊の胃袋 "カラーン" (Ⓚ) に入れて貯蔵する。キルギス人はバターは口にしない。必ず取り出し煮沸してオイル状 "マイ" (Ⓚ) として使用する。交易品の一つとなる。ワヒは同様な造り方をするが、オイル状バター "ルーグゥーン" (Ⓦ) として保存する。

(4) Butter stored in the dried stomach of a sheep

　The butter is stored in the dried stomach (called Karan) of a sheep or goat. The Kyrgyz never eat raw butter. They always boil the butter and turn it into butter oil or Mai, (Ⓚ). Butter is traded. Though the Wakhis use the same method to make butter, they preserve liquid butter (Rogun (Ⓦ)).

75) 乾燥ヨーグルト "クルト" 造り
Making dried yoghurt or "Kurt"

　少量のヨーグルト"アイラーン"を加えながら、煮沸した乳を貯蔵室"アシュハナ イーチェ"で1〜数日静置すると、上部に浮くクリーム"カイマック"と分離し、下部にどろりとしたヨーグルト"アイラーン"（Ⓚ）が出来る。それに充分醗酵したアイラーンを加え、2〜3時間煮沸を続ける。半凝固した部分を掬い出し布袋に入れ、一夜脱水する。それを適当な丸型に作り、天日で2週前後乾燥させる。水で薄めたヨーグルトから造るワヒのそれと違って、味が濃く一流の交易品となる。携行食は勿論、冬期のスープの素にしている。供のサフェーラは1kg/100アフ（邦価約210円）で5kg購入し土産にした。

　A small amount of yoghurt or "ailan" is slowly added to boiling milk. The liquid is left to stand for one to several days in the pantry or "ashukhana eeche". The cream or "Kaimak"（Ⓚ）coagulates on the surface, while below the thick yoghurt or "ailan"（Ⓚ）forms. More yoghurt which has fully fermented is added. Then the liquid is boiled for a further two to three hours. The partially coagulated liquid is scooped out and put into a bag made of cloth, to squeeze the water out. The dehydrated yoghurt is formed into small balls, placed on a dry mat and left to dry in the sun for about two weeks.
　Unlike the "kurt" made by the Wakhi's , who dilute the yoghurt with water, the "kurt" or dry yoghurt made by the Pamir Kyrgyz has a richer taste, and is thus coveted for trade. It is light and easy to take along as food, and can be used as seasoning for soups. Safiullah, my guide, bought 5 kilograms of kurt at 100 Afghani per kilo (which is equivalent to 210 Japanese yen).

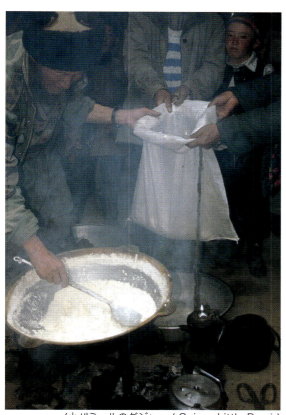

(小パミールのグジャナ / Gujana,Little Pamir)

(1) 煮沸後の半凝固体を一夜の脱水

(1) After boiling the milk, the partially coagulated cream is left to dehydrate for one night.

(小パミールのクール ムックール / Qur Muqur, Little Pamir)

(2) 天日で乾燥

　緑色の塊は緑ネギ入りヨーグルト"クール ゴーン"

(2) The yoghurt is left to dry in the sun. The green colored one is mixed with onion and called "korggon".

(小パミールのグジャナ / Gujana, Little Pamir)

(3) 交易品の一つ

(3) The "kurt" is coveted for trade.

"コゾーン" で少量の "アイラーン" を加え、3時間ほど "チャモージ" で撹拌する。半凝固体を掬い出し、チャモージで圧迫し脱水する。ほくほくとして口当たりも軽い。

動物臭は全くなく、豆腐由来のようなさっぱり味である。"プシュタック"（Ⓚ）と称ばれるカッテージチーズである。"アイラーン" と共に供されることが多い。

A small amount of yoghurt or "ailan" is added into the pan or "kozon", and then agitated with the ladle or "chamoji" for three hours. The partially coagulated liquid is scooped out and pressed down with a ladle or "chamoji" to squeeze out the water. The cheese tastes light and the texture is good. It does not have a meaty smell, and has a refreshing taste that is similar to tofu. It is cottage cheese called "Pushtack" (Ⓚ) and is offered to the visitor along with "ailan".

（1）煮沸後の半凝固体を圧迫脱水

(1) Pressing down on the half coagulated yoghurt to squeeze out the water after boiling

（2）大きな餅大に仕上げる

(2) Forming it into a big ball

（いずれも小パミールのグジャナ / Both fig.s, Gujana, Little Pamir）

　原乳で小麦粉を練り、少量の塩とイースト液を入れ、4〜5cm四方大に切り、バターを溶かしたマイで揚げる。2日ぐらいはふっくらとして、少し甘味があって口触りも良く、クルトと並んで美味しい携行食だ。
　アフガーン内陸部やワハーンでは水で捏ね、塩の代わりに砂糖を入れ、綿実油で揚げる。

Milk, a pinch of salt, and liquid yeast is added to flour and kneaded. The dough is cut into 4-5cm squares and then fried in melted butter.(called mai). In two days the bread rises. It tastes slightly sweet, and has a good texture. As with kurt, it is a delicious food to carry when traveling. In other areas of Afghanistan and in the Wakhan, water is added to the flour, and instead of salt, sugar is added before the dough is fried in cotton seed oil.

(1) 小麦粉を捏ねる

(1) Kneading flour

(2) マイ(バターを溶かしたオイル)で揚げる

(2) Deep-frying the bread in "mai"(melted butter oil)

(いずれも小パミールのセキ / Both fig.s, Seki, Little Pamir)

(1) "シール ブレンジ" Ⓓ Ⓦ Ⓚ

　原乳を2〜3回足しながら1時間余り煮沸する。ミルク煮ライスであるが、出来上がりは粥というよりはむしろ糊状に近い。塩は普通加えない。副食無しで食べる。表面にはクリームが浮かんでいるが、バターを溶かしたオイル"マイ"を掛け口にする。私はマイを除いて口にしている。数本のスプーンで廻し食いをする客人用食の一つだ。シールは乳、ブレンジは米の意味。

(1) "Sir berenj" Ⓓ Ⓦ Ⓚ

　Rice is cooked in boiling fresh milk and churned several times to make rice porridge. The Kyrgyz rarely add salt to the porridge, and eat it without any assortments. Usually there is a layer of cream floating on the surface, and melted butter oil or "mai" is often poured over the pudding.
　I usually remove the melted butter before eating this pudding. A bowl full of "sir berenj", or rice porridge is passed around and shared. It is usually only served when there is a visitor.

（いずれも小パミールのセキ / Both fig.s, Seki, Little Pamir）

（A）原乳を煮沸する

(A) Boiling fresh milk

左から"アイラーン"、"カイマック"と"シール ブレンジ"

（B）出来上がり

(B) The completed state From the left "ailan", "kaimak" and "sir berenj"

(2) "カターマ" Ⓓ Ⓚ

　小麦粉を原乳で捏ね伸ばし、数ヶ所にクリームを挟んで折り曲げ、鋳物か鉄製で蓋付きのコマチドーンに円心状に入れ、ティーゼックやカックの置き火（消し炭）で1時間ほど蒸し焼きにする。砂糖は加えないがほのかに甘みがする。

　キルギスでは岩塩を入れるか、アフガーン内部では砂糖を用いる。

(2) Katama Ⓓ Ⓚ

　The dough is kneaded and rolled out as fresh milk is added. Next, cream is placed on the flattened dough which is then folded, and placed in the center of the circle within the "komachidon", where it is baked in the residual heat of charcoal made from "teezek" and "qack". It is sugerless but is sweet-tasting. The Kyrgyz add salt to the dough, while in the interior areas of Afghanistan sugar is added.

（いずれも小パミールのセキ / Both fig.s, Seki, Little Pamir）

（A）小麦粉を捏ね伸ばす

(A) Stretching and flattening the dough

（B）出来上がり

(B) The dough is completed

（3）脂臀羊　koi（Ⓚ）学名 オビス アリエス ステアトピジア

　アフガーン内部のものより耳が少し短く多毛であるが、形態や大きな臀部は変わりない。

(3) Fat-rumped sheep or "koi" (Ⓚ) Scientific name: Ovis aries steatopygia

The sheep Afghan Pamir have shorter ears and are more hairy than their cousins in Afghanistan. But both types of sheep are physically similar and are fat -rumped.

（いずれも小パミールのセキ / All fig.s, Seki, Little Pamir）

（4）臀部位の脂肪部分

　羊の盛り上がった脂臀 "クーロック"（Ⓚ）は脂肪の塊だ。煮沸すると脂濃くなくサクサクとした舌触りはさっぱり味だ。

(4) The clumps of fat taken from the rump after boiling

"Kulok" is the fatty rump of the sheep, and is actually a clump of fat. The taste of the boiled fat-rump is grainy and surprisingly light. It does not leave an oily taste in the mouth.

（5）羊・山羊の頭と肉

　煮沸した羊・山羊の頭部 "カラー" は、脂臀と並んで最高級品とされ、賓客用として供される。目玉と頬の肉も美味である。他の部分の肉も来客用だ。

(5) The head and meat of the sheep and goats after boiling

"Kara", which is the boiled head of sheep and goats ,and the fatty rump of the sheep are a highly coveted delicacy that are only prepared for guests. The taste of the eyes and meat around the cheeks are particularly delicious. The meat of other parts shown here are also reserved for guests.

（小パミールのイルガ イル / Elgha Eli, Little Pamir）

(1) "シュワック" (Ⓚ) (Ⓓ)

背丈10cm足らずの多根性灌木。非常に燃えつきが良い。火付け用とナーン焼きに繁用される。

(1) "Showaq" (ⓀⒹ)

A shrub with many roots that has a height of less than 10 cm The shrub burns easily and is used predominantly for igniting fire and baking nan.

（大パミールのスティック / Steq, Great Pamir）

(2) ティーゼック" 又は "オーテ"

ヤク糞の天日乾燥品。燃え易い。最も繁用される燃料。

(2) "Teezek" or "Ote"

The sun-dried yak dung. The most popular fuel since it burns easily

（小パミールのイルマヌトツク / Ernanutok, Little Pamir）

(3) "カック"

羊・山羊の糞塊の天日乾燥品。火持ちが良い（図48）参照）。

(3) "Qack"

Sun-dried sheep and goat manure. Once aflame, it will continue to burn for a long time(refer to fig. 48).

（小パミールのイルガ イル / Elgha Eli, Little Pamir）

(4) 火吹き袋

仔羊・仔山羊の縫いぐるみで作った吹子、コーロック（Ⓚ）と称ぶ

(4) A blower to make the fire bigger

The blower, made from the skin of a baby sheep or goat, is called "koroq".

80) ヤク糞は燃料源
The yak dung is used for fuel.

円型に"カック"を下に並べ、上部に"ティーゼック"を重ね、一方に小口を開くと良く燃える。悪臭はない。長時間の暖房用にもなる。

The "qack" is placed in a circle on the bottom, and "teezek" above it. With one small opening for aeration, the fuel burns well. The odor is not bad. It can be burned many hours and is used for heating.

暖かいなー

How warm it is!

（小パミールのクルチン / Qurchin, Little Pamir)

The Afghan Pamirs is contaminated with opium.

ア・パミールのキルギス人は殆んどが阿片常用者と思われる。ここには矯正院がない。ワハーンには一ヶ所設置されていて、中毒者は近年減少してきているとされる。それでも80%ぐらいの吸引率と思われる。

Based on my observations, I would venture to say that most of the Kyrgyz living in the Afghan Pamirs are addicted to opium. There is one drug rehabilitation center that services the entire Wakhan area. Drug addiction is said to be on the decline. Even so, the addiction rate is said to be around 80%.

(小パミールのビルギィット ウヤー / Birgit Uya, Little Pamir)

(小パミールのラボート チラップ / Rabot Chilap, Little Pamir)

(1) 阿片吸引王アパンディ ボイ

ラーマン クル脱国後、ア・パミール随一の富豪となった彼は、筋肉リュウマチからこの道にはまったと話してくれた。一日数gを2日続け、3日目には寝て過ごしていた。私は当地を訪れるたびに、ウィスキーを呈上したが、それがある間は粗製阿片 "タリヤク" は吸わないで済むと云っていた。2008年12月没。

(1) Apandi Boi, the king of the addicts

After Rahman Qul fled the country, Apandi Boi became the richest man in the Afghan Pamirs. When I visited Apandi Boi he confided to me that he had muscle rheumatism and started smoking opium as a pain killer. Before he died in December, 2008, Apandi Boi would smoke a couple of grams of opium per day for two consecutive days, and then be bedridden on the third day. Each time I visited the Afghan Pamirs. I brought him a bottle of whiskey. He told me that as long as the whiskey lasted, he did not smoke opium or "tariyak".

(2) 女性も負けじと

この夫婦は揃って阿片中毒者だ（図37を参照）。

(2) Women become as addicted as men.

This married couple is addicted to opium (refer to fig. 37)).

82) タジキスターンのキルギス人 (小パミール東端)
The Kyrgyz in Tajikistan (the eastern end of the Little Pamir)

パミールのキルギス人と違って、近代的家屋に住まう人々もいる。主食もナーンではなく、固いがパンに似ている。生活圏も他民族と共生している。

Most of the Kyrgyz living in Tajikistan live in modern houses, unlike the inhabitants of the Afghan Pamirs. Hard bread rather than nan is the staple source of food. The ethnic mix of the population is also more diverse.

(いずれもシャイマック / All fig.s, Shaymak)

(1) ユルト式の住居

永住地にもジャイロ - (アイラークに相当) にも見られる。

(1) Yurt housing

Yurt can be observed in both the summer grazing camps (Jailou) and the permanent settlements.

(2) 近代風の家屋

ア・パミールには全く見られない。

(2) Modern houses

Modern houses such as these do not exist in the Afghan Pamirs.

(3) 他民族との共生

ア・パミールと違って同一生活圏に他民族と共生している。クァールパク着用者がキルギス人。

(3) Co-existing with other ethnic groups

In Tajikistan, the Kyrgyz coexist with other ethnic groups, unlike the Afghan Kyrgyz. The Kyrgyz are distinguished by their traditional hats, the Kualpak.

（5）出来上がったパン

　イーストを加えるが、温度が低く充分醗酵しないので、大変硬くて力を入れてナイフで切る。

(5) The baked bread

The cold temperature prevents the yeast from fermenting sufficiently, so the bread is very hard and has to be cut with a knife.

（4）パン焼きはタンドールで

(4) The Tandoor to bake bread

（6）ストーブでも焼ける

(6) Bread can be baked over the stove.

（7）食卓に並ぶ食品とクリーム分離器

　ア・パミールと違って、原乳を手動式器械でクリームを分離する。それをア・パミールと同じく揉んでバターを造る。

(7) Meals, and a cream separator

Unlike the Afghan Pamirs, the cream is separated from the milk manually. Butter is made by agitating the cream, the same process as that of the Afghan Pamirs.

(1) 蝶の分類・同定　酒井成司（日本鱗翅学会会員）Seiji Sakai（The Lepidopterological Society of Japan）

(1) Classification and identification of butterflies

A list of butterflies collected by Dr. Go Hirai in Wakhan Valley Afghanistan 2010
（平位博士が2010年ワハン谷において採集した蝶類リスト: *Melitaea pallas* 1 新亜種の記載。）
The expedition was not well timed, much too late, and much of the material Dr.Go Hirai brought to me was worn. Butterflies were collected mainly at Wakhjir Pass.

A. アゲハチョウ科(Papilionidae)
1. ニセテンザンウスバ
   Parnassius rubicundus baroghila Tytler, 1926
   14♂, 4♀: Wakhjir Pass, 4600m, 18-19. VIII. 2010, Wakhan Valley, Afghanistan. leg. Dr.Go Hirai. in coll. Seiji Sakai

B. シロチョウ科 (Pieridae)
2. エオゲネモンキチョウ
   Colias eogene erythas Grum-Grshimailo, 1890
   1♂, 2♀: Wakhjir Pass, 4600m, 18-19. VIII. 2010, Wakhan Valley, Afghanistan. leg. Dr.Go Hirai. in coll. Seiji Sakai
3. モンシロチョウ
   Artogeia rapae (Linnaeus, 1758)
   29exs., Ismurgh, 3200m, 3. IX, Wakhan Valley, Afghanistan. leg. Dr.Go Hirai. in coll. Seiji Sakai

C. タテハチョウ科 (Nymphalidae)
4. アライヒョウモンモドキ
   A new subspecies of *Melitaea pallas* Staudinger (Lepidoptera: Nymphalidae)
   Melitaea pallas hirai ssp. nov.（新亜種）
   アフガニスタンからは新記録種である。表面の地色はパミールの個体群より赤味が強い。
   表面中央部の黒斑列は大きく目立つ。
   副模試標本は酒井成司により、ロンドン自然史博物館（旧大英博物館）に寄贈された。
   This is the first record of this species from the Wakhan Valley Afghanistan
   It differs from the Pamir race pseudobalbina in the following respects
   (1) The upperside ground colour is much more reddish-brown;
   (2) black discal spots prominent

Holotype ♀: Length of forewing 18mm. Wakhjir Pass, 4600m, 18-19. VIII. 2010. Wakhan Valley, Afghanistan. leg. Dr.Go Hirai. in coll. Seiji Sakai
1 Paratype（♂・♀?）, abdomen: lose.In coll.The Natural History Museum , London , England
5. ギンボシヒョウモン
   Argynnis aglaja vitatha Moore, [1875]
   1♂, 1♀: Wakhjir Pass, 4600m, 18-19. VIII. 2010, Wakhan Valley, Afghanistan. leg. Dr.Go Hirai. in coll. Seiji Sakai

D. ジャノメチョウ亜科 (Nymphalidae: Satyrinae)
6. チビキイロジャノメ
   Hyponephele hilaris hilaris (Staudinger, 1886)
   1♀: Wakhjir Pass, 4600m, 18-19. VIII. 2010, Wakhan Valley, Afghanistan. leg. Dr.Go Hirai. in coll. Seiji Sakai
7. ヒメパミールタカネヒカゲ
   Karanasa bolorica bolorica (Grum Grshimailo, 1888)
   3♂, 1♀: Wakhjir Pass, 4600m, 18-19. VIII. 2010, Wakhan Valley, Afghanistan. leg. Dr.Go Hirai. in coll. Seiji Sakai

Bibliography
酒井成司, (1981) アフガニスタン蝶類図鑑。講談社。東京。271pp. figs.,48pls.
Sakai S.(1981):Butterflies of Afghanistan. Tokyo. 271pp.,figs.,48pls
Kolesnichenko K.A., & Churkin S.V., (2000) Helios, Moscow
酒井成司　他, (2002) パルナシウス大図鑑。講談社。東京。468pp. figs.,pls.,104
Sakai S.,Aoki.,Yamaguchi S.,Watanabe Y.,Inaoka S.(2002):The pamassiology. TheParnassius Butterflies, A Study in Evolution. kodansha Ltd.Tokyo.468pp.,figs.,104 pls
Tuzov V.K., (2003) Nymphalidae part 1. In Bozano, G. C. (Ed.). Milano

A. アゲハチョウ科(Papilionidae)

B. シロチョウ科 (Pieridae)

1. ニセテンザンウスバ　♂
Parnassius rubicundus baroghila

1. ニセテンザンウスバ　♀
Parnassius rubicundus baroghila

2. エオゲネモンキチョウ　♀
Colias eogene erythas

C. タテハチョウ科 (Nymphalidae)

3. モンシロチョウ　♂
Artogeia rapae

4. アライヒョウモンモドキ　♀
Melitaea pallas hirai ssp. nov. (Holotype)

5. ギンボシヒョウモン　♂
Argynnis aglaja vitatha

D. ジャノメチョウ亜科（Nymphalidae: Satyrinae）

6. チビキイロジャノメ　♀
Hyponephele hilaris hilaris

7. ヒメパミールタカネヒカゲ　♂
Karanasa bolorica bolorica

7. ヒメパミールタカネヒカゲ　♀
Karanasa bolorica bolorica

(2) カラビル(黒い峠)の黒い岩石　同定　沖村雄二（広島大学名誉教授）

　岩石名は流紋岩。珪長質の火山岩で粘性が強い。大陸地殻特有の火山から噴出・流動した溶岩で、溶岩・火砕岩は流理構造をもち、凝灰岩は地層を形成する。風化作用のために、周りの岩石に比べて、異様に表面が黒くなっていて、黒い峠と称ばれる所以だろうと想像できる。またガラス質の部分と繊細な鉱物の結晶の部分の割合からすると、この岩石のかけらを打ち合わせると快い金属音が聞こえてくるような気がする。

(2) Stone of Qara Bel (Black Pass)
Identified by Yuji Okimura (Professor Emeritus of Hiroshima University)

The black stone is a rhyolite. It is a volcanic rock that is felsic. It is a remnant of lava that flowed out after a volcano sitting on a continental plate erupted. The pyroclastic rock or lava has a flow structure, while the volcanic ashes ? create the geological stratum. Due to corrosion, when compared to the surrounding rocks, the surface appears to be unnaturally black; hence the name Black Pass. Based upon the ratio of glass and the finely crystallized mineral layer, I could almost hear the tingling sound of metal if I were to hit the pieces of rock together.

(3) ア・パミールの魚類の分類　同定　寺島彰（京都大学学士山岳会会員）

　アフガーンの淡水魚については、まだ十分調査が進んでいないが、これまでに102種類の生息が知られている。そうした状況の中で、今回採取された魚を簡単にいえば、コイである。もちろん日本で見られるコイとは異なり、チベット・ヒラヤマを中心とする地域にだけ分布しているコイの仲間である。このグループの魚に対する日本語名は無いが、中国では裂腹魚学名Schizothoraxとよばれている。尻鰭の付け根に沿った部分の左右に大形の鱗が並んでいるため、魚を裏返して腹側からその部分をみると、まるで腹部が裂けているかのように見える。(中略)。

　アフガーンからは、これまでに3属15種の裂腹魚が記載されているが、今回ワハーン回廊（ア・パミール）で採取された裂腹魚は、この内Schizopygopisi属（中国名：裸裂尻魚）の一種と思われる。これは裂腹魚の仲間の中でも比較的高地環境に適応したグループとされているが、小生がかつてギルギットからチトラールへ抜けるルートの途上で採取した裂腹魚と詳細について現在比較検討中である。(後略)。

(3) The classification of fish in the Afghan Pamirs
Identified by Akira Terashima
(Member of the AACK (Academic Alpine Club of Kyoto University))

Though fresh water fish found in the Afghanistan, have not been sufficiently researched yet, 102 types of species have been identified as of date.

Dr.Hirai was able to bring back a sample of fish species that belonged to the family of carp. Of course the carp that I sampled is of a different variety from those found in Japan. They belong to the family of carp that is only found in Tibet and the Himalayas. Though there is no Japanese name for this type of carp, in Chinese they have been named "the fish with a split stomach". They are formally known as the Schizothorax.

Because the fish have a large scale on both the left and right sides of the base of their fin, if you would turn the fish upside down and look at its belly, it would appear as if the belly were split.

Up to now 15 species belonging to three groups of "fish with a split stomach" have been identified. The fish that Dr.Hirai brought back from his most recent trip to the Afghan Pamirs may belong to the Schizopygopisi group (Chinese name,fish with a split stomach). This type of fish is said to be relatively well adapted to high altitude mountains. Currently I am comparing this fish sample with another fish sample that I found when I was traveling between Gilgit and Chitral.

（4）温泉の分析（2001～2004）　分析　広島市衛生研究所・広島県保健環境センター

(4) Analysis of hot springs (2001-2004)
Analyzed by the Hiroshima City Institute of Hygiene and
Hiroshima Prefectural Technology Research Institute Health and Environment

Location	Items	℃	pH	Na$^+$	K$^+$	Ca^{++}	Mg^{++}	F$^-$	Cl$^-$	NO$_3^-$	SO$_4^-$	CO$_3^-$
Wakhan	Serk	41	11↑	63	0.5	0.5	0.4	10.2	3.9	0	52.4	42
	Sargoz	46	7.6									
	Baba Tangi	33~39	8.0	130	30.	11.0	0.8	7.8	11.1	0	34.0	150
	Sar had	38~39	7.0	95.3	1.7	0.4	0.4	5.1	5.5	0	50.5	108
Little Pamir	Eastof Boqai Gumbaq	37	7.0	800.0	43.5	11.4	7.2	14.8	54.4	0	6.5	1320
	Sar Tash	32	7.6	80	1.0	1.4	0.4	11.3	30.3	0	14.3	60

（温度とpHを除く）（Except for ℃ and pH）

（5）家畜用塩の分析　分析　広島市衛生研究所

　キルギス人が動物用の飼料塩としている"シュラー"（図36(1)）の主成分は重炭酸ナトリウムで、塩分は僅かに2%に過ぎなかった。採取時に舐めたが重曹の味がした。

(5) Analysis of salt fed to livestock
Analyzed by the Hiroshima City Institute of Hygiene

　The main chemical composition of the salt,"shura" (fig.36(1)) that the Kyrgyz feed to their livestock is Na2CO3. The concentration of salt is a mere 2%. I licked the salt when I took a sample but it tasted of baking soda.

構成成分 Breakdown of chemical composition		含有率（%） Concentration(%)
水	H$_2$O	48.3
重炭酸ナトリウム	Na$_2$CO$_3$	41.0
塩	NaCl	2.0
硫酸ナトリウム	NaSO$_4$	1.2
水溶性成分		12.5
	pH	10.7

ア・パミールでは頭痛を訴える人が多い。その人達、頭痛を訴える入域パーキスタン人、馬方のワハーン人達とサフューラ経皮的動脈血ヘモグロビン酸素飽和度をONYXを用いて調べた。いずれも頭痛のない私の値よりも高かった。また最高血圧190mm/Hgの1人（※）（入院加療一年後の再検で正常域）を除いて、いずれも正常域であった。一日の塩分摂取量は8〜10gと思われる。

（1）Many people suffer from headaches in the Afghan Pamirs. I conducted a medical examination of a Pakistani who was in the area from Gilgit, Wakhan inhabitant s who tended my horses, and Safiullah John. I used the Onyx to examine the percutaneous hemoglobin saturating degree of oxygen of the arterial blood. SpO2. All three men showed higher measurements when compared to myself. I did not suffer at all from headaches. Also, the blood pressure level was normal, except for young woman whose systolic blood pressure measured 190mm/.Hg (after hospitalization and treatment, her blood pressure returned to normal.) Salt intake per day is estimated to be around 8-10 grams.

（6）経皮的動脈血ヘモグロビン酸素飽和濃度・SpO2100分率 (1999 〜 2004)

(6) Percutaneous hemoglobin saturating degee of oxygen of arterial blood・SpO2 complaing headach(1999 〜 2004)

地域 Location	症例数 Case Numbers	SpO₂
Wakhjir	1	94
	1	95
	2	96
	2	97
	4	98
Little Pamir	1	94
	2	95
	1	96
	3	97
	2	98
	1	99
Great Pamir	1	94
	1	95
	1	96
	3	97
	3	98
	1	99
Pakistani	1	91
Wakhi	4	94〜96
Safiullah	1	90〜93
(Hirai)	1	86〜90

（7）血圧の分布 (1999 〜 2004)

(7) Distsibution of maximum blood pressure complaing headach

地域 Location	症例数 Case Numbers	値(mm/Hg) Values(mm/Hg)		
		140↑	139〜100	99↓
Wakhjir	17	0	16	1
Little Pamir	25	1(※)	23	1
Great Pamir	24	0	24	0
Pakistani	1	0	1	0
Wakhi	4	0	4	0
Safiullah	1	0	1	0

（8）その他

Vit.Cの欠乏：ワハーンでは夏期は充分量の杏、3種類の豆類や少量の緑野菜を摂っている。秋にはジャガイモも収穫される。

ア・パミールではこれらのものは全くなく、稀に僅少量の野生ネギとチグリと称ぶ緑野草を口にするだけだ。ミルク・紅茶とヨーグルトに含まれる微量のVit.Cを摂取するのみであるが、壊血病や歯肉出血患者を診察した事はない。

地方性甲状腺腫：（沃度含有率が極めて低い）岩塩を撮っているアフガーンでは、以前は内部やワハーンでも、大きな単純性甲状腺腫と思われるものが、地方性甲状腺腫として目についていたが、最近は菓子など欧米の食品の流通によるものか、見かけなくなった。ア・パミールでは1999年の入域以来目にした事がない。

(8) Others

Deficiency of Vitamin C: During the summer months, the residents of the Wakhan can consume sufficient amounts of apricot, three types of beans and small amounts of green vegetables. In the autumn, potatoes are harvested.

In the Afghan Pamirs, these vegetables are unavailable. The Afghans living in the Pamirs consume small amounts of wild onions and a green grass called Chiguri. The Afghans only consume minute traces of Vit.C through milk, tea and yoghurt. However, I have never observed patients with bleeding tooth gums or suffering from scurvy.

Endemic Goiter ：Because the Afghans consume rock salt with minimal iodine content, in the past in the interior regions of Afghanistan and in the Wakhan, one could observe many people with very big goiter. However, in recent years because American or European candies and snacks are being increasingly sold in Afghanistan, I have not encountered people with this symptom. Since 1999, during my travels in Afghanistan, I have not seen any Afghan with large goiter.

ワハーンの回廊部は、文字通り細い帯のような地帯で、北にはパミールの重畳たる高原が、南は東西に続く屏風のようなヒンズー・クシュ山脈が続き、生産的なものはなに一つなく、古来、東西交流ルートにすぎなかった。

ただ、東西どちらからにしてもここを抜けることは大変な危険が伴い、このためもあって地理学的な情報が少ない。具体的な詳しい紹介記事は、ようやく19世紀に入ってからで、ただワハーン回廊部全てについてふれられたものは、きわめてわずかにすぎない。大半は東西のせいぜい入口か出口部分で、西から東、東から西へ全ての紹介記事になると、まさしく暁天の星ほど少ない。

そのためここでは総括的な参考資料と言えるかどうかきわめて疑問であるが、ともかくワハーンの回廊部分にいくらかなりと関わりがあり、参考になりそうなものは、だいたいここに加えてある。ただしパミール北部や中央部については除くことにした。ここでは文献のタイトルだけでなく、それらの抄録を紹介したが、ここから19世紀の時代背景や当時の雰囲気を、わずかながらも偲んでいただけたら幸いである。

ワハーンは、いまなお現地同様に資料の面でも、きわめて歴史的に見ても未知の世界であると思えるからでもある。

<西暦5、6世紀のシナの西域旅行者―法顕・宋雲>
1) Samuel Beal : Travels of Fah-hsien and Sung-yun, 208p, a fold.map, London1869
中国・東普の求法僧法顕と北魏の宋雲・恵生は、399年と518年に各々西域を通り、インドまで行った。この紀行が、『法顕伝』と『宋雲紀行』で、当時を知る貴重な参考資料である。西洋人には漢文のテキストが使えないので、ビールが英訳し大変貴重視された。

<7世紀　玄奘三蔵の西域・インド紀行>
2) Hsüang-tsang's Shi-ui-ji (Chines Ver.)
玄奘『大唐西域記』　ワハーンの回廊部分の記述は、第12巻15の部分にごく短くふれられている。護侶（ワハーン）、縛芻河（オクサス河）、活国（クンドウズ）、葱嶺（パミール）、瀧池（ヴィクトリア湖）、波謎羅川（パミール渓谷）などの地名が見れる。

<唐の将軍、高仙芝のパミール遠征、747年>
3) Sir Aurel Stein: A Chinese Expedition across the Pamirs and Hindukush, A.D.747.G.J.RGS, Feb.1922, p.122-131
唐の将軍、高仙芝は、747年、玄宗皇帝から命ぜられ、吐蕃（チベット）の勢力が増したギルギット遠征に向い、タルゴット峠を越えて小勃律（ギルギット）を制圧した。

スタインはワハーンの現地調査を行い、唐軍の戦闘状況を再現している。

<西暦10世紀のアラブの旅行家イブン・ハウカルの記録>
4) Oriental Geography of Ibn Haukal. Transl. by Sir William Ouseley. xxxvi+327p. London 1800
イブン・ハウカルは、943年、バクダートからスペイン、中東、インドへと広くイスラム社会を旅し、地誌として『道程と諸国への旅』を出版した。この中で、マウェラウンナール（中央アジア）、ジェイホーン（オクサス河）、フェルガーナ、サマルカンド、ボハラ、バルフ、インダス川などが紹介される。

<マルコ・ポーロの東方見聞録>
5) The Book of Ser Marco Polo. 2 vols,Vol. I. cii+462p, Vol. II. xxii+662p. London 1921
13世紀のイタリアの東洋旅行家の旅行体験録は、一般に『東方見聞録』と呼ばれている。マルコは父と叔父と共に東方旅行に出かけたものの、1260年、戦乱のため東方へ向うことになった。この折、約一年バダフシャン地方に滞在し、様々な記録を遺している。ここから12日間ほど行くと、旅の終わりのせいぜい3日もかからぬ狭い地域に入るが、ここをワハーン（Vokhan）と呼んでいるといっている。ここから3日ほど東北に進むと、全てが山岳地帯で、世界で一番高い所という。この高地に2つの山地に囲まれた大湖（ヴィクトリア湖）があり、ここから1条の大河が流れ出ている（パミール河）。この河岸は豊かな平原で、牧草が生え、とくに野生の羊が群生し、この角が大きく立派である。

ただ野生狼がこれを襲って食用にするので、大きな角が辺りに散乱し、これを現地民が拾い集めて積み上げ、道標にしている。この土地をパミールと呼ぶ。野生羊は一般にマルコ・ポーロ羊と呼ばれている。このテキストはヘンリー・ユールの校正本。なお本書ユール版のうち第1巻の第29章以下数章の補注が、大変参考になる。

<14世紀、ヒンズー・クシュを超えたイタリアの修道士の記録>
6) Henry Yule,ed.:Cathay and the Way Thither. 2 vols, Vol.I.3+ccliii+250p. Vol.II.253-596p+cviii. The Hakuyt Society. London 1866
マルコ・ポーコの旅から半世紀たった1328～29年頃、イタリアの修道士オドリコが、シナから中央アジアを通ってペルシアに行き、この折、記録が簡単なため詳しい事は不明だが、ワハーンを抜け、ヒンズー・クシュを超えた可能性が大きい。これを翻訳・編集したヘンリー・ユールは、彼の著『キャセイとそちらへの道』第1巻のOdoric of Pondenone(p.1-162)の章で紹介している。またワハンとオクサス河についても追求さ

れている。

<イブン・バットゥータの三大陸周遊記>

7) The Travels of Ibn Battutah.Translated by Gibb.Vol.Ⅲ, xi+539-771p, Cambridge(The HakluySociety) 1971. And others

　邦訳に『イブン・バットゥータ　三大陸周遊記』(抄)、前嶋信次訳、河出書房、1953。『大旅行記』全6巻、永島彦一訳、平凡社。

　14世紀、アラビアの旅行家。1335年、メッカ巡礼の旅に上る。エジプトから中近東、中央アジアに入り、ブハラ、サマルカンド経由でアム・ダリア(オクサス)河を南に下って、アフガーニスターンのバダフシャン地方に至る。直接ワハーンの実施体験談はないが、当時の貴重な情報を得ることができる。このアラビア語の原本は「町々の珍しさ、旅の驚異について観る人々への贈り物」と題され、古典的名著とされた。

8) 19世紀初期には、英国でアラビア語の原文に英語の解説を付けたテキストが、出版されている。

<15-16世紀、トルキスタン、アフガーニスターン、インド征服者の記録>

9) Memoirs of Zehir-ed-Din Muhammed Baber. Transl.by John Leyden & W.Erskine.lxix+432p.London 1826

　　チムールの血を引くパミール山麓のフェルガーナの領主の子として生まれ、中央アジアの統一を図るが成功せず、アフガーニスターン、インドに遠征し、300年続くムガール帝国の創始者となる。この回想録『バーブルナーマ』は広く中央アジアの歴史を知る貴重な資料を呈供してくれる。オクサスとヤクサルテス河(シル・ダリア)の間の地図(折り込み)が、大変参考になる。

<16-17世紀、インドより　ワハーン、パミール、西域経由で敦煌に旅したベネディクト・ゴエス>

10) Jahangir and the Jesuits. Part Ⅱ.The Travels of Benedict Goes. P.119-182,Transl.by C.H.Panyne.xxix+287p. London 1930

　「シルクロードの歴史から」榎一雄著　研文出版(JNP Ver.)　1979年ベネディクト・ゴエス(1562?-1607)は1584年、インドのゴアでイエズス会に入り、1602年、アクバル帝の援助で首都アグラを発ち、ヒンズー・クシュ山脈を越え、ワハーン回廊を抜け、パミール、天山南路を経由して敦煌に達するが急死。当時は謎であったキタイとシナが同一である事を、この旅によって初めて実証した。

<西域・葱嶺地域の河川誌>

11) 徐松撰:『西域水道記』　全5巻　道光3年(1822)

　清朝時代、徐松による、とくに天山南北路沿いに現地調査を元に纏められた、河川地誌。本書ではパミール(葱嶺)南縁のワハーン地域は入っていないが、パミール

北部のイシック・クル(湖)にも言及され、河川図が貴重である。

<英東インド会社による初のアフガーン使節>

12) Mountstuart Elphinstone : An Account of the Kingdon of Caubul・・・. xxii+675p. a fold map. London 1815. New revised. 2vols. Vol.Ⅰ.xii+422p, Vol.Ⅱ.xii+440p/London Ⅱ.xii+440p, London 1839

　東インド会社は1809年、アフガーニスターンの重要性からエルフィンストーンを代表団長として、初の使節団を派遣し、カーブルでアフガン国王シャー・ジュジャーと会見して、通商条約を締結して帰国する。これが『カーブル宮廷使節記』。北方のヒンズー・クシュ、カラコラム山脈、ワハーンについての情報が初めてもたらされる。大型地図が参考になる。

<ムーアクロフトのアジア旅行>

13) William Moorcroft, & George Trebeck : Travels in the Himalayan Provinnces of Hindustan…from 1819 to 1825. 2 vols.lvi+459p. viii+508p, map. London 1841

　19世紀初め、チベットから広く中央アジアを旅した英国の旅行家。彼は東インド会社から依頼され、インダス河を渉りカーブルに行き、ここから北ヘタシュクルガン、クンドゥズまで訪れたが、ワハーンには入らなかった。このあとアム・ダリア河を渡り、ブハラまで行ったものの、アフガーンに戻ったところで病没してしまった。当時の北アフガーニスターンを知る貴重な書。

<アフガン・ルートの開拓者>

14) Alexander Burnes : Travels into Bokhara. 3 vols.xxiv+356p, xv+473p, xix+332p. maps. London 1834

　英東インド会社の士官アレクサンダー・バーンズは、1832年、インド(カシミール)人の通訳モハン・ラルを伴って、カーブルから北上し、ヒンズー・クシュ山脈を越え、クルム、クンドゥズに至り、ここから反転してバルフ経由でトルキスタンに入り、ブハラまで行った。ただ彼らはワハーンの入り口までには達していたが、それ以上は東に進まなかった。

　インド、アフガーニスターン、西トルキスタン、ペルシャの古典的報告書。

<ウッドのオクサス源流調査>

16) John Wood : A Personal Narrative of a Journey to the Source of the Oxus, 424p. a folding map. London 1841. 2nd ed. cv+280p. 2 fold. maps. London 1872

　1830年代、英東インド会社の交易代表としてアフガーニスターンに赴任したアレクサンダー・バーンズに同行した英国士官ジョン・ウッドはバーンズから派遣され、1837年、ワハーンの回廊を抜け、オクサス源流の水源調査を行った。

1841年に初版が、1872年、ウッドの没後に増補改訂版が出版され、ヘンリー・ユールの詳細な「オクサス渓谷の地理」(84ページ)が入っている。ワハーンの古典的名著。

<19世紀、オクサス、ワハーンをめぐる政治情勢>

17) Suhash Chakravarty : From Khyber to Oxus. A study in Imprial Expansion. vi+280p. maps. New Delhi 1976

1869～1880年のアフガーニスターンをめぐる英露関係を、外交資料から歴史的背景を、インド人研究者が紹介した書。ワハーン回廊がアフガーンに編入された経緯についてもふれられている。

<19世紀中期の十年間の西トルキスタンの支配者と政情>

18) Demetrius Charles Boulger : The Life of Yakoob Beg；
Ameer of Kashgar.ix+344p. a folding map. London 1878

ヤクブ・ベクはフェルガーナのコーカンド出身の軍人。ロシア軍に敗れてカシュガールに移り、ここの支配者となり、西トルキスタンを統治するが、1877年、清の左宗棠軍に敗れる。英露両軍から貴重視され、英フォーサイス、露クロパトキンの各使節団の訪問を受ける。彼の没後、西トルキスタンは新疆省(清国)となる。中央アジアの近代史を調べる上で、ヤクブ・ベクについての情報はぜひ知る必要がある。

<ロバート・ショーとジョージ・ヘイワードの報告書>

19) Robert Shaw : Visits to High Tartary, Yarkand and Kashgar. xvi+486p. London 1871

20) G.J.W.Hayward : Letters. JRGS. vol xv, 1870,xvi,&1871

直接ワハーンの回廊にまで踏み込まなかったものの、1860年代にカシュガールにヤクブ・ベクを訪れ、パミール地域に入ったショーとヘイワードに一応ふれる必要があろう。

19世紀末期、インド北西部のギルギット地方で活躍した英国人のジョージ・ヘイワードは、1818～69年スリナガール経由で、カシュガルに旅し、ヤクブ・ベクに会った。だが、後に1870年ダルコットで現地人に殺された。

<フォーサイス使節団一行の報告書>

21) T.D.Forsyth : Ost Turkestan und das Pamir-Plateau …… 1873 u. 1874. 76s. Petermanns Geo.Mit, Nr.52,Gotha 1877:Autobiography and Reminiscences of Sir Douglas Forsyth. vii+283p. London 1887

英インド政庁は、当時カシュガリアを支配していたヤクブ・ベクの下に、通商協定を結ぶためダグラス・フォーサイスを団長とする使節団を1870年に派遣するが、ヤク

ブ・ベグが不在で果せず、次いで1873～4年、再度使節団をカシュガールに送り込んだ。そして協定は締結されたが、この際、各分野の専門家も参加し、東トルキスタン、パミールを調査し、帰国後、各自が報告書、紀行本を出版した。このうちヘンダーソンの『ラホールからヤルカンド』はフォーサイスの第一回の使節団(1870)に同行したときの記録。あとは第2回のとき。ただトロッターの報告書だけは、未見で参照できなかった。

22) George Henderson & Allan O.Hume : Lahore to Yarkand.
Incidents of the Route and Nature History …. xiv+370p. ills,a fold. map. London 1873

23) H.W.Bellew : Kashmir and Kashghar.xix.419p.London 1875
(このテキストは、著書からゴルドン宛の寄贈本)

<初めてワハーンの回廊部をスケッチした旅行記録>

24) T.E.Gordon : THE ROOF OF THE WORLD. Being the Narrative of a Journey over the High Plateau of Tibet …… and the Oxus sources on Pamir. xiv+172p. a fold map. London 1876

第二回のフォーサイによるカシュガール使節団に同行した、ゴルドンの個人的旅行記。とくに旅行中に描いた66枚(うち4枚はカラー)の素描画が入っていて、大変興味深い。とくに著者が言うように、「インダス河からオクサス河」のルート上では、これまでスケッチされたことのない秘密に鎖された世界だったので、絵を見ているだけでも旅が楽しめる本になった。戦前に邦訳されたことがある。『世界の屋根』田中一呂訳、生活社 1942。

<帝政ロシアが派遣したカシュガールへの外交使節団報告>

25) А.Н.КУРОПАТКИН：КАШГАРИЯ.435p a folding map. С-ПЕТЕРБУРГ.1879

西トルキスタンを制圧した帝政ロシアは、1876-7年に当時カシュガールを統治していたヤクブ・ベクの元に、外交使節団を派遣した。その使節団長がのちの日露戦争時のロシア軍総司令官のクロパトキン将軍だった。すでに英インド政庁がカシュガールに使節団を送り込んでいたので焦燥感があったのであろう。このときの報告書が『カシュガリア』で、歴史・地理・民族などの詳細な記録があり、大型の折込み地図が当時のロシアの情報を知る手掛りとなる。ただワハーンの回廊部分が南縁となっている。英訳がカルカッタから出されている。

26) 英訳がカルカッタから出されている

<カーゾン卿の中央アジア旅行記>

27) George N. Curzon : Russia in Central Asia in 1889. xiii+477p. London 1889 : The Pamirs and the Source of the Oxus. JRGS. Vol.8, 1,2,3.1896

英国の政治家。1888年、下院議員だったとき西トルキスタンを旅し、名高い旅行記を出版。この折、アム・ダリア（オクサス）河を渡り、いつかこの水源地帯への旅を願い、10年後に実現した。邦訳『シルクロードの山と谷』 吉沢一郎訳 あかね書房（世界山岳名著全集、第1巻、5-111p、1967）

＜ヤングハズバンドのパミール、ワハン紀行＞

28) Francise E.Younghusband : The Heart of a Continent. xvii+ 409p. ills, maps. London 1896

英軍人・探検家、ヤングハズバンドは、1890年、インド政府からの要請で、シナ語通訳のマカートニとカシミールからタシュクルガン、ワクジル峠を経て、ワハンの回廊部に入り、ワハン・スー川畔のボサイ・グンバスに行き、ここから反転して大パミールを訪れ、カシュガールに至る。

＜ダンモア卿のパミール紀行＞

29) The Earl of Dunmore : The Pamirs. 2 vols. xx+360p, xi+352p. London 1893

英国のダンモア卿（伯爵）は、1892年、旅仲間のロシュ少佐とインドを訪れ、カシミールからトルキスタンをめぐる。1892年10〜11月にワクジル峠からワハーンの回廊に入り、ヴィクトリア湖を抜けてパミールを旅する。この旅行記を記したのが本書。地図が参考になる。

＜英露パミール国境委員会議事録＞

30) M.G.Gerard : Report on the Proceedings of the Pamir Boundary Commission, 1896. vi+97p, 2 folding maps, Calcutta.1897

1890年代末までに、帝政ロシアは西トルキスタンをほぼ制圧し、パミールも領有下に収め英領インドと国境を接することになったので、1895年6〜8月、ワクジル峠近傍で国境画定委員会が開かれ、ワハーンの回廊部の国境線も決まった。英国代表はジェラード将軍、ロシア側はシュワイコフスキー将軍。47葉の写真。大型地図は大変参考となる。

＜スタインのパミール、崑崙の山岳パノラマ図集＞

31) Aurel Stein : Mountain Panoramas from the Pamirs and Kuen Lun. x+36p. 24 panoramas & map. RGS.1908

オーレル・スタインは、1900〜01年の第一回のシナ・トルキスタンの調査の折、パミールと崑崙山岳のパノラマ写真を撮ってきて、地図作成の資料とした。
本書を編集する上でも、これは大変参考になった。

＜第一次大戦時ドイツの秘密アフガン使節団によるワハーン横断記録＞

32) Werner-Otto von Hentig : Ins verschlossene Land. Ein Kampf mit Mensch und Meile.248 s.map. Berlin 1928

1914年に第一次大戦の勃発により、ドイツ外務省はアフガーニスターンに秘密使節団を派遣し、アフガン国王に反英行動をとらす工作に着手した。そこでペルシア勤務の経験のあるウェルナー・オットー・フォン・ヘンティヒに2人の仲間をつけ、1915年4月、一行はトルコ、バクダット、テヘランを経由し、さらに東へケビール砂漠を横断してアフガーニスターンのカーブルに入った。ここで10ヶ月滞在したもののアフガン側の説得に失敗し、1916年5月21日、カブールを発って北上し、ヒンズー・クシュ山脈を越えて、ワハーンの回廊に入り、オクサス河沿いに東行したが、詳しい現地名が地図上で確認できず、日付も記載がないので、詳しいルートが分からない。ただ無事にロシア軍の追跡を振り切って、シナ・トルキスタンに入り、ヤルカンド経由でカシュガールに着いた。戦後ようやく10年してこの体験録『禁じられた国にて』が出版された。

＜ドイツのルフトハンザ機による空からパミール、ワハーン横断飛行の記録＞

33）Carl August Freiherr v. Gablenz : D-ANOY bewingt den Pamir. 241 s.maps. Berlin 1937

ドイツの航空機メーカーのフューゴー・ユンケルスは、1927年からスヴェン・ヘディンの中央アジア探検を支援するはずだったが、実現に至らず、探検の終了した翌年の1936年、フォン・ガブレンツによるD−ANOY機でアフガーニスターンのカブールから、パミール南縁のワハーン回廊を抜け、二機の編隊を組んでホータン、安西を経由し、最終目的地の西安に向った。ワハーンの空中からの実体験とワハーンの空中写真が貴重である。
邦訳『パミール翔破』 永淵三郎訳、東京（自刊） 1938。

＜ティルマンのワハーンとチトラル紀行＞

34) Harold W. Tilman : Two Mountains and a River.xii+233p. maps. Cambridge 1949

英国の登山家ティルマンは、第二次大戦後二年した1947年、カラコラム山脈の高峰にアタックし、次いでパミールを訪れ、ワクジル峠を西にワハーンの回廊をイシュカシムに抜けた。オクサスの水源地帯の連続写真が大変参考になる。邦訳。『カラコルムからパミールへ』薬師義美訳、白水社 1975年。

35) China to Chitral : xi + 124p. Cambridge 1951

上記の旅のあとすぐ（1949年）、ティルマンはカシュガールからワハーン回廊部の南のヒンズー・クシュ南山麓を抜けて、チトラルへの旅をする。直接関係ないが一応参考になる。

＜第二次大戦後のオーストリア隊のパミール調査報告書＞

36）R.S. de Grancy u. R. Kostka(ed.) : Grosser Pamir. 400 s. Graz 1978

オーストリア隊による、1975年のワハーン、パミール、アフガーニスターンの総合的調査報告書。多数の写真と折り込み地図を含む。

<日本人によるワハーン地域の初の調査報告書>
37）平位　剛著　『禁断のアフガーニスターン・パミール紀行—ワハーン回廊の山・湖・人』488頁、図版・地図、京都（ナカニシヤ出版）2003年。

<わが国で紹介されたアフガニスタンに関する総合文献集>
38）堀込静香編『アフガニスタン書誌—明治期—2003』390p.　金沢文圃閣、2003。
明治初年から2002年まで、日本で発表された単行本、単行書及び雑誌、週刊誌、団体の会報等に公表された記事5161件が収録されている。分類としてA．社会と文化、B．自然、C．文学、D．現代社会等。これに書名索引もついている。日本で過去100年にわたるアフガーニスターンの紹介が概観できる貴重な文献目録といえよう。2003年11月、本書の原稿校了の翌日、編者は享年60歳で死去。この編集者である堀込静香の追悼文集が『文献探索2005、書誌・書誌論』472p.として出版された。深井人詩編、文献探索研究会、金沢文圃閣、2006。

補遺
<19世紀末、英国士官のパミール紀行>
39）Ralph P Cobbold : Innermost Asia. Travel & sport in the Pamir. xviii+345p. ills. a folding map. London 1900
インド政庁よりキルギット、フンザ経由の旅行許可が得られたので、1897−98年にかけて、カシュガールからパミール縦断旅行を行った。政治問題には入らないといいながら、英露のパミールの政治・外交問題にもふれられている。ワハーンには立ち入らなかったが、貴重な資料を呈示してくれる。大型折り込み地図が大変参考になる。

<19世紀末に、インド測量局の編集になる中央アジア（西トルキスタン）地図。4葉から成る>
40) Maps of Turk.stan. Compiled under Survey of India, Dehra Dun, issued in Calcutta, 1833. 4 parts. I. Caspian, II. Samarcand, III. Beluchistan, IV. Afghan. Scale 1 inch=32 miles

<地図：>インド測量局による中央アジア（東トルキスタン）>
40) Sir Aurel Stein : Memoir on Maps of Chinese Turkestan and Kansu.From the Surveys made during Sir Aurel Stein's Explorations, 1900-1, 1906-8, 1913-5, xvi+208p. 14 plans, 30 plates, Dehra Dun. Trigonomerical Survey office. India 1923

中央アジアのうち主にシナ・トルキスタンについては、オーレル・スタインの監修になる測量・製作された地図があるが、ワハーンはアフガーン領のためスタインの地図には入っていない。ただインド、アフガーン、ロシア領中央アジアとの国境地帯については、大いに参考になってくれる。このうち三角測量による地図の製作過程については、上記の報告書が参考になってくれる。

−お詫び−（平位　剛）
長岡正利氏には、これらの書影と付属地図の印刷原稿をご用意頂いたが、残念ながら紙数の為、心ならずも割愛させて頂いた。

A bibliography accompanied by a short summary of books related to the Pamirs and Wakhan which were mainly written in the 19th century (Tamio Kaneko)

As the name implies, the Wakhan Corridor is a narrow strip of land which is bounded to the north by the multi-layered highlands of the Pamirs, and to the south by the Hindu Kush mountains, which are oriented east-west and rise perpendicular from the valley,almost as if it were a screen. The area is barely cultivated, and only served as a conduit through which the East and   West were linked.

Whether one was to enter the region from the East or West, travelers who wished to pass through the Wakhan Corridor were exposed to severe danger. Due to this situation, information pertaining to the geography of the region remains scant. It was only in the 19th century that at long last detailed reports about the region began to appear, but few covered the Wakhan in its entirety. Most of the information was limited to both ends of Wakhan. Ineed rarely has the Wakhan been traversed in its entirety from east to west, or west to east, and therefore, there are few written records about the area.

The bibliography given below therefore does not cover the Wakhan Corridor comprehensively. The books were chosen because they contain information that is related to the Wakhan, and can be a good point of reference for the reader. Books pertaining to the northern parts of the Pamirs and the central parts have been omitted. The titles, abstract of the contents and some maps have been introduced with the hope that the reader will gain some insight of the historical context that the region was placed in during the 19th century, and thus gain an appreciation of what the region was like in those turbulent times. The Wakhan and its history remain as elusive as it has been in the past. One can only hope that the bibliography given below will provide the interested reader with some point of reference to this remote corner of the earth.

<Chinese travelers to the "Western Regieons" of the 5th and the 6th-Century Fa-hsien and Sung-yun with Hwui-sang>

1) Samuel Beal : Travels of Fah-hsien and Sung-yun,208p,a fold.map, London1869

The Chinese monks Fa-hsien and Sung-yun reached India via the " Western Regions" or what is now Central Asia in A.D. 399 and A.D.518 respectively.Their travelogues, 『Travels of Fa-hsien and Sung-yun』 is an invaluable records that provide us with a valuable reference regarding that period. Since most Europeans cannot read the Chinese letters, Samuel Beal' s English translation of the travelogues is invaluable.

<Hsüang-tsang' s travels to the Western regions and India in the 7th Century>

2) Hsüang-tsang' s Shi-ui-ji (Chines Ver.)

Hsüang-tsang gives a brief description of the Wakhan Corridor in Volume 12-7 of the Shi-ui-ji. He mentions Hu-mi (Wakhan) , Fu-chu-fuo (Oxus River), Hou-quo(Kunduz), Tson-Lin(the Onion Mountains or Pamirs) , the Ta-long-chi (Great Dragon Lake, Lake Victoria), and the Po-mi-lo-tsuang (Pamir Valley).

<General Kao Hsien Chih' s Mililtary campaign in the Pamirs 747>

3) Sir Aurel Stein: A Chinese Expedition across the Pamirs and Hindukukush, A.D.747.G.J.RGS,Feb.1922,p.122-131

The Chinese General Kao Hsien Chih of the Tang Dynasty (747A.D.) was ordered by the Emperor lead a campaign against the Tibetans who were strengthening their position in Gilgit. The General successfully lead his troops over the Darkot Pass into "Little Po-lu" (Gilgit) which he successfully conquered. Stein conducted a detailed survey of the Wakhan and provides us with a detailed explanation of the battle lead by Kao Hsien Chih.

<Ibn Haukal' s the Arabian traveler of the 10th century>

4) Oriental Geography of Ibn Haukal. Transl. by Sir William Ouseley. xxxvi+327p. London 1800

Ibn Haukal was an Arabian geographer who traveled much of the Muslim world. Starting in 943 he passed through Bagdad, Spain, the Middle East and India. In his book 『On the Routes and Kingdoms』 . He mentioned Mawara' un-Nahr (Central Asia), Jayhoun (Oxus River), Ferghana, Samarkand, Bokhara, Balkh and the Indus River.

<Marco Polo' s "Travel' s" >

5) The Book of Ser Marco Polo.2 vols,Vol. Ⅰ.cii+462p,Vol. Ⅱ.xxii+662p.London 1921

The Travels of Marco Polo written around the 13th century is more generally known in Japan as the [Travels to the East]. Marco left for the East with his father and uncle. The three proceeded east and found themselves having to proceed even further east in A.D.1260 due to armedconflict.

The three Polos stayed for about one year in Badak h shan, during which time Marco recorded his observations. According to the Travels, "In leaving Bada k h shan you ride twelve days till you come to a province extending indeed no more than three days journey,and this is called Vokhan・・・.When you leave this country and ride three days towards northern east, always among mountains, you get to such a height that tis said to be the highest place in the world. And when you have got to this height you find a great lake (Lake Victoria) between two mountains and out of it a fine river (Great Pamir River) running through a plain, clothed in the finest pasture in the world. There especially are a great numbers of wild sheep, whose horns are a great size and good.

Wolves were numerous and killed many of those wild sheep. Hence quantities of their horns and bones were found, and these were made into great heaps by the ways-side, in order to guide travelers. The plain is called Pamir. The wild sheep are generally known today as the Marco Polo Sheep. This text is edited by Henry Yule. Volume 1 Chapter 29 and the following chapters provide much detailed information regarding this region.

＜A record left by the Italian Friar who crossed the Hindu Kush＞

6) Henry Yule,ed.:Cathay and the Way Thither. 2vols, Vol. I.3+ccliii+250p. Vol. II .253-596p+cviii. The Hakuyt Society. London 1866

Half a century after Marco Polo visited the East, around A.D.1328 to A.D.1329, the Italian Friar Odoric of Pondenone left China and traveled to Persia. Enroute, the friar most probably , passed through the Wakhan and crossed the Hindu Kush. Henry Yule translated and edited the travelogue of Odoric which was published in Volume 1, " Odoric of Pondenone "(p.1-162). Yule also shares his research of the Wakhan and the Oxus River.

＜The Travels of Ibn Battutah to the three continents＞

7) The Travels of Ibn Battutah. Translated by Gibb.Vol. III ,xi+539-771p, Cambridge (The Hakluyt Society)1971. And others

The Travels of Ibn Battutah (abridged) was translated into Japanese by S. Maejima and published by Kawade Shobo Publishing Co. in 1953. Another translation by H. Nagashima was published in six volumes by Heibonsha Publishing Co.

An Arabian Traveler of the 14th century. In A.D.1335 he left Egypt to go on a pilgrimage to Mecca, and then proceeded through the Middle East and Central Asia where he passed through Bokhara and Samarkand. From there he followed the Amu Darya (Oxus) River southwards and entered the Badakhshan region of Afghanistan. Though he does not directly mention the Wakhan, much insight can be gained from his descriptions. The original Arabic script of this classic is titled "The Travels of Ibn Battutah" .

8) In the early 19th century, "The Travels of Ibn Battutah" translated from the abridged Arabic manuscript copies, preserved in Public Library of Cambridge, with English notes, ・ ・ ・ by The Rev. Samuel Lee. xviii+243p. London 1829

＜The records left by the conquerors of Turkestan,Afghanistan and India in the 15th and 16th centuries＞

9) Memoirs of Zehir-ed-Din Muhammed Baber. Transl.by John Leyden & W.Erskine. lxix+432p.

London 1826

Babur' s father was the ruler of the Ferghana Valley on the foothills of the Pamirs, Babur is believed to be a direct descendant of Tamerlane. Having unsuccessfully tried to unite Central Asia, Babur invaded Afghanistan and India where he founded the Mughal Empire. The Mughal Empire lasted for 300 years. His memoire "Babur Nama" is a classic that gives us an invaluable glimpse into the history of Central Asia. The map of the area lying between the Oxus and the Jaxartes River (Syr Darya) is very informative.

＜Benedict Goos traveling to Tun-huang from India via the Wakhan and the Pamirs＞

10) Jahangir and the Jesuits. Part II .The Travels of Benedict Goes. P.119-182, Transl.by C.H.

Panyne.xxix+287p. London 1930

Benedict Goes (1562?-1607) converted to Jesuitism in 1584 in Goa, India. In 1602, he left Agra, the capital of the Mughal Empire. With the support of Emperor Akbal, Goes crossed the Hindu Kush Range, passed through the Wakhan Corridor and reached Dunhuan via the Pamir, and the south route of the Tien-shan Mountains. Upon reaching Dunhuang, Goes died suddenly, but he was the first person who was able to prove that Kitai (Cathay) and China were identical places, a mystery at that time. This book has been translated into Japanese by K.Enoki (Kenbun Publishing Co. 1979).

＜Records regarding the Western Regions and their rivers＞

11) Edited by Shui-suong: 『Shi-ui-sui-tao-ji』 5 Vols. Tao-kuang 3 (1822). (Chinease Ver.)

The book excludes Wakhan region at southern edge of Pamirs , yet refers to the Lake Issik to the north of the Pamirs and its fluvial chart is quite valuable.

<The first mission to Afghanistan sent by the British East India Company>

12) Mountstuart Elphinstone:An Account of the Kingdon of Caubul・・・.xxii+675p.a fold map. London 1815. New revised ed. 2 vols. Vol.Ⅰ. xii+422p, Vol.Ⅱ. xii+440p, London 1839

Elphinstone was appointed the first British envoy to Afghanistan by the East India Company which recognized the importance of that country to British interests. In 1809, Elphinstone led a delegation to Kabul, where he was granted an audience with the King of Afghanistan, Shauh Shujah , with whom he was able to secure a bilateral trade treaty before returning home.

The report of Elphinstone's mission, *Account of the Kingdom of Caubul and its Dependencies in Persia and India* (1815), is credited for being the first book in English to introduce the northern Hindu Kush, the Karakorum Range and the Wakhan. The over-sized map attached to the book is extremely useful.

<The travels of William Moorcroft>

13) William Moorcroft, & George Trebeck : Travels in the Himalayan Provinnces of Hindusstan…from 1819 to 1825. 2 vols.lvi+459p.viii+508p,map.London 1841

Moorcroft was a British who traveled widely in Tibet and Central Asia during the 19th century. Upon the request of the East India Company, he crossed the Indus River to enter Kabul. From here he proceeded north to Tashkurgan and Kunduz but did not venture into the Wakhan. He crossed the Amu Darya, and proceeded to Bokhara. He became ill and died shortly after returning to Afghanistan. This book gives us a description of northern Afghanistan during the 19th century.

<The pioneer who blazed the Afghan trail>

14) Alexander Burnes : Travels into Bokhara, 3vols.xxiv+356p, xv+473p, xix+332p. maps. London 1834

Alexander Burns was an officer of the army of the East India Company. In 1932, together with his interpreter Mohan Lal, Burns left Kabul, headed north and crossed the Hindu Kush Range. From there he passed through Kulm and Kunduz. Turning west, Burns visited Turkistan via Balkh and reached Bukhara. Though he reached the entrance of the Wakhan Valley he did not proceed further east into the valley.

This book is the classic report about India,Afghanistan,Western Turkestan and Persia.

15) Mohan Lal : Travels in Panjab,Afghanistan, & Turkestan …… .vii+528p.a fold map. London 1846

<Wood's survey of the source of the Oxus>

16) John Wood : A Personal Narrative of a Journey to the Source of the Oxus,424p. a folding map. London 1841, 2nd ed, cv+280p. 2 fold. maps. London 1872

In the 1830s, Lieutenant John Wood was sent to survey the Wakhan by Alexander Burns, the representative of the British East India Company who had just arrived in Afghanistan. In 1837, Wood traveled the length of the Wakhan and surveyed the source of the Oxus River.The book was first published in 1841, and later posthumously published in 1872 as an expanded version. The book included a section written by Henry Yule which was 84 pages long and which explained in detail the geography of the Wakhan Valley. The book is highly acclaimed as a masterpiece regarding the Wakhan.

<The political situation of the Wakhan and the Oxus River in the 19th century>

17) Suhash Chakravarty : From Khyber to Oxus. A study in Imperial Expansion. vi+280p. maps.New Delhi 1976

Written by an Indian scholar, this book gives us the historical background of the British-Russian bilateral relationship as it pertained to Afghanistan, based on an analysis of diplomatic documents. The book explains the circumstances that led to the annexation of the Wakhan to Afghanistan.

<The rulers and political situation of West Turkestan during the ten years in mid-19th century>

18) Demetrius Charles Boulger : The Life of Yakoob Beg ; Ameer of Kashgar.ix+344p. a folding map.London 1878

Yakoob Beg was a military figure who came from Kokand in the Ferghana Valley. He was defeated by the Russians and fled to Kashgar, where he became a ruler of Western Turkestan. In 1877, Yakoob Beg was defeated by the General of the Qing army. Both the British and the Russians tried to establish a strategic relationship with Yakoob Beg, with the former sending the Forsyth Mission and the latter sending the Kuropatkin Mission. After his death, Western Turkestan became the Sinkiang Province(China). Any study regarding the modern history of Central Asia cannot ignore information regarding Yakoob Beg.

<Reports by Robert Shaw and George Hayward>

19) Robert Shaw : Visits to High Tartary, Yarkand and Kashgar. xvi+486p London

1871

20) G.J.W.Hayward : Letters.JRGS.vol xv, 1870, xvi, &1871

Though both Shaw and Hayward never set foot in the Wakhan Corridor, both men deserve to be mentioned because they met Yakoob Beg at Kashgar and traveled in the Pamir Region.

George Hayward was a British who was active in Gilgit of the British Northwest Frontier in the end of 19th century. He traveled to Kashgar between 1818 to 1869 via Srinagar where he met Yakoob Beg. In 1870, a native killed Hayward in Darkot.

<The Forsyth Mission -related reports>

21) T.D.Forsyth : Ost Turkestan und das Pamir-Plateau …   … 1873 u. 1874.76s. Petermanns Geo.Mit,Nr.52,Gotha 1877:Autobiography and Reminiscences of Sir Douglas Forsyth. vii+283p. London 1887.

The British Indian government dispatched a mission headed by Douglas Forsyth in 1870 to establish a trade agreement with Yakoob Beg who was ruling Kashgaria at that time. Unfortunately for the British, Yakoob Beg had left Kashgar and could not be located when the mission arrived in Kashgar. Between 1873 to1874 the Second Forsyth mission was sent to Kashgar to successfully conclude the trade pact.Many experts in different fields accompanied the mission to survey Eastern Turkestan and the Pamirs, and upon their return, their reports and travelogues were published.Henderson' s [Lahore to Yarkand] is a report of the first Forsyth mission (1870). All the other reports I have on hand were written by members of the Second Forsyth Mission. I could not obtain Trotter' s report.

22) George Henderson & Allan O.Hume : Lahore to Yarkand.Incidents of the Route and Nature History….xiv+370p.ills,a fold.map.London 1873

23) H.W.Bellew : Kashmir and Kashghar.xix.419p.London 1875

(This text was sent as a gift from Bellow to Gordon.)

<The first travelogue to leave pictorial sketches of the Wakhan Corridor>

24) T.E.Gordon : The Roof of the world. Being the Narrative of a Journey over the High Plateau of Tibet …   … and the Oxus sources on Pamir.xiv+172p. a fold map.London 1876

"The Roof of the World" is a personal narrative of T.E. Gordon who accompanied the Second Forsyth Mission to Kashgar. What is particularly notable about this book is the 66 sketches (of which 4 are colored) that were drawn by Gordon. As the author writes, " up to then there were hardly any sketches of the scenery between the Indus River and the Oxus, so the book is a visual delight that records scenes inaccessible at that time.

The book will transport any reader on an imaginary trip to the area. This book was translated into Japanese in 1942 by Ichiro Tanaka,Seikatsusha Publishing Co.

<The Report of the Diplomatic Misseon to Kshgar sent by Czarist Russia.>

25) A.HKYYPO○ΕATK○NH:KAⓌ○RAP○N○R 435p.a folding map. C-ETEP ○○○○○PYP ○○ .1879.

Kashgaria (Eastern or Chinese Turkestan) Transl Walter E.Gowan viii+255p Calcutta 1882

Imperial Russian which had by then conquered Western Turkestan, sent a diplomatic mission to Yaqub Beg, the ruler of Kashgaria in 1876-1877. The mission was led by Kuropatkin, who subsequently became the commander- in- chief of the Imperial Russian Army during the Japan-Russo War of 1905. By that time the British had already dispatched a similar mission to Kashgar, so the Russians must have been hard pressed to follow suit. The report published by the mission, titled "Kashgaria" ,contained detailed records of the history, geography and people, etc. of Kashgar. The over-sized map provides us with a guide to the information that was collected by the Russians. The Wakhan Corridor is shown to be lying on the southern fringe of Kashgar. The English version of the map was published in Calcutta.

26) Kashgaria. (Eastern or Chinese Turkestan). Transl. by Walter E.Gowan. viii+255p. Calcutta 1882.

＜Curzon' s Travelogue of his trips in Central Asia＞

27) George N. Curzon : Russia in Central Asia in 1889. xiii+477p. London 1889 — : The Pamirs and the Source of the Oxus.JRGS.vol.8,1,2,3.1896

George N. Curzon was a statesman of Great Britain. In 1888 in his capacity as a parliamentarian of the House of Commons, Curzon traveled to Western Turkestan and published a most reputable travelogue. During his first trip to Western Turkestan, Curzon dreamed of crossing the Amu Darya (Oxus River) and exploring its source. That dream was fulfilled ten years later. "The Pamirs and the Source of the Oxus" has been translated into Japanese by Ichiro Yoshizawa. (Akane Publishing Co. The World Mountaineer-ing Series. Volume 1, pp. 5-111,1967)

<Younghusband' s travelogue on his trip to the Pamirs and the Wakhan>

28) Francise E.Younghusband : The Heart of a Continent. xvii+409p.ills,maps.London 1896

Francis Younghusband served in the British military and was an explorer. In 1890, Younghusband was sent by the Indian British government together with McCartney, his Chinese language interpreter, to survey the area north of India up to Kashgar. The two traveled from Kashmir to Tashkurgan, and then crossed over the Wakhjir Pass to enter the Wakhan Corridor. They followed the Wakhan Su (River) up to Bozai Gumbaz. They then turned back east and proceeded to Kashgar.

<Earl Dunmore's trip to the Pamirs>
29) The Earl of Dunmore : The Pamirs. 2 vols. xx+360p,xi+352p.London 1893

Earl Dunmore of Great Britain travelled with his compatriot Major Roche to India. They then proceeded on a (big game hunting) trip from Kashmir to various areas in Turkestan. From October to November 1892, they entered the Wakhan Corridor, passed through Lake Victoria and traveled around the Pamirs. Earl Dunmore's travelogue and the map that accompanies this book provides good reference.

<The minutes of the Russo-British Boundary Commission>
30) M.G.Gerard : Report on the Proceedings of the Pamir Boundary Commission,1896. ,vi+97p ,2 folding maps, Calcutta.1897

By the end of the 1890's, having almost conquered all of Westen Turkestan, including the Pamirs, the Russian Empire was effectively sharing a border with British India. Between June and August 1895, the Russo-British joint Pamir Boundary Commision was held near the Wakhjir Pass, where the boundary of the Wakhan Corridor was delineated. General M.G. Gerard headed the British commission, and General Jewaikoski headed the Russian commission. 47 photographs are included in this work. The over-sized map is invaluable.

<Stein's panoramic pictures of the Pamirs and Kuen Lun Range>
31) Aurel Stein : Mountain Panoramas from the Pamirs and Kuen Lun.x+36p.24 panoramas & map. RGS. 1908

Aurel Stein took panoramic pictures of the Pamirs and the Kuen Lun Range during his first visit to Chinese Turkestan between 1900 to 1901. He then prepared maps based on these photographs.

In editing this work, Aurel Stein's work provided invaluable reference.

<A secret German mission to Afghanistan and their report regarding the Wakhan>
32) Werner-Otto von Hentig : Ins verschlossene Land. Ein Kampf mit Mensch und

Meile.248 s. map. Berlin 1928

Shortly after the start of WWI in 1914, The Foreign Ministry of Germany dispatched a secret mission to Afghanistan to convince the King of Afghanistan to turn against the British. Mr. Werner Otto von Hentig who was entrusted with the mission, left Germany in April 1915 with two compatriots, and headed for Afghanistan via Turkey, Baghdad and Teheran. The group crossed the Kebil Desert and entered Kabul, where they stayed for 10 months. Having failed to win over the King, the three departed Kabul on May 21st 1916. After crossing the Hindu Kush, they entered the Wakhan Corridor, and proceeded east along the Oxus River. The exact route which they followed is difficult to determine because of the lack of place names on their maps, and because the group failed to leave any records regarding the dates they traveled. Pursued by the Russians, the three fled into Chinese Turkestan where they reached Kashgar via Yarkand. The book was published ten years after the end of WWI under the title 『In the Forbidden Land』.

<The German Lufthansa flight across the Pamirs and Wakhan>
33) Carl August Freiherr v. Gablenz : D-ANOY bewingt den Pamir.241 s.maps.Berlin 1937

The German aircraft manufacturer Fugo Yunkel was supposed to provide Sven Hedin support for his 1927 Central Asian expedition but the collaboration did not materialize. In 1936 the year after Sven Hedin had completed his exploration, Fon Gablenz flew the D-ANOY aircraft from Kabul in Afghanistan over the Wakhan Corridor on the southern fringe of the Pamirs, reaching Xian via Khotan and Anxi (he was accompanied by another airplane). His record of the flight over the Wakhan and the aerial photographs he took are very valuable.

A Japanese translation was published by Saburo Nagafuchi in Tokyo in1938.

<Tilman's trip to the Wakhan and Chitral>
34) Harold W. Tilman : Two Mountains and a River.xii+233p.maps.Cambridge 1949

The British mountaineer, Harold W. Tilman climbed the peaks of the Karakorum Range two years after the end of WWII in 1947. He then proceeded to travel in the Pamirs and entered the Wakhan over the Wakhjir Pass. He traveled the length of the Wakhan until he reached Ishkashim. The continuous photographic shots that he took of the source of the Oxus River are extremely interesting as a reference. The book was translated into Japanese by Yoshimi Yakushi and published by the Hakusuisha

Publishing company in 1975.

35) China to Chitral : xi + 124p. Cambridge 1951

Soon after the above in 1949, Tilman travled from Kashgar to Chital through the southern foot of the Hindu Kush Range along the southern side of the Wakhan Corridor.

Though Tillman is not directly associated with the topic of interest, I mention him just for reference.

<A report by the Austrian team regarding their survey of the Pamirs>
36) R.S. de Grancy u. R. Kostka(ed.) : Grosser Pamir. 400 s. Graz 1978

This book is a comprehensive report written by an Australian expedition team that surveyed the Wakhan, Pamirs and Afghanistan in 1975. The work includes many photographs and oversized maps.

<The first survey report written by a Japanese regarding theWakhan>
37) Go Hirai: Travels in the Forbidden Land of the Afghan Pamirs- The mountains, lakes and people of the Wakhan Corridor. 488 pages, figures, drawings, and maps. Kyoto. (Nakanishi Publishing Company) 2003.(JPN Ver.)

<A comprehensive books translated into Japanese regarding Afghanistan>
38) Edited by Shizuka Horigome. [Bibliography of Afghanistan- Meiji Period-2003, 390 pages(JPN Ver.),Kanazwa Bunkaku.2003

A compendium of 5161 books, articles and reports that were published in Japan in paperback form, monographs, magazines, weekly magazines and academic society journals during the period 1868 to 2002. The publications are categorized into A. Society and Culture, B. Nature, C. Literature, D. Modern Society, and others. It includes an index of the titles of these publications. The bibliography is exceptionally useful since it introduces books and articles that were written over the last 100 years in Japan regarding Afghanistan. The editor passed away in November 2003 one day after he finished proof reading the work.

The editor in chief, Shizuka Horigome wrote an eulogy titled " Exploration of Publications 2005. Bibliography and theory p.472." Published by Fukai Jin, Bunkenntannsaku Kenkyukai, Kanazawa Bunkokaku, 2006.

A saplement
<Travels to the Pamirs by British Military Personnel during the end of the 19th century>
39) Ralph P Cobbold : Innermost Asia.Travel & sport in the Pamir.xviii+345p.ills.a folding map. London 1900

Having received permission from the British Indian government to travel via Gilgit and Hunza, Cobbold traveled from 1897 to 1898 from Kashgar across the Pamirs. Despite his vow to refrain from commenting on political issues, Cobbold made references to the political and diplomatic positions of Britain and Russia. Though he did not set foot in the Wakhan, he has provided us with invaluable information. The oversized folding map is very informative.

<Maps of Central Asia (West Turkestan) produced by the Trigonomerical Survey Office of India in the end of the 19th century. Four Areas>
40) Maps of Turkistan. Compiled under Survey of India, Dehra Dun, issued in Calcutta, 1883. 4 parts. I .Caspian, II . Samarcand, III . Beluchistan, IV. Afghan Scale 1 inch=32 miles

<Maps of Central Asia (Eastern Turkestan) produced by the Trigonomerical Survey Office of India>
41) Sir Aurel Stein : Memoir on Maps of Chinese Turkestan and Kansu.From the Surveys made during Sir Aurel Stein' s Explorations, 1900-1, 1906-8, 1913-5,xvi+208p.14 plans, 30 plates, Dehra Dun. Trigonomerical Survey office.India 1923

Though Aurel Stein supplied the data for and supervised the production of maps of Chinese Turkestan, he did not produce any maps of the Afghan Wakhan. However, much information can be obtained regarding the borderland between Afghanistan and Russian Central Asia. The above report gives an interesting insight into the process of map production based on trigonometrical surveys.

—Apology— (Go Hirai)
Mr. Masatoshi Nagaoka kindly prepare the photographs of the covers and attached maps of the books introduced above.However due to limited space, I had to make the unfortunate decision to omit them from this work. I would like to express my sincere apologies.

あとがき・謝辞

ワハーン、ア・パミールの名を知ったのは、11才・1942（昭和17年）の時であった。当時未踏の最高峯エヴェレストの頂上直下の急雪氷斜面で、吹雪に包まれて姿を消すマロリーかアーヴィンの後姿が、ラストシーンとなる実録映画を見ての帰り、本屋に立寄った。そこで"世界の屋根"のタイトルに魅かれて、求めたのが最初で、それが1886年ゴートン中佐著、田中一呂訳、生活社刊、1942（昭和17）年であった。当時僅か60年前に、恰も中世かと思えるような圏が、世界にはまだ実在していたことに、非常な驚きを覚えた。この本は現在も座右の書となっている。

1944（昭和19）年旧制広島一中に入学し、その地方が漫画西遊記で見た三蔵（玄奘）法師やマルコ　ポーロが辿った途である事を習い、憧れの地になった。だがそこは夢の夢の永却の彼方の圏であった。

当時、その25年後にワハーンを、55年後にア・パミールを踏めるとは、全く夢想だに出来なかった。それが10度にも及ぶ現実の世界となった。その括めを記している今、多くの方々との偶然の出会い、その方達から頂いた思いがけない大きな幸運の賜である事を心から感謝申し上げます。

1967（昭和42）年の夏に、広島大学山岳部OBを主体とする、ヒンズークシュ遠征隊に参加した。この時、2年後にワハーン入域許可のきっかけになる、兼松江商カーブル駐在所長高田善雄氏の知己を頂いた。この隊に参加できたのは、2名いた同行予定の医学部山岳会の候補者が都合がつかなくなり、連絡役をしていた私が代替りとなって参加したのであった。1969（昭和44）年の春、広島大学西部カラコルム・中部アフガニスタン学術調査隊北部支隊員として、先発交渉のため2月に現地入りをした。パーキスターンでは、カラチで今川好則領事（後総領事、スーダン大使などを圣て退官）のご尽力で、当時は膨大な関税を要したテレビなどを無税通関して頂いた。次いでイスラマバード行きの機内で、偶然・隣席となった商社員の方が、アユブ・ハーン大統領の選挙事務局長を紹介して下さり、テレビを利用して交渉の結果、異例的に申請期限が昨年6月であった（フンザへの）入域申請を、3月末まで受け付けて頂く許可を得た。例外的に当年度のフンザ入域の申請が認められた。次いでアフガーンに飛び、帰路の3月中旬に、当時中国によるカラコルム ハイウエイ建設中で、関係の中国人以外の外人は入域が規制されていたギルギットへ、(漢字とひら仮名で記された日本語の）大学の

身分証明書（漢字が混じっているので中国人と間違われて）で飛ぶ事ができた。そこで偶然外遊から帰国途中のフンザ藩主に謁見でき、無税輸入の高級アクセサリーが役立ち、当時フンザ入域の有力手段であった招聘状を入手した。これらは3月に起きたクーデターで、立ち消えとなった。もし、クーデターがなく、フンザ入りが実現していたならば、（予備的に考えていた）ワハーンとは全く無縁になっていたであろう。何が幸運をもたらすのか、全く不思議である。

2月下旬にカーブルに入ったが、外務省の窓口では、ワハーンと口にするだけで、門前払いの毎日であった。厳寒のカーブルで、温湯の出ない安ホテルの冷水シャワーを浴びたため、風邪をひき、高熱に悩まされていた私は、暖かい高田善雄氏の事務所で時間を費やしていた。そこにある日、カーブル博物館長令夫人のモタメディ遙子女史（現土谷遙子上智大学名誉教授）が、勤務先のユニセフで使用する日本製の駆虫剤の注文に見えた。その医学用語などのお手伝いを少しばかりしたのが縁で、知遇を頂き、ファルハーディ外務次官をご紹介頂いた。早速外務省の窓口担当官が驚く程、短時間にワハーンのハンドゥードゥ周辺での登山許可が頂けた。

ワハーンへは中部アフガニスタン学術調査隊北部支隊の名称でなく、別隊の医学部山岳会小パミール遠征隊として許可された。それで隊は広島大学中部アフガニスタン学術調査隊とに2分された。

その数日後、アフガーン入国時にカーブル空港で、入国手続きの僅かばかりのお手伝いをした、森繁杏子女史（俳優森繁久彌氏夫人、いずれも故人）の依頼で、雪のサーラング峠の写真撮影に同行した。

その足で、コロンボ プランで陶器製造指導のため、クンドゥズに滞在中の橋本亮一氏を訪ねた。そこで高熱のため臥床していた、パシュトゥーンの青年の診察・治療を求められた。幸い持参のペニシリンが著効し、3日目にはカーブルに帰宅できた。

青年はサーダート・サマード・ワルダック氏（カーブル大学農学部学生）で、父は最高国会のローヤ・ジルガの有力議員、長兄はガズニー州知事、次兄はカーブル市警察司令官、叔父は内務大臣という名門の子息であった。彼は3ヵ月後と2年後に、私達のワハーン登山隊に同行してくれる事になる。私は一回目

のワハーン遠征の翌年、彼を日本に招聘した。約1ヵ月の間八幡、川西（後の八幡夫人）の両医学部山岳部員が、彼の案内などをしてくれた。

　アフガーンでは当時も現在でも、カーブルなどから一定以上の距離を離れる際には、警察（内務省）の通行許可が必要である。内務省に強いパイプを持つ彼の同行という事は、ファラハディ次官の知遇を得た事と併せて、まさに鬼に金棒である。

　1971年には、モタメディ遥子夫人と高田善雄氏のそれぞれ公私に汎るご援助で、ファラハディ次官より、ババ・タンギ西方のヒンドゥクシュ山脈での登山許可を得た。私達の目標であるワハーン山脈での登山は、すでに次官の盟友であるイタリアのピネリー教授隊に許可したので、私達は次回にという事である。それで次官から頂いた公的許可地域以遠は、サマード氏一家の顔パスで検門を通過でき、ワハーン山脈入域の矩矢となり得た。

　1973年の共和革命以降、交渉ルートを失った私達から、アフガーンは遠くに去った。1974（昭和49）年晩秋、第6回日本ヒンズー・クシュ会議が、パーキスターンのチトラール周辺で日本の登山隊がご援助を頂いていた、旧チトラール王国（パーキスターンに併合後の前北西辺境州・現 Khyber Pakhtunkhwa）の最後の摂政官であった、ブルハーン・ウディーン・ハーン殿下を招聘した。

　ヒンズー・クシュ会議にご出席の後、殿下は広島の原爆慰霊碑に参拝をご希望され、私達はそれまでご縁のなかった殿下のご訪問をお世話させて頂いた。これが20年近く後に、私のア・パミール探踏への扉になろうとは、夢想だにしなかった。因みに同殿下は1942（昭和17）年2月英印軍空軍少尉の時にシンガポールで日本軍に降伏後、インド国民軍・INA(Indian National Army)に参加し、後インド独立の志士スバス・チャンドラ・ボースの高級副官・大佐として活躍。敗戦後英国女王に対する反逆罪で1947年まで在獄。同年秋チトラールをパーキスターンに合併する了諒のもと解放された親日家である（1995・平成7年事故死）。

　ワハーンへの途を閉ざされていた私達は、知遇を頂いた同殿下のご助力で、1976（昭和51）年と1979（昭和54）年に、ワハーンの南側に位置するチトラール北部の未踏峰への登山活動（試登）ができた。

　1980（昭和55）年春に同殿下の広大な敷地の一隅に、侵攻ソ連軍と戦う、ア

ーメード・シャー・マスゥド（以下マスゥド）総司令官摩下のムジャヒディーン達のテントが多く見られた。当時大学病院から女子大学に転勤し、時間的余裕のできた私は、春・夏・冬の休暇には、そこで医療サービスなどをしていた。

　そのうちチトラールの街なかに、パンジ・シェール渓谷の一般難民用の国連キャンプが建設され、管理責任者である同殿下の直弟のフシャメード・ウル・ムルク殿下（以下ムルク殿下）を紹介された。キャンプを介して、ムルク殿下とマスゥド総司令官は実懇であった。

　ムルク殿下には、チトラール北部の東部ヒンドゥクシュ山脈での登山を支援する、トレッキング会社を経営する息子さん・マクスード・ウル・ムルク（以下マクスード）氏がいる。1993（平成10）年ムルク殿下を介して、2人のマクスード氏の社員と共に、東部ヒンドゥクシュ山脈を越えて、ワハーンに入りサルハッド手前までの小トレッキングをした。この時はバロギールの2峠を経由した。帰路チトラールでフランス人夫婦に、ペシャワールまでの航空券入手の手助けをした。2人はグラデュー夫妻で、イシュカーシェム南東で、5000m前後の峠を越えワハーンに入り、オクサス河本流沿いに、チャクマク・ティン湖辺りまでを往復したと語った。

　その話と再び熱く燃え上がったワハーン、ア・パミールへの想いを、ムルク殿下にお伝えしたところ、"ワハーン回廊を統治下に置く北部同盟のマスゥド総司令官に頼んでみる"と快諾して頂いた。ムルク殿下の知遇を頂けた事こそ、私のア・パミール踏査の途が開かれたのである。

　それで翌1999年、マスドー総司令官の庇護の下に最初のア・パミール入域が実現し、3夏続けてマクスード氏の社員2人と共に、バロギール、その西のカーンフーンとイシュカーシェム南方のドーラの各峠越えで、ワハーン、ア・パミールに入れた。供の一人は叔父にマスード総司令官の側近者を持っていた事も有利に働いた。他の一人がコックのサフューラ君で、同君は母国のアフガーンに帰った2004年以後も、常に私に同行して、コックは勿論、通訳、渉外、採蝶、採魚やガイド役も務めてくれた。同君の同行がなければ、私の踏査行は極めて困難であったであろう。またマクスード氏には、私の2005年・2006年の2夏に汎る、タジキスターン側のビクトリア湖・ゾル クルへの途を拓いて頂いている。

　なお2000年以降の私のワハーン回廊行は、1999年、最初のア・パミール入

域時に知遇を頂いた、ワハーン回廊一帯の国境警備の最高責任者であるミール・ワイド・ハーン総司令官のご援助によるものと感謝している。

この様に多くの方達から頂いた幸運で、ワハーン回廊探踏ができた。

1941年出版の成書に、ワハーン・達摩悉鐵帝 Da-mo-shi-tie-ti に該当するDarmarakなる地が、オクサス河の西方に現存すると記してあり、イシュカーシェム周辺で、"西方"を重点にして長年尋ねたが解らず、ある年"ダルマ…"と問いかけた。するとイシュカーシェムから北折下行するオクサス河の70kmばかりの左岸"(西畔)"に、Darmorakh、そのすぐ南にDarmadarという古くからの大村落が在る事が解った。ハンドゥードゥでは、長年"仏教"遺趾の存在を訊いても解らず、村長や古老を集め、松田徳太郎氏(アフガン研究会員)から、教えて頂いた文献に載っている、"仏教"遺趾の地名・場所を尋ねても解らず、単に"遺跡"と尋ねると、翌日案内してもらえた。文献にある地名は現地で用いられているものではなく、調査隊が独自に付けたものであった。スタインが記録している、サルハッド対岸のチベット軍の"監視塔"も、永年"タワー"として尋ねたので解らなかったらしく、単に"壊れた建物"と聞いたところ、壊れた"平屋"に案内され判明した。ワフジール峠に南接する、オクサス河の真の源であるかも知れない小湖は、ワハーンの山座同定のご教示を頂いている宮森常雄氏から、ほぼ年中凍結しているパミール最高位の湖として、所在と登路をグーグル　アースを基にした示唆頂き、到達する事ができた

このようにして、質問の表現をいろいろ変えて聞いても、今だに答を得られないのが、1940年代の成書にある、ワハーンと東部のワハーンをそれぞれ指すと思われる、"Komedhと伽倍ジヤペイ又はジヤパイ"である。また多くない高山植物も、カラ ビル東面やワフジール峠で見かけても、知識のない私にはエーデルワイスやサクラ草ぐらいしか区別できず心残りである。

本書の完成も多くの方々から頂いた温かいご支援の賜である。とりわけ次の皆様には特別なご尽力を頂いた。

中央アジア史の碩学金子民雄博士には、早々にパミールの美少女のスケッチ付きと序文を頂き、ご所蔵の得難い19世紀の関連原書のご開示とそれらの抄録を頂き、更に印刷・出版までご高配などを賜り、感謝の言葉もありません。

本書に収載した精密地図をご高配頂いた、長岡正利氏には心より御礼申し上げます。

採集した蝶の分類・同定と、タテハチョウ科ヒョウモンモドキ属の一亜種をロンドン自然史博物館 The Natural History Museum(旧大英博物館)の所蔵品にご高配頂いた酒井成司氏、採取した岩石を同定頂いた沖村雄二博士、採取した魚類の同定を頂いている寺島彰博士、採取した温泉水などの分析を頂いた広島市衛生研究所、広島県保健環境センターの関係研究員の皆様、マルコ ポーロ羊の説明に、学術的添削を頂いた伊藤敏男博士に篤く御礼申し上げます。

複雑な山座同定・標高などを御教示頂いた宮森常雄氏、J・Wala氏(1,971年)に大なる敬意と謝意を表します。

絶妙な英文対訳を頂いた井手マヤ女史に深湛な謝意を表し、オクサス河の説明文にご助言を頂いた本多海太郎氏(前学研編集長)、文献収集にご尽力頂いた福山市中央図書館および関係図書館に御礼申し上げます。

なお、度重なるア・パミール踏査に、その度に長期の休暇を与えて頂いた紅萌会理事長・藤井功博士(広島大学医学部山岳会パミール遠征隊1971副隊長、広島大学医学部山岳会員、日本山岳会員、第53次日本南極地域観測隊員)、当初より刊行に関して、いろいろと御高慮頂いた柏木暁氏(環境アセスメント研究室)、盟友の広島一中時代の同級生・吉田韶三氏(東京商工会議所員)に心よりお礼申し上げます。

乱雑な原稿を整理・整頓して頂いた渡邉彰子女史、田中三香子嬢、板屋紘司氏、中村影紀氏、英訳の整理にご協力頂いたシェパード由美女史および印刷と発行の労をお取り頂いた上毛印刷様にもありがたく御礼を述べます。

最後になりましたが、年余に汎り多くの写真・和英両説明文の繁雑な撰定・構成・編集など本書製作すべてにご尽力頂いた紺野昇氏に心から謝意を呈します。また本の装訂にご尽力頂いた中村信子女史に深く御礼を申し上げます。

I was only eleven years old when I first heard about a place called Wakhan and the Afghan Pamirs. It was in 1942, when I saw a documentary film that showed either Mallory or Irvin struggling up Mount Everest, almost on the brink of being conquered by either of the two.

The last scene of that movie showed the climber disappear in a snowy blizzard. Leaving the cinema, I visited a bookstore where I was drawn to a book titled, "The Roof of the World. " Written in 1886 by Lieutenant Colonel Gordon, I happened to notice the Japanese language translation which had just been published (translated by Ichiro Tanaka, published by Seikatsu Sha 1942). Sixty years ago, I was greatly surprised to learn that there was a country in some remote corner of this world that still lived in the Middle Ages. "The Roof of the World" remains my favorite book to this day.

In 1944, as a junior high school student in Hiroshima, after learning that the Chinese monk Hsüang Tsang, and Marco Polo had passed through Wakhan, I became strongly attracted to this region, which was then completely inaccessible to me.

At that time, little did I imagine that 25 years later I would be making my first entry to the Wakhan, nor that 55 years later, I would be exploring the Afghan Pamirs. Over the course of 10 visits, Wakhan has become a reality that is close to my heart. As I write this book as a tribute to the nature and inhabitants of Wakhan, I feel extremely fortunate that I was able to encounter so many who have kindly supported my travels to the region.

In the summer of 1967, I joined the Alpine Club of Hiroshima University Hindu Kush mountaineering expedition, whose members were mostly alumina. During the expedition, I had the good fortune of meeting Mr. Yoshio Takada, the Kabul branch manager of Kanematsu Gosho Company at that time. Two years later, Mr. Takada helped me obtain the permission for my next visit to the Wakhan.

I was fortunate in being able to participate in the Hiroshima Expedition, because I was chosen to replace two original members from the Medical Alpine Club of Hiroshima University who could not accompany the expedition due to urgent business. At that time I was acting as a liaison for the expedition. On February, 1969 I entered Kabul as a member of the Hiroshima University Scientific Expedition to the West Karakorum and Central Afghanistan.We had been entrusted to negotiate the preparation for the summer expedition. In Pakistan, thanks to the support of Mr. Yoshinori Imagawa, the Consulate of Japan in Karachi. (later Consulate General, and Ambassador to Sudan before retiring) I was able to bring Japanese television sets and other equipment into Pakistan tariff free, a considerable savings since these types of goods carried heavy import duties.

On the flight from Karachi to Islamabad, a Japanese working for a trading firm happened to be seated next to me. He introduced me to the manager in charge of President Ayub Khan' s election.

After negotiating with the authorities, I was informed that though the actual deadline for sending the application to enter Hunza had been June of the previous year, our deadline for submission would be extended till March of the following year. We were thus able to receive the permission to enter Hunza as scheduled that year. We presented the Japanese television as a show of appreciation.

After my visit to Afghanistan ended, mid-March I flew back to Pakistan and visited Gilgit , which was a restricted area for all foreigners except the Chinese at that time. I was able to fly to Gilgit by just showing my identification card which was written in both Chinese and Japanese hiragana characters. The Pakistani police therefore, mistook me to be a Chinese, who had free access to the area. By pure coincidence, I happened to meet the ruler of Hunza who was returning from an official visit abroad. My present of valuable jewelry which I had brought to Pakistan duty-free helped us obtain a letter of invitation to visit Hunza. But in March, a coup-de-tat occurred, and we lost our chance to visit Hunza. If a coup-de-tat had not occurred and we had been able to proceed to Hunza, I might never have visited the Wakhan. (Wakhan had been only an alternative destination, since the main goal of the expedition was to enter Hunza). This turned out to be a blessing in disguise.

I entered Kabul at the end of February, but each time I visited the Afghanistan Ministry of Foreign Affairs to seek a permit to visit the Wakhan, they rejected my application. In the bone-chilling cold of Kabul, I was staying in a cheap hotel where the shower was cold. I was suffering from high fever, so I spent much of my time in the warm office of Mr. Yoshio Takada. One day, Mrs. Haruko Motamedi (currently Dr. Haruko Tsuchiya, Professor Emeritus of Sophia University who was at that time working for UNICEF) stepped by the office to order pesticide on behalf of UNICEF. I helped her sort out the medical terms. Having made my acquaintance with Mrs. Motamedi, she introduced me to the Deputy Minister of Foreign Affairs, H.E. Dr. Farahdi, who issued us a mountaineering permit that would allow us to climb the mountains surrounding the Khandud area of the Wakhan. The permit was issued not for the original Hiroshima University Scientfic Expedition to Central Afganistan but to the Medical Alpine Club of Hiroshima University Expedition to the Little Pamir 1969. As a result, the University Expedition was divided into two groups.

A few days later, I accompanied Mrs. Kyoko Morishige (wife of the actor, Hisaya

Morishige, a famous Japanese actor, both are the departed) to figure the Salang Pass in the snow. I had helped her pass through immigration at Kabul Airport.

On that leg of the journey we continued on to Kunduz to meet Ryoichi Hashimoto who was providing technical guidance to pottery manufacturers under the Colombo Plan. On reaching Kunduz, Mr.Hashimoto asked me to treat a Pashtun youth who was bedridden with a high fever. Fortunately, a shot of penicillin which I had brought with me from Japan, cured him of his ailment, and the youth was able to return home to Kabul three days later.

The young man, Sadaat Samad Waldaq, happened to belong to a very reputable family. A student of the Agricultural Department of Kabul University then, his father was a prominent member of the Loya Jirga, the supreme national assembly of Afghan. His eldest brother was the governor of Ghazni Province, and another brother was a commander of the Kabul Police. His uncle was the Minister of Interior. Mr. Samad accompanied our Wakhan mountaineering expedition twice; the first time was three months after we first met him, and the second time was two years after that first trip with him.

One year after my first visit to the Wakhan, I invited Mr. Samad to visit Japan for one month, during which time two students who were members of the Medical Alpine Club of Hiroshima University, Mr. Yahata and Ms. Kawanishi (subsequently Mrs. Yahata) guided him around.

In those days, as is true today, to travel outside of Kabul, a travel permit issued by the police (by the Ministry of the Interior) was required, so having the niece of H.E. Ravan Farhadi, Deputy Foreign Minister accompanying us, coupled with the support of the deputy minister himself, effectively gave us unlimited access to travel outside of Kabul.

In 1971, thanks to the public and personal support extended to us by Mrs. Haruko Motamedi and Yoshio Takada, Deputy Minister Ravan Farhadi issued us a travel permit for climbing the Hindu Kush Mountains west of Baba Tangi. Our original goal had been to climb the Wakhan Range but the Deputy Minister had already issued a permit to his good friend, the Italian, Professor Pinelli, so we were told to wait till the next opportunity arose. We were however, able to travel to regions and pass the military checkpoints that were not covered by the public travel permit, thanks to our connection with the Samad Family.

After the Republican revolution of 1973, I lost our my connection with the Afghan authorities, and once again, Afghanistan became a far and inaccessible country for us.

In the late autumn of 1974, His Royal Highness Bruhan uddin Khan, the last regent of the Kingdom of Chitral, former North West Frontier Province (current Khyber Pakhtunkhwa of Pakistan) was invited to attend the 6th Japan Hindu Kush -Karakorum Society Meeting. The regent had given assistance to the Japanese mountaineering expeditions who visited the vicinity of Chitral. Regent Bruhan uddin Khan wished to pay homage to the cenotaph of the A-bomb victims in Hiroshim, so we were asked by the society to guide him there. I could hardly imagine then that my cquaintance with the regent would pry open the opportunity to explore the Afghan Pamirs 20 years later.

Regent Bruhan uddin Khan, as an air vice marshal of the British Indian Royal Air Force, surrendered to the Japanese Imperial army after which he participated in the INA (Indian National Army). Regent Bruhan uddin Khan served as a senior adjutant and colonel under Subhas Chandra Bose, who fought for the independence of India with the Japanese army. When World War II ended, he was imprisoned as a traitor against the Queen of England until 1947, and was released on condition that he cede Chitral to Pakistan. He remained a Japanophile until he died in 1997.

Thanks to the support of Regent Bruhan uddin Khan, we were able to enter the hitherto forbidden area of Wakhan in 1976 and 1979, where we climbed the mountains that lie south of the Wakhan.

In the spring of 1980, we were able to observe many tents that had been set up in the spacious compound of Regent Bruhan's residence to accommodate the mujahedeen leader, Ahmed Shah Mussoud and his followers who were at that time fighting against the Russian occupation of Afghanistan. I had some time on my hands then, having left my position at a university hospital to work for a women's university. I spent the spring, summer and winter holidays offering medical services on a volunteer basis in Chitral. Eventually, a UN refugee camp was set up in Chitral to accommodate the refugees from the Panjiser Valley. At that time I was introduced to the younger brother of Regent Bruhan, His Royal Highness Khushahmed ul Mulk (henceforth H.R.H.) and the Mujahedeen leader, Mussoud were acquainted through the camp.

H.R.H. had a son by the name of Maqsood ul Mulk (henceforth Maqsood) who owned a travel agency that specialized in mountaineering tours in the eastern Hindu Kush around Chitral. In 1998, I was introduced to this travel agency by H.R.H, and trekked over the Eastern Hindu Kush to a point just before Sarhard, together with two employees of his son's company. At that time, I trekked over the two passes of Baroghil.

When I returned to Chitral, I helped Mr. and Mrs. Gradue, a French couple, to obtain airplane tickets to Peshawar. The two had climbed over a 5000 meter class pass near Ishkashim to enter the Wakhan, and had proceeded along the Oxus River all the way to Chaqmak-tin Lake and back. They gave me a detailed map of the Afghan Pamirs later.

Upon hearing about their feat, my desire to visit the Afghan Pamirs was reignited strongly so I appealed to H.R.H.. He readily agreed to talk to his friends General Mussoud who was the supreme commander of the Northern Alliance which effectively controlled the Wakhan Corridor region. Through his support, H.R.H had opened up the Afghan Pamirs to me. Subsequently, I had the immense pleasure of climbing to the top of the Darkot Pass with H.R.H..

The following year in 1999, I entered the Afghan Pamirs for the first time under the protection of Commander Mussoud. For three consecutive summers together with two employees of Mr. Maqsood's travel company, we climbed over the passes in Baroghil, the Kand Khun Pass, which lies to the west of the passes in Baroghil, and the Dorah Pass which lies to the south of Ishkashim to enter the Wakhan Corridor. Passage was made even easier because one of the employees who accompanied me had an uncle who was the right hand man to Commander Mussoud, The other employee who was the cook, Safiullah John, subsequently accompanied me during all of my travels to the Wakhan Coridor even after 2004 when he returned to his homeland in Afghanistan. He supported me in his role as a cook, interpreter, communication officer, and guide. Without his assistance, I would have faced many more difficulties during my explorations to the Wakhan Corridor. Safiullah John also helped me gather butterfly and fish samples.

Mr. Maqsood also helped arrange my travels in the summers of 2005 and 2006 to Lake Victoria (Zor Kul) on the Tajikistan side.

Since 2000, my explorations in the Wakhan Corridor have been assisted by Mir Wahid Khan, commander in charge of border control along the Wakhan Corridor whom I came to know in 1999 when I first entered the region. I am deeply indebted to him. I am grateful for the support extended to me by many people. Without them, I would never have been able to explore the deepest and most remote parts of the Wakhan Corridor,

For many years, I surveyed the areas around Ishkashim focusing on the west side of the Oxus River, because I had read a book published in 1941, which described a land known as Darmarak (which corresponds to Da-mo-shi-tie-ti) that lies west of the Oxus River.

I had not been able to find evidence of such a place until one day when I asked whether there was a place called Darma something, I was told that there was a large village known as Darmorakh that lay on the left side (west side) of the Oxus, 70km from the point where the river takes a sharp turn to the north as it flows downstream. In Khandud, for many years I could not find the remains of an ancient Buddhism site. Though I queried the headman of the Khandud village and the elderly, about the name of an ancient Buddhist site mentioned in a book introduced to me by Mr. Tokutaro Matsuda (a member of the Afghan Research Society) my queries led nowhere until one day I was led to an archeological site. The site of the ancient Buddhism temples had been named arbitrarily by the French archeological team and therefore did not have a local name. For many years I could not get any information about a Tibetan watch tower that Stein had reported was located across Sarhad. Only when I asked for an ancient, destroyed structure, rather than a tower, did the locals guide me to a crumbling one-storied structure which clearly corresponded to the ancient Tibetan watch tower.

With the support of Mr. Tsuneo Miyamori I was able identify the small lake that lies adjacent to the southern side of the Wakhjir Pass, and which might be the true source of the Oxus. Together we plotted the location and route to the lake using Google Earth and discovered that it was the highest lake in the Pamirs, being ice-bound most of the year.

Though I raised many questions and phrased the questions in many different ways, I could not ascertain the locations of Komedh, Chihpei or Chipai, which are all supposed to represent the eastern areas of the Wakhan. I observed many high altitude plants growing on the eastern slopes of the Qara Bel and the Wakhjir Pass, but due to my limited knowledge of botany, I could only recognize the edelweiss and woodland primrose.

This book could never have been published without the warm support and kind cooperation of many.

I am especially indebted to Dr. Tamio Kaneko, one of the most knowledgeable persons regarding Central Asian history in Japan, who promptly sent me a sketch of a beautiful Pamiri girl together with the introduction to this book. Dr. Kaneko very generously not only allowed me to peruse his valuable collection of 19th century books mainly related to Afghanistan and the Pamirs, but also wrote a short summary of the works listed in the bibiliography. Based on his experience as an author, Dr. Kaneko also offered me his advice regarding publishing and printing.

I owe my thanks to Mr. Masatoshi Nagaoka for his advice in preparing the detailed map shown in this book. Special thanks goes to Mr. Seiji Sakai, who kindly identified and categorized my butterfly collection and was instrumental in submitting the Paratype Melitaea pallas hirai Sakai to the London Natural History Museum (The former British Museum). My gratitude goes to Dr. Yuji Okimura who identified my rock collection from the Afghan Pamirs

I am also indebted to the researchers of the Hiroshima City Institute of Hygiene, Hiroshima Prefectural Technology Reserch Insutitute Health and Environment for analyzing the chemical properties of the water samples taken from various hot-springs in the region.

I would like to thank Dr. Toshio Ito for checking the academic accuracy of my explanations regarding the Marco Polo Sheep. I would like to thank Mr. Tsuneo Miyamori and Mr. J. Wala (1971) for undertaking the complex task of identifying the names and the altitude of the mountains.

I would like to express my deep appreciation to Ms. Maya Ide for her competent translation of the original Japanese into English.

I would like to thank Mr. Kaitaro Honda (former chief editor with Gakken Publishing Co.) who kindly advised me on the explanations regarding the Oxus River, and the Fukuyama Central Library and affiliated libraries for searching the relevant documents on my behalf.

I am deeply indebted to Dr. Isao Fujii, trustee of the Kouboukai who generously granted me many long vacations so that I could travel to the Afghan Pamirs. Doctor Fujii was the deputy leader of the Medical Alpine Club of Hiroshima University Expedition to the Pamir 1971, a member of the Medical Alpine Club of Hiroshima University ,a member of the Japanese Alpine Club and a member of the 53rd Japanese Antarctic Research Expedition. Special thanks goes to Mr. Satoru Kashiwagi (Environmental Assessment Research Laboratory) and to Mr. Shouzou Yoshida (a member of the Tokyo Chamber of Commerce) ,a close friend of mine since my days as a student of the Hiroshima First Junior High School (The First Middle School), for helping me produce this book. I would also like to thank Ms. Akiko Watanabe , Ms. Mikako Tanaka, Mr. Kouji Itaya and Mr.Kageki Nakamura for organizing the untidy draft of this book, Ms.Yumi Shepherd for reconciling the order of the photo captions between the draft English translation and the original Japanese, and the Joumon Publishing Company which took the great trouble to print and publish my book.

Last but not least, I would like to express my deep gratitude to Mr. Noboru Konno for going through the entire painstaking task of selecting, proof reading and editing the Japanese text and the English translation, and for organizing the layout of the numerous figures. I would also like to express my gratitude to Ms. Nobuko Nakamura for binding the book.

参考文献
Bibliography

1. http://www.mofa.go.jp/mofaj/area/afghanistan/data.html(2010)：(JPNVer.)
2. Kabul Museum (1971)：Bulletin board gate floor
3. http//www.Geocities.jp/waera-tikyujin/afghanistem/afghan.html 2012/01/ 05：(JPN Ver)
4. 産経新聞(2011)：自立への喘ぎ5(2月7日、13版6頁)
   Sankei Shimbun (2011)：A struggle for independence (JPN Ver)5, Feb. 7th, 13th edition. p.6
5. http//www.afbb.com/article/life-culture/life/2273/71/2049627 (JPN Ver.) (2012/05/08)
6. M.G.Gerard (1897)：Report on the Proceedings of the Pamir Boundary Commission 1896
7. 白鳥庫吉(1941・昭和16)：西域史研究　上　130,131頁
   Koukichi Shiratori (1941)：Saiiki Shi Kenkyu (JPN Ver.) Vol. 1 pp. 130,131
8. 白鳥庫吉(1944・昭和19)：西域史研究　下　27頁
   Koukichi Shiratori (1944)：Saiiki Shi Kenkyu (JPN Ver.) Vol. 2 p.27
9. 白鳥庫吉(1944・昭和19)：西域史研究　下　28頁
   Koukichi Shiratori (1944)：Saiiki Shi Kenkyu (JPN Ver.) Vol. 2 p.28
10. 白鳥庫吉(1941・昭和16)：西域史研究　上　132頁
    Koukichi Shiratori (1941)：Saiiki Shi Kenkyu (JPN Ver.) Vol. 1 p.132
11. 足立喜六(1943・昭和18)：大唐西域記の研究　下巻　972頁
    Kiroku Adachi (1943):Daitousaiikiki No Kenkyu (JPN Ver.)Vol.2 p. 972
12. 白鳥庫吉(1941・昭和16)：西域史研究　上　134,135頁
    Koukichi Shiratori (1941)：Saiiki Shi Kenkyu (JPN Ver.) Vol.1 pp. 134,135
13. J.Wood(1872)：JOURNEY TO THE SOURCE OF THE RIVER OXUS　p.333
14. T.E.Gordon(1876)：THE ROOF OF THE WORLD　p.142
15. G.N.Curzon(1896)：THE PAMIRS AND THE SOURCE OF THE OXUS　p.30
16. The New encyclopaedia Brittanica Vol.I. p.358
17. 白鳥庫吉(1941・昭和16)：西域史研究　上　121頁
    Koukichi Shiratori (1941): Saiiki Shi Kenkyu (JPN Ver.) Vol. 1 p. 121
18. 白鳥庫吉(1944・昭和19)：西域史研究　下　27頁
    Koukichi Shiratori (1944): Saiiki Shi Kenkyu (JPN Ver.)　Vol. 2 p.27
19. A.Stein(1928)：INNERMOST ASIA　Vol.IIp.859
20. J.Wood(1872)：JOURNEY TO THE SOURCE OF THE RIVER OXUS　p.306
21. 足立喜六(1943・昭和18)：大唐西域記の研究　下巻　963頁
    Kiroku Adachi (1943): Daitousaiikiki No Kenkyu (JPN Ver.) Vol. 2 p.963
22. A.Stein(1921)：SERINDIA Vol.I. pp.62,63
23. 玄奘、水谷真成訳(1972・昭和47)：大唐西域記 中国古典文学大系22巻 381頁
    Genjou, translated by Shinjo Mizutani (1972)：Daitousaiikiki, Chugoku Kotenbunngaku Taikei (Classical Chinese Literature Series) (JPN Ver.)Vol. 22 p. 381
24. W.Ball(2008)：THE MONUMENT OF AFGHANISTAN　pp.233,234
25. T.E.Gordon(1876)：THE ROOF OF THE WORLD
26. J.Wood(1872)：JOURNEY TO THE SOURCE OF THE RIVER OXUS p.317
27. T.E.Gordon(1876)：THE ROOF OF THE WORLD　p.131
28. J.Wood(1872)：JOURNEY TO THE SOURCE OF THE RIVER OXUS　p.329
29. T.E.Gordon(1876)：THE ROOF OF THE WORLD　p.152
30. Wood(1872)：JOURNEY TO THE SOURCE OF THE RIVER OXUS　p.332
31. J.Wood(1872)：JOURNEY TO THE SOURCE OF THE RIVER OXUS　pp.354,355
32. 足立喜六(1943・昭和18)：大唐西域記の研究　下巻　973頁
    Kiroku Adachi (1943)：Daitousaiikiki No Kenkyu (JPN Ver.) Vol. 2 p. 973
33. Marco Polo，愛宕松男訳注 (1972・昭和47)：東方見聞録1　107頁
    Marco Polo, translated and annotated by Matsuo Otagi(1972)：Toho Kenbunroku (JPN Ver.)Vol. 1, p. 107
34. 劉昫等 撰 (後晋1975復刻)：舊唐書第10冊巻104　3203頁　中華書局
    Edited by Ryu-shen et al (Hu Chin・Late Chin 936~946 A.D.)：Chu Tang-su・Old Tang Annals (Chinese Ver.) .Vol. 10 Part 104 p.3203 (reprinted 1975) Chun Howa Su Chui
35. A.Stein(1921)：SERINDIA VOL.I pp.53,54
36. 劉昫等 撰(後晋，1975復刻)：舊唐書第10冊巻104　3204頁　中華書局
    Edited by Ryu-shen et al (Hu Chin・Late Chin936~946A.D.)：Chu Tang-su・Old Tang Annals (Chinese Ver.). Vol. 10 Part 104 p.3204 (reprinted 1975) Chun Howa Su Chui
37. A.Stein(1921)：SERINDIA VOL.I p.68
38. A.Stein(1921)：SERINDIA VOL.I p.69
39. A.Stein(1921)：SERINDIA VOL.I p.67
40. T.E.Gordon(1876)：THE ROOF OF THE WORLD　p.129
41. D-Naumann(1978)：Die Kirghisen des Afghanischen Pamir　p.2
42. A.Stein(1921)：SERINDIA Vol.1　p.70,71
43. A.Stein(1921)：SERINDIA Vol.1　pp.72
44. F.E.Younghusband(1896)：THE HEART OF A CONTINENT　pp.329,330
45. INYATULLAH Faizi(1996)：WAKHAN　p.44
46. M.N.M.Sharani(1976)：The Kirghiz and Wakhi of Afghanistan Introduction　p.xx.
47. INYATULLAH Faizi (1996)：WAKHAN　p.65
48. モタメディ遥子(1976)：シルクロードの十字路で　203,204頁
    Haruko Motamedi(1976)：At a crossroad on the silk road (JPN Ver.)pp. 203,204

49. INYATULLAH Faizi (1996)：WAKHAN p.67

50. F.E.Younghusband(1892) : PROCEEDINGS OF THE ROYAL GEOGRAPHICAL
    SOCIETY VOL.XIV p.231

51. G.N.Curzon(1896)：THE PAMIRS AND THE SOURCE OF THE OXUS p.31

52. G.N.Curzon(1896)：THE PAMIRS AND THE SOURCE OF THE OXUS p.56
    : Revised, and reprinted from *'The Geographical Journal' for July, August, and
    September,* 1896. KRAUS REPRINT Nendeln/Liechtenrtein

53. Elizabeth & Nicholas Clinch (2,008)：THROUGH A LAND OF EXTREMES
    THE LITTLEDALES OF CENTRAL ASIA p. 56

54. 足立喜六(1943・昭和18)：大唐西域記の研究　下巻　974頁
    Kiroku Adachi (1943)：Daitousaiikiki No Kenkyu (JPN Ver.) Vol. 2 p. 974

55. Marco Polo：THE TRAVELS OF MARCO POLO EVERYMANS LIBRARY p.91

56. G.N.Curzon(1896)：THE PAMIRS AND THE SOURCE OF THE OXUS p.57
    : Revised, and reprinted from *'The Geographical Journal' for July, August, and
    September,* 1896. KRAUS REPRINT Nendeln/Liechtenrtein

57. G.N.Curzon(1896)：THE PAMIRS AND THE SOURCE OF THE OXUS p.43
    : Revised, and reprinted from *'The Geographical Journal' for July, August, and
    September,* 1896. KRAUS REPRINT Nendeln/Liechtenrtein

58. Map J-43-XX(1:200,000) published by the Soviet Union General Staff Office

59. 足立喜六(1942・昭和17)：大唐西域記の研究　上巻　12頁
    Kiroku Adachi (1943) Daitousaiikiki No Kenkyu (JPN Ver.) Vol.1 p.12

60. T.E.Gordon(1876)：THE ROOF OF THE WORLD p.156

61. Marco Polo：THE TRAVELS OF MARCO POLO EVERYMANS LIBRARY p.90

62. ブリタニカ国際大百科辞典18巻781頁
    The International Encyclopaedia Britanica (JPN Ver.)Vol.18. p781

63. A. Stein(1907)：ANCIENT KHOTAN VOL.I pp.30,31

64. 酒井敏明(2000・平成12)：旅人たちのパミール　80頁
    Toshiaki Sakai (2000)：THE PAMIRIS AND THE TRAVELLERS (JPN Ver.) p.80

65. A.Stein(1928)：INNERMOST ASIA VOL.Ⅲ Fig.360

66. A.Stein(1928)：INNERMOST ASIA VOL.Ⅱ pp.859～861

67. A.Stein(1921)：SERINDIA VOL.I Fig.25

索引

太数字は図又は表と関係深い頁を示す

Index

The **bold number** indicates the page that corresponds most with the figure or table.

著者プロフィール
平位 剛（ひらい ごう）

昭和 6 (1931) 年　　広島生まれ
昭和 32 (1957) 年　　広島大学医学部医学科卒
昭和 33（1958)年　　医師（産婦人科）
広島大学医学部助教授，広島女子大学教授，新潟県立加茂病院
などを経て，
平成 9 年 (1997) 年　広島市立安佐市民病院長を定年退職
現在　紅萌会福山記念病院を経て同グループ老健施設ビーブル春秋苑施設長
中国重慶第三人民医院名誉院長

医学部在学中に医学部山岳部入部。北アルプスを中心に夏山，
冬山を始める

昭和 42 (1967) 年　　広島大学ヒンズークシュ遠征隊員
昭和 44 (1969) 年　　広島大学中部アフガニスタン・西部カラコルム
　　　　　　　　　　学術調査隊員 (広島大学医学部山岳会 (MACH)
　　　　　　　　　　小パミール遠征隊 1969 隊長)
昭和 46 (1971) 年　　MACH パミール遠征隊 1971 隊長
昭和 51 (1976) 年　　MACH チトラール北西探踏隊 1976 隊長
昭和 54 (1979) 年　　MACH チトラール北西探踏隊 1979 隊長
　　以後、平成 9(1997) 年までダルコット峠とバロギール周辺の
　　4 峠を含むチトラール北部山岳地帯を 8 回トレッキング
平成 10 (1998) 年　　バロギールの峠を経てワハーン入域
平成 11 ～ 13 (1999 ～ 2001) 年　三夏に亘りアフガーン パミール縦・横断
平成 16 (2004) 年　　アフガーン パミール縦・横断
平成 17 (2005) 年　　タジキスターン　ワハーン, 小パミール東南端
平成 18 (2006) 年　　タジキスターン　ワハーン, ビクトリア湖, 小パミール
　　　　　　　　　　東南端探踏
平成 19 (2007) 年　　アフガーン パミール縦・横断
平成 21 (2009) 年　　同上
平成 22 (2010) 年　　同上
平成 23 (2011) 年　　(大) パミール河左岸再遡上
広島大学医学部山岳会員, 日本山岳会員, 日本山岳会元広島支部長

Profile of Author Hirai Go:

1931　Born in Hiroshima
1957　Graduated from Hiroshima University Faculty of Medicine, School of Medicine
1958　　Medical Doctor, Obstretrics and Gynecology
　　　After working at the Niigata Prefectural Hospital, Dr. Hirai joined the Hiroshima City Asa-Hospital.
1997　Retired from the position of Hospital Director of Hiroshima City Asa Hospital.
Dr. Hirai also served in the following posts during 40 years of service before he retired from the Hiroshima City Asa Hospital.
◆Hiroshima University Hospital,
◆Futami Chyuuou Hospital,
◆Associate Professor of Hiroshima University Faculty of Medicine,
◆Professor of Hiroshima Women's University ,
◆Niigata Prefectural Kamo Hospital
Current position:
　After working at Kouboukai Fukuyama Memorial Hospital, he has been working as the Director of Geriatric Health Service Facility, Vivre Syunjuuen (a medical facility that belongs to the Kouboukai Fukuyama Memorial Hospital Group),
Hospital Director Emeritus of Chongqing Number Three People's Hospital, China
Dr. Hirai joined the Medical Alpine Club of Hiroshima University (MACH) after entering Hiroshima University and started climbing mainly the Northern Japanese Alps, both in the summer and winter.
1967　Member of the Hiroshima University Hindu Kush Expedition
1969　Member of the Hiroshima University Scientific Expedition to Central Afghanistan and the Western Karakorum 1969 (leader of MACH Expedition to the Little Pamir 1969)
1971　Leader of the MACH Expedition to the Pamirs 1971
1976　Leader of the MACH Expedition to Northwestern Chitral 1976
1979　Leader of the MACH Expedition to Northwestern Chitral 1979
Subsequently trekked the northwestern parts of Chitral including four passes of Baroghil region and Darkot Pass 8 times until 1997.
1998　Visited Wakhan (near Sarhad) via the Pass of Baroghil region
2005 Spent the summer exploring the Tajikistan Wakhan and The Little Pamir southeasternmost
2006 Spent the summer exploring Zor Kul (LakeVictoria), and The Little Pamir south-easternmost
1999-2011　Spent eight summers traveling the length and width of the Afghan Pamirs
Member of the MACH and Japanese Alpine Club, Former Director of the Japanese Alpine Club Hiroshima Section

あとがきにかえて

　本書がようやく出版のめどがついたのは、2014 年の年も終わる 12 月 29 日のことだった。そして出版計画が実行に移ったのは、年が明けた 2015 年の 1 月早々だった。私の古くからの友人でもある霞ヶ関出版㈱の加藤敏雄氏にふと話をしたとき、早速、実行に移って下さったのである。そして氏の知り合いのモリモト印刷が一切を引き受けてくださるとのことだった。

　詳しいことはもう忘れたが、本書の計画が平位先生と出来たのは、もう 6、7 年以上昔のことではなかったかと思う。それから平位先生は毎年のようにアフガーン国境のワハーン回廊一帯を訪れ、新しい記録の採集につとめられた。もうそろそろ止められたらと思いながら、なかなか思い切りがつかなかったようで、こちらはむしろ半分以上諦めていた。しかしアフガーン情勢が悪化する一方で、もうこれ以上無理と判断されたのは、2014 年の頃のだったようである。

　そこでやっと 2 人で最終案を相談し、なんとか出版のめどを考えたのが 2014 年の末であった。しかし、本書の完成準備のためにかかった費用も大変なものだったので、すんなり決断できなかったのである。

　しかし、なんとか原稿も出来上がったので、ただちに着行しようということになった。これが実行に移れたのは、霞ヶ関出版㈱の加藤敏雄氏のお陰である。改めてお礼を申し述べたい。

　ところがなんと 2 月 6 日の本書の初校のゲラが出来た当日に、予想外の事件が起こったのだった。平位兼子夫人からの、連絡でなんと平位氏本人が過労で倒れ入院されたとのことだった。深刻な事態であるものの、本はもう 8、9 割方は完成しており、なんとか無事にしたいというのが、こちらの心からの願いである。

　そこで一切をモリモト印刷にお願いすることにした。このことがこのような予想もしていなかった ＜ あとがき ＞ を取り急ぎかくことになった理由である。本当に辛いことではあるが、これもまたわれわれが体験しなくてはならない、人生の一齣なのかもしれない

2015 年 2 月 9 日　金子民雄

玄奘（三蔵）法師やマルコポーロも辿った

ワハーン回廊
自然と棲む人たち

発行日	平成 27（2015）年 2 月 25 日
初版発行	
著　者	平位 剛
	広島市中区小町 3-31　ルミナス小町 1102
	電話 084-928-5884
監修者	金子 民雄
英　訳	井手 マヤ
編　集	紺野 昇
製　丁	中村 信子
発行者	平位 剛
発売所	霞ヶ関出版株式会社
	〒174-0056　東京都板橋区志村 1-35-2-902
	電話 03-3966-8575　ファックス 03-3966-8638

定　価　　　（4,500 円＋税）
印刷・製本　モリモト印刷株式会社
ISBN978-4-7603-0419-6 C3625 ¥4500

In the Footeps of Hsüang-tsang and Marco Polo
The Wakhan Corridor -
Nature and Inhaboitants

First Edition	Feb.2015
Author	Go Hirai
Editor	Tamio Kaneko
Translation	Maya Ide
Editing	Noboru Konno
Design	Nobuko Nakamura
Publisher	Go Hirai
Distributer	Kasumigaseki Publishing Co., Ltd.
Printer	Morimoto Printing Co., Ltd.
Price	4,500 Japanese yen + tax